Not
Your Mother's®
Casseroles

Not
Your Mother's®
Casseroles

Faith Durand

The Harvard Common Press
Boston, Massachusetts

THE HARVARD COMMON PRESS
535 Albany Street
Boston, Massachusetts 02118
www.harvardcommonpress.com

Printed in the United States of America
Printed on acid-free paper

Library of Congress Cataloging-in-Publication Data
Durand, Faith.
  Not your mother's casseroles / Faith Durand.
     p. cm.
  Includes index.
  ISBN 978-1-55832-483-1 (hardcover : alk. paper)
  ISBN 978-1-55832-484-8 (pbk. : alk. paper)
  1. Casserole cookery.   I. Title.
  TX693.D97   2011
  641.8'21—dc22   2010013248

Special bulk-order discounts are available on this and other Harvard Common Press books.
Companies and organizations may purchase books for premiums or resale, or may arrange a
custom edition, by contacting the Marketing Director at the address above.

Cover recipe: Oven Paella with Chicken, Shrimp, and Chorizo, page 250
Spine recipe: Bacon and Lentils with Egg, page 58
Back cover recipe: Winter Vegetable and Comté Gratin, page 111

Book design by Ralph Fowler / rlf design
Cover photography, food styling, and prop styling by Sabra Krock
Author photograph by Michael Durand

10 9 8 7 6 5 4 3 2 1

Not Your Mother's is a registered trademark of The Harvard Common Press.

To my husband, Mike,
who so graciously washed a parade of casserole dishes,
and who so ably performed the duties of
first (and best) taste-tester.

Contents

Acknowledgments

Deep thanks are in order to the many, many people who helped me write this book. I am grateful to the team at The Harvard Common Press for encouraging me to write my first book and develop these recipes. From Avi Kramer and Christine Cox, who first approached me with an idea and an invitation, to Valerie Cimino and Jane Dornbusch, who brought so much energy and care to the editing, to Bruce Shaw, who gave me the opportunity, this has been a wonderful group of people to work with, and many thanks are due.

Thank you to my fellow writers and cooks at Apartment Therapy and The Kitchn, from Sara Kate (who gave me my first food-writing job) to Emma, Elizabeth, Emily, Kathryn, Joanna, Nora, (the other) Nora, Sarah Rae, and Dana, for their constant inspiration and encouragement. Thank you especially to Sabra for her lovely photos and enthusiasm for this project.

Thank you to all the friends and family, too, who ate casseroles nonstop at dinner parties and potlucks for more than a year. My parents were unfailingly encouraging, and my brothers and sisters gladly received casseroles and gave great feedback, too. Thank you to the Tuesday dinner crowd (John, Allie, Cat, Zoltán, Ryan, and Henry) for their enthusiastic support of casseroles, and to the Friday dinner group (Pavi, Jeanne, Hannah, Micah, Ray, Jeanie, Ethan, Evan, Dorothy, Lilian, April, and Alan) for their encouragement.

My husband washed casserole dishes large and small seemingly without end, and was my biggest supporter—a full participant in all the shopping, prepping, eating, and giving away of casseroles that occurs when you test more than 200 recipes.

Thanks so much to each and every one of you. As I hope you know, I couldn't have written this book without you.

Why Casseroles?

On any given weeknight, in any given city in the United States (and probably throughout the world), you will find mothers and fathers, grandmothers and young professionals, single college students and newly married couples staring blankly into the refrigerator as they ponder the age-old question: *What should we eat for dinner?*

These days, the answer to this question isn't simple. On the one hand, we *need* to eat quickly—that appointment, soccer practice, or late-night study session won't wait. On the other hand, we *want* to eat fresh food that has some connection to the current season, is grown not too far away from us, and is likely to be good for our bodies.

Old ways of growing and gathering food, as well as eating in rhythm with the seasons (ripe tomatoes from the vine, young chickens from the farm, new eggs and smoked ham, spring peas and summer zucchini), are becoming popular again as urban gardening gains new footing and families look for fresher sources of good food. These are old ways of eating, and we celebrate them.

And yet the old ways are slow ways, and our modern lives have sped up. How do we cook sensible and reasonably fresh food in simple and delicious dishes that still allow us time for other things? How do we nourish our families and find balance in the modern conflict of freshness versus convenience?

One way to resolve this conflict is with a return to the casserole.

Casserole! Like turkey Tetrazzini?

Casserole! That much-maligned word carries connotations of four-day-old turkey, paired unfortunately with mayonnaise and mushy vegetables. Perhaps visions of cream-of-whatever-soups dumped over canned peas and tuna flash in front of your eyes. *Casserole* should signify easy comfort food, but let's face it: It's come to be a bad word in many households.

Let's talk about mine, for instance. I grew up in a huge family, one of eight children. Life was busy and noisy in such a full household, and getting dinner on the table every night was not an easy task for my mother. She often turned to baked dishes that could be mixed up quickly and put in the oven to stew, letting her turn her attention to more pressing things (like arbitrating disagreements among her many children).

And yet my five brothers and two sisters wouldn't have been happy to hear that casserole was on the menu. My mother, being a wise cook, didn't often call her baked dishes *casseroles*. Many favorite dishes at our table were actually casseroles in disguise—Creamy Cheesy Potatoes, for instance, which makes an appearance later in this book.

As I grew up and learned to cook for myself, I rejected the casserole and my mother's baked dishes, too—so old-fashioned and bland! so full of fat and canned ingredients! No thanks.

Life became full. I got a job, got married, got a house, got really busy. Even though cooking was part of my job, I often found myself turning to easy baked pastas and quick one-pot dishes. If I could squeeze my starch, meat, and vegetable into one dish, I was a happy cook.

Then one day I had an epiphany: I had been making casseroles all along!

But I had tools and a range of ingredients that weren't available to my mother 20 years ago. Canned soups were off the ingredient list, and I wanted to bring my favorite flavors and preference for the freshest foods to the one-dish meals I enjoyed so much.

Casseroles had the potential to be easy, delicious, and quick—but I didn't want to make the recipes I grew up with. I also had friends with vegan, vegetarian, and gluten-free eating preferences, and I wondered if casseroles could stretch to accommodate their eating needs as well.

What Is a Casserole?

For the purposes of this book, a casserole is a baked dish. Historically, the category includes classics from around the world like Italian lasagna, Indian rice biryani, French bread panade, American macaroni and cheese, and breakfast favorites such as cherry clafoutis and egg-and-ham bake.

The casserole has its roots in humble peasant meals made by cooks who were using what was near to hand in frugal, thrifty recipes that let nothing go to waste. Constraints of time and money often yield the best kinds of creative cooking, so the wide range of dishes that could be called *casserole* are part of a long history of hearty deliciousness.

The latter half of the twentieth century marred this history with years of too-prepackaged recipes involving chemical-laden canned soups, unearthly combinations of ingredients, and unfortunate preservatives, all in the name of supposed convenience. I wanted to take the casserole back to its roots: a humble baked dish using fresh, readily available ingredients. Casseroles should be among the most welcome and delicious dishes in your repertoire, and they should use what is available to you without giving in to manufacturers' insistence that their products will make your cooking easier.

The casserole is also *easy*. Yes, there are complicated dishes like the French cassoulet and proper Italian lasagna, and these are wonderful indulgences of time and ingredients for special occasions. Putting together an entire lasagna from scratch is incredibly rewarding—not to mention delicious—but it's not something that we all have time for every week.

Most casseroles by their very nature should be frugal dishes you can throw together with minimal advance notice and slide away into the oven to cook. The everyday casserole is a dish that makes you look like a hero when you take out a bubbling pan filled with hot pasta and cheese or sweet cherries and eggy custard.

What Kind of Casseroles Are in This Book?

This book has more than 200 recipes that are designed to extract the maximum goodness from your oven and that also give starchy, too-fatty casseroles the boot. You won't find any canned soups or strange combinations of fake cheese and noodles. Instead, I depend on simple, fresh ingredients and wisely chosen preserved foods to give us easy baked meals.

What you will find are down-to-earth dishes that take advantage of seasonal vegetables, like Summer Vegetable and Fresh Mozzarella Gratin (page 114). There are also super-quick one-dish dinners like Smoked Sausage and Sage Pasta Casserole (page 188) and vegan recipes like Baked Quinoa with Sweet Potatoes and Almonds (page 209). The casserole is king of make-ahead breakfasts, so you'll find plenty of breakfast dishes, such as Basic Baked Steel-Cut Oats (page 24) and Savory Bread Pudding with Bacon and Mushrooms (page 36). You'll also find many updated classics, because I am still secretly fond of that old green bean casserole—although in the version here, the ingredient list is revamped to be friendlier to our bodies. (But it's still delicious, I assure you.)

I've created several fresh interpretations of old-fashioned casseroles, such as an updated tuna casserole with artichoke hearts and capers (and again, no canned soup!), but there's also a healthy selection of recipes here that will teach you that certain dishes and ingredients are, surprisingly, easier and more hands-off in the oven. Even if you bake regularly, you may not realize that your oven holds hidden potential for cooking many, many things. Did you know, for instance, that rice is foolproof when cooked in the oven? Or dried beans? The modern casserole can be a revelation, not just an easy, delicious way to put meals on the table.

Tradition and Improvisation

Classic casseroles, as I mentioned earlier, are often very time- and work-intensive. The traditions of French, British, and Italian cooking have produced some amazing recipes freighted with the weight of hundreds of interpretations and culinary significance. Contrast this with the three-ingredient, canned-mushroom-soup-with-noodles school of American casseroles, and you have two extremes.

My own style tries to strike a balance between these two extremes, in a very improvisational way: You take your own likes and dislikes and the food you have readily available to you, and you bake it into something fresh and delicious. I like cooking that keeps me alert, always testing and changing things. This isn't exclusive to casseroles; I improvise in all my home cooking. And in that improvisation I always hope to find a balance between the solid advice and weight of historic recipes and the quick, corner-cutting recipes of modern convenience.

The writer and cook John Thorne talks about this balance in his deliciously crotchety and entertaining book *Mouth Wide Open* (North Point Press, 2007), where he reviews another casserole cookbook, James Villas's *Crazy for Casseroles* (The Harvard Common Press, 2003).

Villas's book is a deep collection of classic casseroles. He gives us everything from shroups to pandowdies, and it's a great look back at historic American cooking, especially that of the South.

Thorne first talks about his pleasure in the idea of casseroles as a communal sharing, which Villas expresses beautifully in his well-researched book. This sense of communal sharing is also something that convenience foods brought to the table. They made any recipe seem accessible and immediately doable by any new cook; recipes were suddenly able to be shared and disseminated widely without too much personal idiosyncrasy, thanks to standardized ingredients such as canned soups and the test kitchens of big American food corporations.

But while sharing of recipes is, of course, a good thing, Thorne then goes on to talk about his discomfort with the resulting attitude of "convenience food cookery." He writes that "just as the invention of the personal deodorant transformed body odor, until then a mere fact of life, into a universal embarrassment, so could casserole cookery, which impressed cooks with its unthreatening easiness, make the uncertain work of preparing something pleasing from scratch seem rife with potential discomfiture. Convenience food cookery frees the cook of responsibility of the dish, and freedom from responsibility is such a delicious experience that it becomes part of the dish itself. . . . These dishes are not what makes me want to cook."

What does make him want to cook? It's the same thing that makes me want to cook: recipes that get reinvented every time I make them, with a pinch of this or a new way of cooking that. It's dishes, as Thorne puts it, that "demand more from us than to be just thrown together."

It seems to me that an over-slavishness to the historic recipes of the past, as well as to "convenience cookery," loses sight of the real pleasure in cooking: the cook's own responsibility for a dish. This is where the fun lies in cooking the recipes in this book. You try a dish, test, and taste. Maybe you fiddle with the herbs I specify; maybe you want more salt, or no onion, or another type of pasta altogether. Maybe your cupboard is bare of one ingredient so you substitute something else.

This is what these recipes are designed for. They have been tested and tried in my kitchen, but they are still blank slates for you. You have to take responsibility for your own cooking, which seems a matter of course to most cooks, but it is indeed something that "convenience cookery" takes away.

This book is not a historical treatise on the casserole and its evolution throughout history. You won't find a traditional three-day cassoulet or the most old-fashioned of American hot dishes. The weight of all that history is beautiful, but it's too much for me and my kitchen, and there are several other well-written casserole cookbooks that focus on this sort of recipe. The aforementioned book by James Villas is one, and another is *Bake Until Bubbly*, by Clifford A. Wright (Wiley, 2008). I highly recommend both.

This book, on the other hand, is one that is sometimes inspired by those traditional dishes but also calls for convenience ingredients from time to time. It's primarily a list of dishes that I like to cook and eat, made with ingredients that I enjoy putting together. They come from my improvisation with what is available to me, and I hope they stimulate the same sort of improvisation and creativity in your own kitchen.

My hope is that you discover fresh ways of cooking in your own kitchen and even progress to making up new dishes through cooking some of these recipes. They're not blueprints to be followed to the letter. They are, I hope, inspiration for fresh cooking on your own and templates for recipes that will be re-created in your own kitchen.

Casseroles and Convenience

It's easy to mock those not-so-appealing mixes of canned soup and mushy vegetables, but honestly, they were, and are, very convenient—hence their continuing popularity. I often find labor-intensive casserole recipes to be somewhat beside the point. If you have to slave for two hours creating multiple components for a dish before you even slide it into the oven, then why not just make something quicker on top of the stove?

I have gone out of my way in this book to develop recipes that are truly "mix and bake." Not every recipe is this way; many call for a little sautéed onion and garlic or a pound of cooked pasta. But I have tried to cut out unnecessary or fussy steps wherever possible and to find combinations of ingredients that bake together well. Take the Harvest Mixed-Grain Pilaf with Mushrooms on page 210, for instance. It's a mix of mushrooms, wild rice, barley, millet, lentils, and a few other things. And yet they aren't cooked before you put them in the oven; you toss it all together with some hot broth and bake, and, like magic, an hour later you have a healthy, hearty dinner.

I also call for many different kinds of packaged ingredients, but I've strived to do this in a judicious way. Frozen vegetables (I prefer organic ones) are flash-frozen in a way that preserves their freshness well. There's nothing wrong with using frozen peas, spinach, or corn—especially in winter, when finding high-quality fresh vegetables is more difficult and expensive.

Canned low-sodium chicken broth, canned beans and olives, and frozen potato cubes all make appearances, too. But these are still whole foods; they aren't too processed or cooked. For me, they are good compromises between the (sometimes) opposite poles of fresh and quick. By all means, if you have homemade chicken stock, use it! But if you don't, don't let that stop you from cooking a homemade meal. It's fine to substitute a packaged ingredient.

How This Book Is Organized

The recipes are organized by course; you'll find breakfast and dinner recipes, along with plenty of side dishes. But these groupings are fluid; many of the meat dishes can be made in vegetarian versions, and many of the vegetable dishes can accommodate a little meat or double as a main dish. There are recipes in the breakfast chapter that would easily do for a supper main dish, and others that could serve as dessert.

The casserole is often meant to be a one-dish meal, and these recipes reflect that in their flexibility. I encourage you to tweak and improvise! For times when you want something in addition to your casserole, there is also a chapter of quick breads and salads that can be made either ahead of time or while your casserole bakes, so you should be able to put together many meal combinations with these recipes.

Your Cooking Equipment

In my day job as managing editor of a large website on food and cooking, I hear a certain question over and over: What equipment do I need to cook, and what are the essentials for setting up a kitchen? Now, I love fun kitchen gadgets and shiny new tools as much as the next cook. But in the end, I always return to the basics.

Following are the items that I use constantly. You probably have all of the essential tools and baking pans already. If so, great! They are all you really need. I've also included a couple of extremely helpful but not quite as common tools that

I use just as often as the recommended essentials.

Your Oven

Obviously, when it comes to casseroles, your oven is the most important piece of equipment in your kitchen. Whether you have a gas or electric oven, and whether you have one with a convection setting or not, the most important accessory for your oven is an oven thermometer.

You can buy an oven thermometer for less than $5 at the grocery store. Pick one up, hang it in your oven, and always double-check it. Even new ovens are rarely compliant with their thermostats at all times. If you install an oven thermometer you can always be sure that your temperature is right. It's cheap and easy, and there's no reason not to do it.

A note on convection cooking: I did not test any of the recipes in this book in a convection oven. If you are so lucky as to have a convection setting on your oven, you can cut down the baking time for some of the recipes. But experimentation in this area is up to you! Let me know it goes.

Essential Tools

These are the basic tools for cooking casseroles, or any other everyday meal, for that matter.

Chef's knife: You really need only one or two good knives. I use a couple of chef's knives, and I have them professionally sharpened at least once a year.

A chef's knife, paring knife, and high-quality peeler are the main pieces of cutlery I use.

Large wooden cutting board: You'll do a lot of chopping for these recipes, so at least one big cutting board is useful. I prefer wood, especially bamboo for its strength and beauty. A nice wooden cutting board can also double as a cheese platter or serving dish for bread. Plastic cutting boards can go in the dishwasher, so they are convenient in this respect. But a plastic cutting board tends to hold on to germs more tenaciously, and it isn't as aesthetically pleasing as wood.

Metal or Pyrex mixing bowls: I have a few large mixing bowls, and I use them frequently for tossing pasta casseroles and mixing up grain pilafs.

Colander or mesh strainer: Draining pasta and rinsing rice is best done in a large colander or strainer.

Wooden spoons: Where would our kitchens be without a few good wooden spoons for stirring and tasting?

Spatula: Make sure you have at least one spatula for swiping raw ingredients out of bowls into pans.

Whisks: Whisks are good for so many things: beating eggs (although a fork can do this, too) and whisking white sauces smooth, to name just two. I admit to a bit of a whisk addiction; I have many of them, but you really need only one large stiff wire whisk.

Deep sauté pan: Many of the recipes in this book call for cooking a little onion or garlic, then stirring in the rest of the ingredients before pouring it all into a baking dish. It's helpful to have a sauté pan with a flat bottom and high sides for this step. I use a 3-quart pan (about 10 inches across) or, on occasion, a huge 6-quart pan (about 14 inches across). But a 3-quart sauté pan should be sufficient for everything in this book.

Cast-iron skillet: A cast-iron skillet is a great tool for browning meat and caramelizing onions.

Extremely Helpful Tools

Here are two more tools that I highly recommend for everyday use in making casseroles.

Microplane: A basic Microplane is a long, handheld zester and grater that produces fine zest and grated cheese very quickly. I adore my Microplane. It's one of the most-used tools in my kitchen. This book calls for a lot of grated cheese and quite a lot of lemon zest, too. A Microplane is the best tool for both of these.

Benriner mandoline: A mandoline looks like a fussy tool, something you'd see in a Japanese restaurant or French cooking school. Well, you might find this inexpensive slicer in both places, but it should have a spot in your cupboard, too. This razor-sharp slicer slices up potatoes, fennel, onions, carrots, and more in a tiny fraction of the time it would take to do it by hand. It also makes very even and consistent slices, which is important for many of the dishes in the vegetable chapter. The Benriner slicer can be had for less than $30 online, and I highly recommend it.

Essential Baking Pans

The word *casserole* probably originated from the actual pan used to cook these hot baked dishes, and a casserole may still be defined as much by the dish it's baked in as by anything else.

Here's a look at the baking pans (casseroles!) that are called for throughout this book. There is a wide array of beautiful casseroles and cooking pots out there, but this list focuses on the basics. Also, many recipes mention the approximate liquid capacity of the dishes they call for, to help you substitute other sizes if necessary.

Metal or glass 9 × 13-inch baking dish (3 quarts): The ultimate baking dish, right? It's practically synonymous with the casserole itself, and it's great to have at least two of these. Don't buy flimsy or thin metal pans; they're not worth it. Even heavy, commercial-grade aluminum or stainless-steel pans can be found for less than $20 at cookware shops and restaurant supply stores. Pyrex and ceramic versions are fine, too. It's helpful if they have lids that can be snapped on after baking for easy storage of leftovers.

Glass 8 × 8-inch baking dish (1½ quarts): This is another very common size of baking dish. Pyrex glass dishes in this size often come in a set with a 9 × 13-inch pan.

Metal 9 × 9-inch baking dish (2 quarts): For some reason, the square glass baking dishes are usually 8 inches square, while commercially available square metal pans are usually slightly larger, at 9 inches square. For the purposes of this cookbook, these two pans are practically interchangeable. Yes, there is a volume difference between the two, so casseroles baked in the smaller pan will be slightly thicker and may take a little longer to bake. If the recipe calls for one size and you have only the other, don't worry about it.

Metal 9-inch round cake pan (2 quarts): A 9-inch round cake pan can be substituted for an 8-inch or 9-inch square baking dish. I like baking some egg dishes in a round pan, then serving them in wedges. Some tortilla casseroles are also good baked in a round cake or pie pan.

3-quart Dutch oven or other stovetop-to-oven pot with lid: The 3-quart Dutch oven is perhaps my second-most-used pan, after the 9 × 13 workhorse. A good 3-quart Dutch oven with a lid can be used for nearly any casserole in this book, and it's essential for some of the rice and braised meat dishes, where keeping in moisture and heat during cooking is important. I use a Le Creuset Dutch oven, but any enameled cast-iron Dutch oven will do. And of course you can use a regular 3-quart ovenproof stainless-steel pot, too.

5- to 7-quart Dutch oven or other stovetop-to-oven pot with lid: A larger Dutch oven is good for bigger batches of oven stews, baked curries, and a few other dishes. And of course, smaller recipes can be made in here as well. A large Dutch oven can also be used as a pasta pot or to sauté vegetables and onions.

Those are the basics! Are there many, many more pans, pots, and casserole dishes made out of earthenware, cast iron, ceramic, glazed and unglazed porcelain, and stainless steel? Yes. Do you have to assemble a big collection just for these recipes? No. Most will work in a 9 × 13-inch pan or another 3-quart dish.

You can adjust most of these recipes to fit into any dish that is approximately the size called for. Just keep the proportions in mind; a tall, narrow pot will change how the food cooks (that is, more slowly than in a very wide and shallow dish). This is common sense, though; don't be afraid to make changes and use your ingenuity and whatever baking dishes you have on hand. One favorite trick of mine is to mix up everything I need for a casserole in my 3-quart ovenproof sauté pan, then clap the lid on and put the whole thing in the oven.

Having said all those sensible and practical things, I do need to add one note. The casserole dish has always been something intended to go from oven to table. (And sometimes from fridge to stove to oven to table, then back to the fridge, the microwave, and the table again.) So the dishes I reach for first are often the most beautiful ones I own. Clay and earthenware have the edge here; clay pots such as those found at the clay cookware shop Bram in Sonoma, California (bramcookware.com), are really beautiful, with organic shapes and a porous material that some say helps the food taste even better.

So, I do believe that aesthetics can be important in casserole dishes. When you can, buy things that you feel are beautiful. I have one heavy stoneware lasagna pan decorated with delicate curls and swoops;

it was made by hand in South Africa, and I treasure it. Everything I bake in it seems just a little extra-special.

Your Pantry

Chefs and cookbook authors can exhort us to eat fresh, local, and seasonal foods, but it all starts to sound a little wearying after a while—especially in the dead of winter in the Midwest, where I live. I do garden, I love finding local farmers, and I have a favorite local dairy that I adore. But in the end, in the real world, my daily cooking is made up of a mix of compromises.

There are the eggs from a small farm in a suburb of my city, and then there is the frozen corn from a big agricultural conglomerate. There's the meat from the butcher up the street, who raises his own goats and beef cattle, and then there are the cans of diced tomatoes from Mexico.

Our pantries are all made up of such decisions and compromises formed around our own priorities and budgets. The ingredients that I recommend in these recipes reflect that. I try not to be overly controlling about ingredients (use this brand of chicken stock or that specific sort of cinnamon), but there are a few things that I think will really strengthen your cooking, and this book's recipes depend upon those things.

Here's a look at some of the most common ingredients in these recipes and my thoughts about each of them.

Pantry Essentials and Helpers

Salt: What's more essential than salt? Unless otherwise specified, I mean fine table salt. Chunky kosher salt and flaky sea salt are best for finishing dishes, not seasoning them directly before cooking.

Pepper: Freshly ground pepper gives great flavor, so make sure you have a pepper grinder filled with whole peppercorns. I assume, in these recipes, that you can eyeball pepper quantities; I generally direct you to add pepper to taste. If you are uncomfortable with this, or do not use a pepper grinder, then start with ¼ teaspoon of ground pepper and work up from there. You can always add more seasoning to a finished dish.

Olive oil: When I specify olive oil in this book, I generally mean extra-virgin olive oil. But honestly, if you have another sort of olive oil and don't have any extra-virgin around, use what you've got.

Butter: I do not call for great amounts of butter, but when I do, I mean unsalted butter.

Nonstick cooking spray: I use a basic cooking spray to grease many of my casserole dishes. It's even better to get a small spray bottle, fill it with your olive oil or canola oil of choice, and use it for lightly greasing pots and pans.

Onions and garlic: The holy duo of the kitchen! There are many, many onions in these recipes, and you can use any sort you like. I use inexpensive white onions and small Spanish onions, which are quite pungent, although sometimes I call for yellow or red. With fresh garlic, I usually use fresh cloves from whole heads. But one of my own private compromises is peeled garlic cloves, which you can buy in tubs at the grocery store. I love these, and I find that in stews and oven-baked dishes, the difference in flavor between these and freshly peeled garlic is minimal.

Spices: It's always helpful to check and make sure your spices are fresh, as they really do lose their flavor quickly. One spice that you may not be familiar with and that I call for frequently is smoked paprika. Smoked paprika isn't any spicier than its more familiar sweet cousin, but it does have an incredible depth of smoki-ness that permeates anything you add it to. It's not too assertive but still very im-portant in many of the dishes in this book. It's worth seeking out!

Fresh herbs: Many of the casseroles in this book call for fresh herbs. Using fresh herbs is one of the single most effec-tive (and inexpensive) ways to make your cooking more bright and flavorful. I do not recommend substituting dried herbs for fresh, although, as I've said elsewhere, these recipes are just templates for you to experiment with, and if all you have avail-able are dried herbs, go for it.

Eggs: Unless otherwise specified, use large eggs. But once again (sense a theme?), if you have small eggs, medium eggs, or extra-large eggs, put them in. Try them. It will all probably turn out just fine.

Meat: Meat is the one ingredient I am very picky about. If you can find a good local source of meat that's been raised and butchered humanely, then buy that; it's

worth the higher price tag. I prefer using a smaller quantity of better quality meat.

Frozen vegetables: Frozen peas, spin-ach, corn, potatoes, and artichoke hearts all make appearances here.

Canned low-sodium broth: Many reci-pes in this book call for chicken, vegetable, or beef broth. Of course it would be won-derful if we all had freezers full of home-made broth and stock, but good-quality canned or aseptically packaged broth is a perfectly acceptable convenience in baked casseroles. Look for organic broth, though; it does make a difference in taste here. Also, always choose low-sodium broth; the alternatives are far too salty and are often inferior in taste and quality to their lower-sodium counterparts.

Make-Ahead: Preparing and Storing Unbaked Casseroles

Many of the casseroles in this book can be prepared up to the baking stage, then refrigerated until you are ready to bake them. I prefer to let a refrigerated, un-baked casserole come to room temperature before baking. A chilled casserole may still require up to 15 additional minutes to bake, though. When I note that a cas-serole can be refrigerated before baking, assume that you need to pay a little extra attention to the bake time. If you have refrigerated a casserole, then be prepared to let it cook a little longer and to check it carefully before you take it out of the oven. But keep in mind, too, that a refrigerated casserole will not always take too much longer to bake, and some will still bake up in the usual amount of time, especially if they're brought to room temperature before baking.

You can always double-check a casserole's status by inserting a table knife in the center near the end of the bake time. If the knife comes out feeling lukewarm or cold, then the casserole is definitely not ready yet.

Some casseroles are particularly well suited to this make-ahead, bake-later treatment. I've tried to note those in the instructions where appropriate.

Some casseroles can be prepared and then frozen before baking. The more moisture a casserole has, the better it will freeze. The rule of thumb says to avoid freezing potatoes, rice, and pasta, although I have frozen and then baked some pasta dishes (especially lasagna) with particular success. Other things to avoid freezing are milk, tofu, and all-vegetable dishes. The best casseroles to freeze are stews and meat dishes, as well as some fruit desserts. To bake, thaw an unbaked casserole in the refrigerator overnight, let it come to room temperature, then bake as directed in the recipe.

Overall, it's best to freeze unbaked casseroles rather than cooked ones, although I do freeze some baked leftovers, especially stews and braised meats. To reheat leftovers, frozen or not, bake covered at a slightly lower temperature than the original recipe called for until heated through.

Happy Casseroles!

Whether you call it a tian, a biryani, an oven stew, a gratin, or a casserole, these baked dishes are a return to classic, thrifty cooking, while at the same time recognizing that we still want to eat fresh, contemporary foods. This is not your mother's casserole book, but I bet she'd find a lot to like in here.

My goal is to help you cook fresher, cook more often, and discover that nourishing your family and yourself through the classic dish called the casserole is easier than you ever imagined.

Baked for Breakfast

In my household, breakfast is essential. We never skip breakfast; it fuels the whole day! This chapter gives you lots of options for starting your day well. Nearly every recipe can be prepared the night before and baked in the morning. Many of these dishes make great leftovers and reheat well, too, so breakfast the next day is even easier.

The oven is surprisingly effective at making extra-delicious hot cereal—it's easy to make pearly, chewy, steel-cut oatmeal with dried fruit and spices (see Baked Steel-Cut Oats with Dried Fruit, Coconut, and Spices, page 25) or hearty barley with Persian flavors (Breakfast Barley with Pistachios and Dried Apricots, page 27). These baked cereals also reheat beautifully! I often make a big pan and refrigerate the leftovers.

The oven is also my favorite tool for making easy eggs that please everyone. Try the Summer Egg and Potato Breakfast Bake (page 46) for a delicious vegetar-ian casserole that comes together in less than an hour, or the Herbed Egg and Bacon Quiche (page 60) for a rich pie that just gets better the next day.

And then there are bread, fruit, and sweet casseroles layered and baked with milk and eggs. Some of these are special-occasion treats, like the sweet and nutty Flaky Almond Croissant Bake (page 39) or the incredibly delicious Cinnamon Roll Breakfast Bake (page 44). Others are simpler and more suited to a weekday break-fast, like the Whole-Grain Almond-Apricot Bread Pudding (page 43).

Plum Spice Clafouti

HAVE YOU EVER HAD A CLAFOUTI? Sometimes it's called a German pancake, or a *flognarde*, or a Dutch baby. It's an eggy pancake batter poured over fruit, usually in a hot skillet with a little butter, and then baked until golden and puffy—deliciously crispy on top and custard-soft underneath. It's a very easy oven breakfast, and it's even better with a dusting of confectioners' sugar. This recipe is particularly good with the small Italian prune plums that appear in late summer and early fall, although you can make it with any sort of plum. Cherries are another traditional choice. ○ *Serves 4 to 6*

CASSEROLE DISH: 10-inch cast-iron skillet
BAKE TIME: About 1 hour

¼ cup (½ stick) unsalted butter, softened
1 pound prune plums (or regular red or black plums)
1½ cups milk
4 large eggs
¾ cup all-purpose flour
¼ cup sugar
1 teaspoon Chinese five-spice powder
½ teaspoon ground nutmeg
1 teaspoon ground cinnamon
1 teaspoon salt
Zest of ½ orange
Confectioners' sugar, for serving

1. Preheat the oven to 350°F. Smear the butter in the cast-iron skillet, buttering it all the way up the sides.

2. Cut each prune plum in half and remove the pit. (If you are using red or black plums, which are larger, cut each pitted plum into quarters.) Set aside.

3. Beat the milk and eggs thoroughly in a large bowl. Sift the flour, sugar, five-spice powder, nutmeg, cinnamon, and salt into another bowl, and beat the mixture with a whisk or beaters into the milk and eggs until smooth, without any lumps. Beat in the orange zest. Pour about one-third of the batter into the buttered cast-iron pan. Cook over a medium-hot burner just until set, about 10 minutes. Remove from the heat.

4. Arrange the sliced plums on the cooked batter in a spiral pattern. Pour the remaining two-thirds of the batter over the top and bake until puffed and firm, about 1 hour.

5. Let cool on a rack for at least 15 minutes before serving. Dust with confectioners' sugar just before serving.

Variation: Prunes are also very good in this clafouti. If you want to plump them up a little, soak them in hot water or orange juice, draining the liquid before adding them to the batter.

Baked Buttermilk Pancakes

THIS IS A TRUE AMERICAN PANCAKE. A true American pancake, that is, without all the hassle of pouring, flipping, and griddles. It's just a pancake batter baked in the oven, and it's much easier than flipping pancakes for a crowd! But you don't have to forego the maple syrup; serve this in long strips with real maple syrup, warmed up in the microwave. ◦ *Serves 4*

CASSEROLE DISH: 10½ × 15½-inch jelly-roll pan
BAKE TIME: 15 minutes

1 cup all-purpose flour
1 teaspoon baking powder
½ teaspoon baking soda
½ teaspoon salt
2 tablespoons sugar
1 large egg, beaten
1½ cups buttermilk
½ teaspoon vanilla extract
3 tablespoons unsalted butter, melted
Pure maple syrup, for serving

1. Preheat the oven to 400°F. Lightly spray the pan with nonstick cooking spray.

2. Whisk together the flour, baking powder, baking soda, salt, and sugar in a medium-size bowl. Add the egg, buttermilk, vanilla, and butter. Whisk to combine. Do not overmix; the batter will have small lumps.

3. Pour into the prepared pan. Bake for 15 minutes, or until light golden brown and firmly set.

4. Slice into long strips and serve hot, with warm maple syrup.

Variations: Mix a handful of fresh blueberries into the batter, or sprinkle the top of the unbaked pancake with sugar mixed with cinnamon. Or delight the kids by using cookie cutters to cut fun shapes out of the hot baked pancake.

Use the Good Stuff

Pure maple syrup is an essential at the breakfast table. A little goes a long way, since it has much more flavor than the imitation stuff. Yes, it's more expensive, but it tastes so much better. A small bottle will last longer than a larger quantity of the imitation, too-sweet syrups. You can also look for the new combinations of agave and maple syrups, which are still all-natural but a little less expensive.

German Apple Pancake

THE SUBLIME AND DELICIOUS German apple pancake recipe comes from my friend Jennie and her family. It's a classic breakfast dish for them, and it was even instrumental in her parents' courtship. You'll fall in love, too, when you try it. It's similar to the plum clafouti on page 16, but the tender apples and sweet cinnamon sugar give this its own irresistible quality. o *Serves 4*

CASSEROLE DISH: 9-inch square baking dish
BAKE TIME: About 20 minutes

2 or 3 tart apples
4 tablespoons granulated sugar
1 teaspoon ground cinnamon
½ teaspoon ground ginger

⅓ cup unsalted butter
½ cup brown sugar
5 large eggs
¾ cup all-purpose flour
¼ teaspoon salt
1 cup milk
½ teaspoon vanilla extract

FOR THE CINNAMON SUGAR:
⅓ cup granulated sugar
1 tablespoon ground cinnamon

1. Preheat the oven to 400°F. Peel and slice the apples; you should have about 3 cups. Mix 3 tablespoons of the granulated sugar, the cinnamon, and the ginger in a small bowl and set aside.

2. Put the butter in the baking dish and put it in the oven for 2 minutes to melt. Take it out and tilt the pan to coat the bottom and sides with melted butter. Add the brown sugar to the butter in the bottom of the pan. Spread the apples on top of the sugar and sprinkle the spice-sugar mixture over the apples. Put the pan back in the oven so the apples will start cooking.

3. In a large bowl, beat the eggs with a whisk until foamy. Add the flour, salt, and remaining 1 tablespoon of granulated sugar, whisking constantly, and then add the milk and vanilla. Beat just until smooth. There may still be a few small lumps of flour; this is okay.

4. Carefully take the pan out of the oven and pour the batter over the apples. Bake for about 20 minutes, or until the center is set and the sides are lightly browned. If the top browns before the center sets, tent with foil for the duration of the baking. The pancake will puff up dramatically but fall after you take it out of the oven.

5. Let cool for at least 15 minutes before serving. Whisk together the sugar and ground cinnamon, and sprinkle over the dish just before serving.

Variation: You can easily double this recipe for a bigger breakfast crowd or to have leftovers. Leftovers reheat beautifully; I actually prefer them to the fresh-baked pancake! If you double it, use a 9 × 13-inch casserole dish.

Prune and Ricotta Oatmeal Breakfast Pudding

OATMEAL AND PRUNES both have dull reputations; oatmeal is plain and healthy, but rather mushy, and prunes have their own connotations, none too attractive. But put away your old perceptions of prunes and oatmeal! Prunes are dried plums with the mellow richness of long summers and sunlight. They're sweet and melting when treated with respect. See if they don't change your mind when they're baked in this delicately rich oatmeal pudding with plenty of whole-grain nuttiness and creamy ricotta. ● *Serves 4*

CASSEROLE DISH: 9-inch square baking dish
BAKE TIME: 50 to 55 minutes

2 cups prunes, cut into quarters
3 cups boiling water
2 cups old-fashioned rolled oats
2 large eggs
2 cups ricotta cheese
1 cup milk
⅓ cup sugar
2 tablespoons rum or brandy (optional)
1 teaspoon vanilla extract
1½ teaspoons ground cinnamon, plus more for dusting
½ teaspoon ground nutmeg
½ teaspoon salt
Cinnamon sugar (page 19), for sprinkling
Heavy cream or whipped cream, for serving

1. Preheat the oven to 325°F. Lightly grease the baking dish with butter or non-stick cooking spray.

2. Put the prunes in a small bowl and pour 1 cup of the boiling water over them. Set the prunes aside to plump up. In a large bowl, pour the remaining 2 cups of boiling water over the oats. Set aside to cool.

3. In a large bowl, whip the eggs until frothy. Blend in the ricotta cheese, milk, sugar, rum or brandy (if using), vanilla, cinnamon, nutmeg, and salt. Whip until smooth.

4. Stir the oatmeal and drain off any excess liquid. Stir the oatmeal into the ricotta mixture. Drain the prunes of excess liquid, and stir the drained prunes into the oat and ricotta batter. Pour the batter into the prepared baking dish. (At this point the dish can be covered and refrigerated for up to 24 hours.) Dust liberally with ground cinnamon and place in the center of the oven.

5. Bake, uncovered, for 50 to 55 minutes, or until it is golden and the center is set and no longer wobbly. Let cool on a rack for 5 minutes before serving, then slice into thick squares and serve with cinnamon sugar and cream.

Oat and Raisin Breakfast Bars

THIS IS A CLASSIC RECIPE for eggy and moist breakfast bars with oats and raisins. In my household, they are made often and well loved. They are the perfect item to prepare at the beginning of the week. Slice into long bars and wrap each individually, so you can grab one on your way out the door in the morning. That way, you can have your morning oatmeal no matter how busy you are! ○ *Serves 8*

CASSEROLE DISH: 9 × 13-inch baking dish
BAKE TIME: 55 minutes to 1 hour

2½ cups old-fashioned rolled oats
½ cup dark brown sugar
¾ cup raisins
1 apple, cored and chopped
½ cup hazelnuts, toasted and coarsely chopped
1 teaspoon ground cinnamon
½ teaspoon ground ginger
1 teaspoon salt
2 large eggs
3 cups milk
1 teaspoon vanilla extract

1. Preheat the oven to 350°F. Lightly spray the baking dish with nonstick cooking spray.

2. In a large bowl, combine the oats, brown sugar, raisins, chopped apple, nuts, cinnamon, ginger, and salt. Mix well. Beat the eggs thoroughly in a separate small bowl or large measuring cup. Whisk in the milk and vanilla, then pour into the oat mixture and stir until combined.

3. Pour the mixture into the baking dish, spreading out the oats, fruit, and nuts as necessary so that they are evenly distributed. Bake for 55 to 60 minutes, until the center is set and firm to the touch.

4. Let cool for at least 10 minutes on a rack before slicing and serving. Refrigerate or freeze leftovers.

Variations: Try experimenting with the fruits and nuts in this recipe: dried blueberries and crystallized ginger with almonds; dried, sweetened cranberries with orange zest, chopped pears, and walnuts; fresh blackberries with lemon zest and chopped apples; or sliced bananas, pecans, and a dash of rum flavoring.

Stock Up on Convenience

Breakfast bars can be frozen in individually wrapped slices. Put a slice in the fridge to thaw overnight, or microwave a frozen slice for 30 seconds in the morning to warm it up.

Baked Oatmeal with Raisins and Pecans

USUALLY WHEN YOU THINK OF HOT BREAKFAST cereal you think of a pot on the stove. But the oven is just as good for some breakfast cereals, and it lets you put everything in to cook and then go take a shower without worrying about oatmeal scorching or overflowing on the stovetop. This oatmeal is more than just a convenience food, though; it turns out creamy and fragrant with spices.

o *Serves 4*

CASSEROLE DISH: 9-inch square baking dish
BAKE TIME: 25 to 30 minutes

2 cups old-fashioned rolled oats
1 teaspoon ground cinnamon
¼ teaspoon ground nutmeg
½ teaspoon salt
¼ cup sugar
2½ cups milk, plus more for serving (optional)
1 cup raisins
½ cup toasted pecans
Brown sugar, for serving

1. Preheat the oven to 350°F. Lightly grease the baking dish with nonstick cooking spray.

2. Combine the oats, cinnamon, nutmeg, salt, sugar, milk, raisins, and pecans in a large bowl and mix. Pour into the baking dish. Bake for 25 to 30 minutes, or until all the liquid is absorbed.

3. Serve hot, with additional milk, if desired, and brown sugar.

Feeling Your Oats

Old-fashioned oats, quick-cooking oats, instant oats, steel-cut oats—what's the difference? There are several sorts of oats called for in this chapter. The most common kind of oat is rolled, where the grains have been rolled flat so that they will cook faster. Old-fashioned oats and quick-cooking oats are both rolled oats. Quick-cooking oats are chopped up so that they cook a little bit faster, but they are basically interchangeable with old-fashioned oats.

Instant oats are also rolled, but they have been precooked as well. You usually see these only in those little packets of sugary instant oatmeal, and they are almost never called for in recipes.

Steel-cut oats, on the other hand, are not rolled at all. They are the unflattened grain of the oat, chopped into small bits. (They are also called pinhead, Irish, or Scottish oats.) Uncooked, they look like nubs of grain instead of flat flakes. Steel-cut oats take longer to cook, but a bowl of cooked oats has a creamy texture, with distinct chewy grains. It's wonderfully delicious, and the opposite of mushy oatmeal.

Basic Baked Steel-Cut Oats

STEEL-CUT OATS are one of the greatest breakfast pleasures I know. They take a little longer to cook than flat rolled oats, but oh, are they worth it! When cooked slowly in the oven they become creamy and a little chewy, without any of the mushiness that puts some people off regular oatmeal. Their distinct grains, pearly and delicious, are preserved even when cooked. Steel-cut oatmeal also reheats nicely, so you can make a big batch at the start of the week and quickly reheat a bowl every morning. These will also cook a little faster if you mix everything and put it in the fridge overnight. It isn't necessary, but it is helpful.

◦ Serves 4

CASSEROLE DISH: 8- or 9-inch square baking dish
BAKE TIME: About 30 to 40 minutes

1 cup steel-cut oats
¼ teaspoon salt
2 cups water
1 cup milk, plus more for serving
Brown sugar, for serving
Butter, for serving

1. Lightly grease the baking dish with butter or nonstick cooking spray. Mix the oats, salt, water, and milk in the baking dish and cover with aluminum foil. If time allows, refrigerate 8 hours or overnight.

2. When ready to bake, preheat the oven to 375°F. Place the baking dish on a baking sheet (to catch any overflow) and put it in the oven. Bake for 40 minutes, or 30 minutes if you've refrigerated the oatmeal overnight. Remove the baking dish from the oven, stir the oatmeal once, then let it sit for 5 minutes. (Be careful when you pull back the aluminum foil, as there will be a great deal of hot steam underneath.) The oats will look quite soupy at first, but they will thicken into a more familiar oatmeal consistency after they have cooled for a few minutes.

3. Stir the oatmeal once more before serving, and serve hot, with brown sugar, milk, and a little butter.

Baked Steel-Cut Oats with Dried Fruit, Coconut, and Spices

'VE GIVEN YOU ONE BASIC RECIPE for steel-cut oats, but now the sky's the limit with mix-ins, fruit, nuts, and other ways of jazzing up your morning bowl of cereal. Here's one easy favorite that's good all year round, even when there's no decent fresh fruit to be found. I toast the oats, which adds a step to the process. This gives a darker, toastier flavor to the oatmeal, but you can skip it if you're short on prep time. These will cook a little faster if you prepare through step 2, then put the pan in the fridge overnight. ○ *Serves 4*

CASSEROLE DISH: 9-inch square baking dish
BAKE TIME: About 25 to 35 minutes

1 tablespoon unsalted butter
1 cup steel-cut oats
2 cups water
1½ cups milk
⅓ cup brown sugar
1 cup mixed dried fruit, such as raisins, currants, cherries, or blueberries
½ cup unsweetened dried coconut
1 teaspoon ground cinnamon
½ teaspoon ground ginger
½ teaspoon salt

1. Lightly grease the baking dish with butter or nonstick cooking spray. Melt the 1 tablespoon butter in a saucepan over medium heat and add the oats. Cook, stirring frequently, for about 3 minutes, or until the oats start smelling toasty. Add the water and milk and bring to a light simmer. Remove from the heat.

2. Stir in the brown sugar, dried fruit, coconut, cinnamon, ginger, and salt. Pour into the baking dish and cover with aluminum foil. If time allows, refrigerate 8 hours or overnight.

3. When ready to bake, preheat the oven to 375°F. Place the baking dish on a baking sheet (to catch any overflow) and put it in the oven. Bake for 35 minutes, or 25

minutes if you've refrigerated the oatmeal overnight, until the oats have absorbed all the liquid and are creamy. (The oats will look quite soupy at first, but they will thicken into a more familiar oatmeal consistency after they have cooled for a few minutes.) Stir the oatmeal before serving, and serve hot.

Savory Baked Oats with Scallions and Turkey Bacon

SAVORY OATMEAL? INDEED! Savory oatmeal has become rather popular lately. I've seen several versions of it pop up, and the thought of a whole-grain breakfast that still manages to incorporate bacon is very welcome. Here's one version that relies on steel-cut oats, a healthy helping of garlic, and some good turkey bacon. ● *Serves 4*

CASSEROLE DISH: 9-inch square baking dish
BAKE TIME: 25 to 35 minutes

4 slices turkey bacon, chopped into small pieces
2 cloves garlic, minced
4 to 6 scallions (white and green parts), minced
1 cup steel-cut oats
2 tablespoons soy sauce
Freshly ground black pepper
3½ cups water
1 cup grated Parmesan cheese

1. Lightly grease the baking dish with nonstick cooking spray.

2. In a large pan, cook the turkey bacon over medium-high heat until crisp and browned. Turn the heat down to medium and add the garlic, scallions, and oats. Cook for several minutes, or until the oats are toasted and the garlic is fragrant and golden.

3. Add the oat mixture to the baking dish, and stir in the soy sauce, a few turns of black pepper, the water, and Parmesan cheese; cover the dish with aluminum

foil. (At this point the dish can be covered and refrigerated for up to 24 hours.) When ready to bake, preheat the oven to 375°F and bake for 35 minutes, or 25 minutes if you've refrigerated it for several hours, until the liquid is absorbed and the oats are fully cooked. (The oats will look quite soupy at first, but they will thicken into a more familiar oatmeal consistency after they have cooled for a few minutes.) Serve hot.

Breakfast Barley with Pistachios and Dried Apricots

BARLEY IS AN ANCIENT GRAIN; people have been eating it for thousands of years, and that's not just because it's healthy. It also has a pleasantly toasty flavor and a chewy bite. Its flavor is fuller and richer than oatmeal's, with a nutty aftertaste. This recipe is a little more involved than the simple breakfast cereals earlier in the chapter, but it yields a deliciously exotic, Persian-inspired breakfast porridge. o *Serves 4*

CASSEROLE DISH: 8-inch square baking dish
BAKE TIME: 35 to 45 minutes

1½ cups pearl barley
1 tablespoon unsalted butter
½ teaspoon salt
2 cups milk
2½ cups water
3 tablespoons honey, plus more for serving
1 large egg, beaten
¼ cup chopped dried unsulphured apricots
¼ cup shelled pistachios
½ cup unsweetened dried coconut
1 teaspoon orange zest (optional)
Heavy cream, for serving (optional)

1. Preheat the oven to 350°F. Lightly grease the baking dish with nonstick cooking spray.

2. Rinse the barley in water and drain. Heat the butter over medium heat in a 4-quart pot and cook the drained barley for 3 to 5 minutes, or until it smells toasty. Add the salt, milk, water, and honey and bring to a boil over medium heat.

3. While the barley and milk are coming to a boil, beat the egg thoroughly in a small bowl. When the milk comes to a boil, immediately turn off the heat and move the pan off the burner. Pour a spoonful of the milk into the beaten egg and whisk to combine. (Mixing the hot milk and egg tempers the egg so that it doesn't scramble when it's added to the pan.) Whisk the egg mixture into the pan.

4. Stir in the apricots, pistachios, coconut, and orange zest, if using. Pour everything into the prepared dish.

5. Bake, uncovered, for 35 to 45 minutes, or until the top is lightly brown and the casserole is no longer liquid. Serve warm, with honey and a little cream, if desired.

Basic Baked Polenta with Maple Syrup

P OLENTA, which is made from coarse-ground yellow cornmeal, is just one version of a dish served all over the world. It may be called polenta in Italy, but in the United States it's known as "grits," and in eastern Africa it goes by "ugali." You can serve polenta straight from the stovetop like porridge, hot and creamy, but you can also go a step further and bake it until it's firm and a little crispy around the edges. Cut into slices and serve hot, with warm maple syrup and fresh fruit. ○ *Serves 4*

CASSEROLE DISH: 10½ × 15½-inch jelly-roll pan
BAKE TIME: 25 to 35 minutes

4 cups water
1 teaspoon salt
Olive oil
1 cup polenta or yellow cornmeal
Butter, for serving
Pure maple syrup, for serving

1. Bring the water, salt, and a drizzle of olive oil to a boil in a 4-quart pot. Add the polenta very slowly, 1 tablespoon at a time, whisking constantly. If you whisk it in very slowly, then lumps will not form and you will not have to stir frequently as the polenta cooks.

2. When the polenta is fully incorporated, continue whisking for another minute. Reduce the heat to low, cover, and simmer the polenta until quite thick, about 30 minutes. Stir every 10 minutes or so.

3. Preheat the oven to 400°F. Grease the jelly-roll pan with nonstick cooking spray.

4. When the mixture is very thick, carefully pour all of the polenta into the prepared pan. Smooth it out evenly with a spatula. Bake for 25 to 35 minutes, or until quite firm and slightly crispy around the edges.

5. Slice and serve hot, with butter and maple syrup. You can also cut leftovers into pieces and fry them lightly in butter.

About Polenta

Polenta is often regarded as a rarified ingredient best bought from Italian specialty shops. Don't be fooled; it's just cornmeal. You can make polenta dishes out of nearly any ground cornmeal—from fine cornmeal to coarse stone-ground cornmeal—although I personally prefer the coarser grinds. You can find this in bags at the grocery store or in the area of the market that sells grains in bulk bins.

Polenta Bake with Ham, Tomatoes, and Eggs

ONCE POLENTA HAS BEEN COOKED, it will solidify as it cools into a thick, firm mass. This cornmeal mush can be sliced and fried or baked again with toppings piled on. It's like a quick breakfast pizza! This particular recipe is very flexible and calls for the precooked polenta that comes in tubes and is found in supermarkets. Top the baked polenta rounds with whatever strikes your fancy. Spinach, Parmesan, and bacon crumbles are another very good combination.

o *Serves 6*

CASSEROLE DISH: Baking sheet and twelve 6-ounce ramekins or baking cups

BAKE TIME: 15 to 20 minutes, plus 10 minutes to broil the polenta slices

One 11-ounce tube prepared polenta
About 2 tablespoons olive oil
1 cup shredded Asiago or Parmesan cheese
1 plum tomato, diced
¼ cup fresh basil, minced
4 slices (2 to 4 ounces) cured ham, chopped
Freshly ground black pepper
12 large eggs
Salt

1. Preheat the broiler. Lightly grease the ramekins with nonstick cooking spray.

2. Unwrap the tube of polenta and slice into 12 even slices. (You can also use left-over Basic Baked Polenta, page 28, sliced into squares or rounds.)

3. Arrange the slices on the baking sheet. Brush each slice with a little olive oil. Broil for 10 minutes, or until the tops are crispy and turning golden brown. Remove the baking sheet from the oven, and turn the oven down to 400°F.

4. While the polenta slices are baking, in a small bowl combine ¾ cup of the Asiago cheese, the diced tomato, basil, and chopped ham. Add 1 tablespoon of the olive oil and 2 to 3 turns of freshly ground black pepper.

5. Press each hot, broiled polenta slice into a ramekin. Top each slice with a spoonful of the cheese and ham mixture. Crack an egg on top. Sprinkle on a little salt and pepper, then top with the remaining Asiago cheese.

6. Bake on the middle rack for 15 to 20 minutes, or until the eggs are done to your liking. Place 2 ramekins on each plate and serve immediately.

The Baked Egg Bar

Planning a brunch for a crowd can be a little overwhelming; after all, most of us aren't at our best in the morning, and cooking for a big crowd of family members or friends on a holiday weekend might not be your favorite way to start the day. Baked eggs are a really lovely answer to that menu challenge. You can create a baked egg bar, with baking cups ready to be filled with a selection of ham, herbs, cooked bacon, polenta, or vegetables. Let everyone fill up his or her own cup, then crack eggs on top and slide them into the oven as they're wanted. It's elegant, quick, and easy.

Baked Cheesy Chile Grits

CHEESY GRITS are an absolute breakfast necessity in the South. This baked recipe makes spicy, cheesy grits that may be a little different from the classic Southern version, but they're easy and quick, with a zing all their own. Serve with eggs, sausages, and fruit. ❍ *Serves 6 to 8*

CASSEROLE DISH: 9 × 13-inch baking dish
BAKE TIME: 45 minutes

4 cups milk
1 cup water
1 teaspoon salt
1 tablespoon unsalted butter
1 cup quick-cooking grits
1 cup shredded extra-sharp cheddar cheese
½ teaspoon freshly ground black pepper
One 4-ounce can chopped chiles, drained (see Note on page 32)
¼ cup minced fresh chives
5 large eggs, separated
¼ teaspoon cream of tartar

1. Preheat the oven to 350°F. Lightly grease the baking dish with nonstick cooking spray.

2. Combine the milk, water, salt, and butter in a large saucepan over medium-high heat. Bring to a boil. Slowly add the grits to the boiling liquid, whisking rapidly. When the grits are fully whisked in, cover the pot and turn the heat to low. Cook for 8 minutes, or until all the liquid is absorbed.

3. Remove the grits from the heat and stir in the cheese, black pepper, chile peppers, and chives. Set aside to cool.

4. Put the egg whites and cream of tartar in a large clean bowl or the bowl of a stand mixer. Beat the egg whites at high speed until stiff peaks form. (The tips should not flop over when you make peaks with the beaters or a spoon.)

5. Gently fold the grits into the egg whites until mostly combined. Stir in the egg yolks, then spoon the mixture into the baking dish and bake for 45 minutes, or until browned. The grits will still be quite soft, almost like a tender custard or a stiff pudding. Serve hot.

Note: There are several kinds of canned chile peppers you can use in this recipe. The canned green chile peppers found in the supermarket are rather mild, with a light zing. But you can also use canned jalapeño or chipotle chiles (adjusting the quantities as desired), either of which will give this dish quite a kick.

Breakfast Brown Rice with Blueberries and Almonds

HAVE YOU EVER EATEN RICE FOR BREAKFAST? This is a great way to start. Brown rice makes a very nutritious breakfast, full of whole-grain goodness and with plenty of minerals and vitamins. Don't eat brown rice just for the health benefits, though; this dish is nutty and flavorful, with sweet blueberries, too. Serve with honey, maple syrup, or milk. **o** *Serves 4*

CASSEROLE DISH: 9-inch square baking dish
BAKE TIME: 1 hour

1 cup short-grain brown rice
½ cup dried blueberries
½ cup chopped raw almonds

½ teaspoon salt

Zest of 1 orange

2 cups water

1 cup milk

2 tablespoons unsalted butter

¼ cup brown sugar

1. Preheat the oven to 375°F. Lightly grease the baking dish with butter or non-stick cooking spray. Stir together the rice, dried blueberries, almonds, salt, and orange zest in a medium-size bowl. Spread the rice mixture evenly in the pan.

2. Bring the water, milk, and butter to a boil in the microwave or on the stove. Immediately pour over the rice. Cover the dish tightly with a lid or with a double layer of foil and bake for 1 hour.

3. Remove the dish from the oven and uncover carefully. It will be hot, with plenty of steam under the foil. Fluff the rice with a fork, stir in the brown sugar, and let it sit for 5 minutes before serving.

Variations: Try dried currants or dried cranberries instead of the blueberries, and lemon zest instead of the orange. Hazelnuts and dried figs are a very good combination, too.

The Best Rice to Use

Short-, medium-, and long-grain rices differ in their ability to absorb and hold moisture. Short-grain rice will absorb more liquid and hold it well without drying out, whereas long-grain rice stays drier. (Think of the loose, dry, long-grain basmati rice, for instance, that's served with Indian dishes.) Short- or medium-grain brown rice is necessary for this dish, since brown rice is already a little more difficult to cook than white rice and long-grain brown rice will take more time to get really tender and right. Short-grain, on the other hand, has a pearly, chewy texture that is perfect for this breakfast dish.

Baked Basmati Rice with Saffron, Cashews, and Raisins

BASMATI RICE is the only sort of rice you will find in an Indian restaurant. It's long-grained and fragrant, and it stays dry and loose, with distinct grains, even when cooked. In this breakfast dish, the rice is moistened with extra milk, and it's enriched with Eastern flavors of saffron, cinnamon, and cardamom. The flavor is rich, and the pale yellow of the saffron makes this just special enough for a treat, but the dish is also very nutritious. Leftovers reheat beautifully.

o Serves 6

CASSEROLE DISH: 9 × 13-inch baking dish
BAKE TIME: 50 minutes

1½ cups basmati or long-grain rice
½ cup raw cashew pieces
½ cup golden raisins
2 tablespoons hot water
¼ teaspoon saffron threads
2 tablespoons unsalted butter
2 cardamom pods
1 cinnamon stick
2 cups milk
⅓ cup sugar

1. Preheat the oven to 350°F. Lightly grease the baking dish with a little butter or nonstick cooking spray. Spread the rice evenly in the dish and toss with the cashew pieces and raisins.

2. Crumble the saffron threads into a small bowl and pour the hot water over them. Let soak.

3. Heat the butter in a saucepan over medium heat. When it melts and foams, add the cardamom pods and cinnamon stick and cook for 2 to 3 minutes, or until the butter smells fragrant. Add the milk and sugar, and bring to a simmer. As soon as it comes to a boil, turn off the heat and stir in the saffron and its steeping liquid.

4. Pour the hot milk mixture over the rice in the baking dish. Cover tightly, put the dish on a baking sheet in case of any overflow, and place in the oven. Bake for 50 minutes. Remove and let sit, covered, for 5 minutes. Carefully remove the foil and serve immediately. Leave the whole spices in for authenticity, but do not eat them. If you are concerned about accidentally biting into a cardamom pod, you can remove them before serving.

Breakfast Fruit with Granola Streusel

R EALLY GOOD GRANOLA is the key to this easy breakfast casserole made with whatever sort of fruit you have on hand. This is especially good for using up mushy pears, wrinkled apples, and random dried fruit lurking in the cupboards. Toss them together with this crunchy oat topping and bake, and you'll have transformed your leftover fruit into something really special. A hot spoonful of this over plain, creamy yogurt is a simple yet sublime way to start the day. **o** *Serves 6*

CASSEROLE DISH: 9 × 13-inch baking dish
BAKE TIME: 30 minutes

2 apples, cored and chopped into 1-inch pieces
2 pears, cored and chopped into 1-inch pieces
Zest and juice of 1 lemon
½ cup dried cranberries or raisins
½ cup dried apricots or prunes, sliced in half
½ cup walnut pieces
½ cup brown sugar
1 teaspoon ground cinnamon
½ teaspoon freshly grated nutmeg
½ cup fresh orange juice
2 cups granola of your choice
Pinch of salt
¼ cup unsalted butter, melted

1. Preheat the oven to 350°F. Lightly grease the baking dish with nonstick cooking spray.

2. Toss the apples and pears with the lemon zest and juice in a large bowl. Mix in the cranberries, apricots, and walnuts. Toss with ¼ cup of the brown sugar, the cinnamon, and nutmeg, and spread the fruit mixture in the baking dish. Pour the orange juice over the top.

3. In a medium-size bowl, mix the granola, a pinch of salt, the remaining ¼ cup of brown sugar, and the butter, and drop spoonfuls over the fruit. Bake for 30 minutes, or until the streusel is golden brown and the fruit is bubbling. Let stand for 10 minutes, then serve hot.

Savory Bread Pudding with Bacon and Mushrooms

GOOD BREAD, SAVORY MUSHROOMS, and crackling bacon—it's a luxurious weekend breakfast for autumn or winter when you want something hot to start the day. Try different kinds of whole-grain bread in this recipe; I love using hearty, chunky breads that incorporate oats, barley, nuts, or sunflower seeds. o *Serves 6*

CASSEROLE DISH: 9 × 13-inch baking dish
BAKE TIME: 45 to 50 minutes

12 ounces whole-grain bread, including crust, chopped into 1-inch cubes (about 8 cups)
8 slices bacon, chopped
1 pound white or cremini mushrooms, sliced
2 teaspoons fresh thyme leaves
¼ cup minced fresh chives or scallions
5 large eggs
2 cups milk
¼ cup cottage cheese
2 cups shredded Swiss cheese

1 teaspoon salt

½ teaspoon freshly ground black pepper

1. Preheat the oven to 350°F. Lightly grease the baking dish with nonstick cooking spray. Spread the bread cubes in the dish.

2. Cook the bacon over medium-high heat in a large skillet until crisp, stirring occasionally. Line a plate with paper towels, and remove the bacon pieces from the pan to drain. Leave the bacon drippings in the skillet.

3. Turn the heat to high, and add the sliced mushrooms to the skillet in a single layer. Do not stir or move the mushrooms in the first 4 minutes of cooking. When they are quite brown on the bottom, flip them all over and cook without turning for another 3 to 4 minutes. Stir and sauté for an additional 2 to 3 minutes, or until tender. Sprinkle the thyme leaves and chives over the mushrooms and cook for another minute.

4. Whisk the eggs in a large bowl, then whisk in the milk, cottage cheese, Swiss cheese, salt, and pepper. Stir in the cooked mushrooms and bacon. Pour over the bread cubes. (At this point the casserole can be covered and refrigerated overnight.)

5. Cover the casserole with foil and bake for 30 minutes. Uncover and bake 15 to 20 minutes more, or until light golden brown. Serve hot.

Baked Croque Madame
with Ham and Cheese

A CROQUE MADAME is a twist on the *croque monsieur*, the classic French ham-and-cheese egg-battered sandwich. The *croque madame* is topped with an egg, and this casserole takes its breakfast cue from that delicious twist on ham and cheese. ○ *Serves 6 to 8*

CASSEROLE DISH: 9 × 13-inch baking dish
BAKE TIME: 40 minutes, plus 2 to 3 minutes to broil the English muffins

6 English muffins

2 tablespoons unsalted butter, softened

8 ounces (about 8 thick slices) country ham, finely diced

4 ounces Grana Padano cheese

8 large eggs

1 cup sour cream

2 cups milk

1 teaspoon salt

1 teaspoon freshly ground black pepper

1 tablespoon Dijon mustard

1. Preheat the broiler. Split the English muffins and place, cut side up, on a baking sheet. Broil for 2 to 3 minutes, or until just light golden brown. (Watch carefully!) Take out of the oven and spread lightly with the butter. Turn the oven down to 375°F.

2. Cut the English muffins in half, to make half-moons. Lightly grease the baking pan with nonstick cooking spray, and arrange half the English muffin pieces in the bottom of the dish. Spread the diced ham over the muffins, then shave the Grana Padano cheese over the top, using a vegetable peeler to create long strips of cheese. Top with the rest of the toasted English muffins, overlapping them to create a solid top layer.

3. Whisk the eggs, sour cream, milk, salt, pepper, and mustard together in a large bowl. Pour over the English muffin layers. (At this point the casserole can be covered and refrigerated overnight.)

4. Bake, uncovered, for 40 minutes, or until puffed and set in the center. Let stand for 10 minutes before cutting and serving.

Grana Padano Cheese

Grana Padano cheese is similar to the more familiar Parmigiano-Reggiano; they are both produced in northern Italy from cow's milk. But Grana Padano is made from partially skimmed milk, so it's a little lower in fat. It is also usually less expensive than Parmigiano-Reggiano, but still full of flavor.

Flaky Almond Croissant Bake

ONE OF MY VERY FAVORITE PASTRY TREATS is the almond croissant. A long time ago I learned to make this bakery delight at home using day-old croissants and a rich filling of butter, crushed almonds, and sugar. Decadent, right? Well, this casserole is a take on that favorite treat, with flaky, sweet layers of tender croissant, sweet almonds, and custard. It's a special-treat breakfast and utterly delicious. ● *Serves 6*

CASSEROLE DISH: 9 × 13-inch baking dish or 3-quart oval gratin dish
BAKE TIME: 35 minutes

8 to 10 large day-old croissants

FOR THE ALMOND FILLING:
¾ cup unsalted butter, softened and cut into tablespoons
¾ cup granulated sugar
2 large eggs
1 teaspoon vanilla extract
2 cups almond meal

FOR THE MILK CUSTARD:
3 large eggs
1¼ cups milk
⅓ cup granulated sugar
1 teaspoon vanilla extract
¼ teaspoon salt

About ¼ cup sliced toasted almonds
Confectioners' sugar, for serving

1. Preheat the oven to 350°F. Lightly grease the baking dish with butter.

2. Cut each croissant in half crosswise, then split each piece in half like a sandwich. Layer half of the pieces in the bottom of the baking dish, overlapping them so they make a solid layer.

3. To make the almond filling, in a food processor or the bowl of a stand mixer, cream the butter and sugar together. Beat in the eggs thoroughly, then mix in the vanilla and almond meal. Whip until creamy.

4. Spread the filling evenly over the croissants layered in the dish. Layer the remaining croissant halves on top, again overlapping them to make a solid layer.

5. To make the milk custard, beat the eggs thoroughly, then beat in the milk, sugar, vanilla, and salt. Pour over the layered croissants. Sprinkle the dish with the toasted almonds. (At this point the casserole can be covered and refrigerated for up to 24 hours.)

6. Bake, uncovered, for 35 minutes, or until the filling is set and no longer gooey, and the top is golden brown. While the casserole is hot, dust it liberally with confectioners' sugar and more toasted almonds. Let it stand for an additional 10 minutes to cool, then cut into squares and serve warm.

Almond Meal

Almond meal can be purchased in health food stores and at Whole Foods Market; it is often found in the gluten-free section since it is frequently used in GF baking. Look for Bob's Red Mill almond meal or a similar product. You can also make almond meal yourself by grinding almonds in a food processor until they form a gritty powder. The consistency of ground almonds probably won't be as fine as that of commercial almond meal, but it will be perfectly suitable for this recipe. I have used both types of almond meal in almond croissants, and they are equally good.

Lemon Brioche French Toast

FRENCH TOAST is made by pan-frying thick wedges of bread dipped in an egg-and-milk mixture with a little sugar (and nutmeg too!). Baked French toast is very similar, with slices of rich, eggy bread soaked and baked in a light custard. This one has plenty of tangy lemon to cut through the sweetness, and it's a great make-ahead dish for morning brunch guests. ○ *Serves 6*

CASSEROLE DISH: 9 × 13-inch baking dish
BAKE TIME: 30 minutes

One 16-ounce loaf brioche, challah, or other egg-enriched bread
Zest and juice of 2 lemons
3 large eggs
¼ cup brown sugar
3 cups milk
1 teaspoon vanilla extract
¼ teaspoon salt
½ teaspoon ground nutmeg
½ teaspoon ground cinnamon
1½ cups confectioners' sugar, plus more for dusting

1. Preheat the oven to 425°F. Grease the baking dish with nonstick cooking spray or butter.

2. Slice the bread into thick slices, then cut each slice in half. Arrange half of the bread in overlapping layers in the baking dish, then sprinkle the bread with a pinch or two of lemon zest.

3. Whisk the eggs in a large bowl until well beaten, then whisk in the brown sugar. Whisk in the milk, vanilla, salt, nutmeg, cinnamon, and remaining lemon zest. Pour half of the custard over the bread, turning each slice to coat. Layer the rest of the bread on top, and pour the rest of the custard over to coat. (At this point the casserole can be covered and refrigerated for up to 24 hours.)

4. Bake, uncovered, for 30 minutes, or until the top is golden brown and the custard is firm and no longer liquid. Let the casserole sit for at least 10 minutes before serving.

5. Whisk the lemon juice into the confectioners' sugar and drizzle the glaze over the hot casserole. Put a few teaspoons of confectioners' sugar in a small sieve or strainer, and dust the top of the casserole by tapping the strainer lightly over it. Serve in large slices.

Autumn Fruit Strata with Apples, Pears, and Raisins

A STRATA IS AN EASY AND DELICIOUS TAKE on bread pudding—but for breakfast. It's less sweet than the rich baked dessert, but it also calls for a light custard of eggs and milk. This version relies more on fruit and spices for its sweetness and flavor; there isn't very much sugar in it. ○ *Serves 6*

CASSEROLE DISH: 9 × 13-inch baking dish
BAKE TIME: 40 to 50 minutes

1 apple, peeled, cored and diced
1 pear, cored and diced
⅔ cup raisins
Zest and juice of 1 lemon
One 12- to 16-ounce loaf crusty French-style bread, such as a baguette
5 large eggs
2 cups milk
¼ cup sugar
1 teaspoon ground cinnamon
½ teaspoon ground nutmeg
½ teaspoon ground ginger
¼ teaspoon salt

FOR THE CINNAMON SUGAR:
⅓ cup sugar
1 tablespoon ground cinnamon

1. Preheat the oven to 350°F. Lightly grease the baking dish with butter or non-stick cooking spray.

2. In a large bowl, toss the diced apple and pear with the raisins and lemon juice. Cut the bread into 1-inch cubes and toss with the fruit.

3. Whisk the eggs in a medium-size bowl until thoroughly beaten, then whisk in the lemon zest, milk, sugar, cinnamon, nutmeg, ginger, and salt. Pour over the bread and fruit and mix. Pour the mixture into the prepared dish. (At this point the casserole can be covered and refrigerated overnight or for up to 24 hours.)

4. Make the cinnamon sugar by mixing the sugar with the cinnamon; sprinkle evenly over the top of the strata. Bake, uncovered, for 40 to 50 minutes, or until golden brown and fully set. Let cool for 10 minutes before serving.

Whole-Grain Almond-Apricot Bread Pudding

MANY BREAKFAST BREAD CASSEROLES are eggy, rich, and very, very sweet. Casseroles like these are great for special weekend treats but perhaps too rich for every day. This breakfast bread pudding, on the other hand, is made with hearty whole-grain bread and no sugar except for the apricot jam and a bit of honey drizzled over the top. It comes together in a flash, and it's less sweet than those richer casseroles but still deeply satisfying. ● *Serves 6*

CASSEROLE DISH: 3- or 4-quart round baking dish
BAKE TIME: 1 hour

16 ounces hearty whole-grain bread
1 cup apricot jam
1 cup chopped or sliced almonds
5 large eggs
2 cups milk
2 teaspoons vanilla extract
½ teaspoon ground nutmeg
¾ teaspoon salt
Honey, for drizzling

1. Preheat the oven to 350°F. Lightly grease the baking dish with butter or nonstick cooking spray.

2. Cut the bread, including crust, into ½-inch cubes. In a large bowl, toss the bread cubes with the apricot jam and almonds. Spread the mixture in the prepared baking dish.

3. Whisk the eggs in another bowl until thoroughly beaten, then whisk in the milk, vanilla, nutmeg, and salt. Pour over the bread and jam. Press down so the bread is fully moistened and submerged. (At this point the casserole can be covered and refrigerated overnight or for up to 24 hours.)

4. Bake, uncovered, for 1 hour, or until golden brown and fully set. Drizzle a little honey over the casserole when you take it out of the oven. Let cool for 10 minutes before serving.

To Soak or Not To Soak

Bread-based casseroles will be somewhat changed by an overnight soak before baking. If you leave a casserole like this one in the fridge overnight, it will absorb the eggs and milk a little more evenly, resulting in a more uniform final texture. This isn't necessarily a better thing; it's just a difference in texture. This casserole and the others like it in this chapter are equally good when assembled, baked, and eaten in one morning. But the layers will be more distinct and will retain more of their bread texture.

Cinnamon Roll Breakfast Bake

THIS IS A TOTAL WINNER of a breakfast casserole, eye-rollingly sweet and rich, with flaky layers of bread and creamy cinnamon-flavored cream cheese sandwiched together. It's just as good as a tray of hot cinnamon rolls, and while it's not an everyday dish, it is definitely the one to pull out for Christmas morning or when company comes for brunch. ○ *Serves 6*

CASSEROLE DISH: 9 × 13-inch baking dish
BAKE TIME: 50 minutes

One 12- to 16-ounce loaf good-quality white bread (such as Italian or French bread from the bakery), crusts removed, cut in half lengthwise and then into thin slices

FOR THE CUSTARD:
5 large eggs
2¼ cups milk
2 tablespoons granulated sugar

1 teaspoon vanilla extract

1 teaspoon ground cinnamon

½ teaspoon ground nutmeg

¼ teaspoon salt

FOR THE CINNAMON CHEESE FILLING:

8 ounces cream cheese, softened

2 tablespoons unsalted butter, softened

1 large egg

1 tablespoon ground cinnamon

¼ cup granulated sugar

Ground cinnamon, for sprinkling

Confectioners' sugar, for sprinkling

1. Preheat the oven to 325°F. Lightly grease the baking dish with butter or non-stick cooking spray.

2. Layer half of the bread slices in the baking dish, overlapping and wedging them in tightly so they are in an almost solid layer.

3. To make the custard, whisk the eggs until fully beaten, then whisk in the milk, sugar, vanilla, cinnamon, nutmeg, and salt. Pour half of this custard over the bread in the baking dish, letting it settle in and soak the bread thoroughly. Set aside the rest of the custard.

4. To make the filling, in the bowl of a stand mixer or with a handheld mixer, beat the softened cream cheese with the butter, egg, cinnamon, and sugar. Beat until very soft and whipped. Spread over the layer of bread and custard in the pan. Layer the rest of the bread over the cream cheese filling and pour the rest of the custard on top. (At this point the casserole can be covered and refrigerated for up to 24 hours.)

5. Sprinkle with extra cinnamon. Bake, uncovered, for about 50 minutes, or until it is firmly set. Cool for 15 minutes, sprinkle with confectioners' sugar, and serve.

Summer Egg and Potato Breakfast Bake

EGGS AND POTATOES make a simple and economical breakfast—or supper! This recipe does not call for any meat, so it's suitable for vegetarians and omnivores alike, but if you like you can add a cup of cooked, crumbled sausage or a half cup of cooked, crumbled bacon. ◦ *Serves 6*

CASSEROLE DISH: 9 × 13-inch baking dish
BAKE TIME: 35 minutes

1 tablespoon olive oil
1 small onion, diced
2 cloves garlic, minced
⅓ cup sun-dried tomatoes (dry or oil-packed), chopped
1 yellow bell pepper, cored and diced
1 red bell pepper, cored and diced
2 teaspoons salt
8 large eggs
1 cup milk
1 teaspoon freshly cracked black pepper
2 cups shredded Monterey Jack cheese
One 32-ounce bag cubed frozen potatoes (see Note)

1. Preheat the oven to 350°F. Lightly grease the baking dish with nonstick cooking spray or butter.

2. In a large skillet, heat the olive oil over medium heat. When hot, add the onion and cook for about 5 minutes, or until it starts to look translucent. Add the garlic, sun-dried tomatoes, bell peppers, and 1 teaspoon of the salt, and cook over medium heat until all the vegetables are fragrant and soft, about 5 more minutes. Turn off the heat and let cool slightly.

3. In a separate bowl, beat the eggs thoroughly and whisk in the milk. Stir in the remaining 1 teaspoon of salt and the black pepper. Mix in the cheese, frozen potatoes, and the vegetables from the skillet. Transfer the mixture to the prepared baking dish. (At this point the casserole can be covered and refrigerated for up to 24 hours.)

4. Bake, uncovered, for 35 minutes, or until the eggs are firm and the top is slightly golden. Serve immediately.

Note: This recipe calls for frozen potatoes for the sake of convenience. But if you don't have frozen potatoes or would prefer to use fresh potatoes, substitute 1 medium-size potato for each cup of frozen potatoes. Prick the potatoes several times with a fork, then place in the microwave on a paper towel. Cook on HIGH until the potatoes are just barely tender (the time will vary depending on your microwave and how many potatoes you do at a time). Dice and proceed with the recipe.

Gruyère and Spinach Egg Puff

L IKE MOST OF THE OTHER EGG CASSEROLES in this book, this egg puff has no meat (who needs meat, with all those eggs?), and it's very inexpensive to make. It's also just as good for dinner as it is for breakfast; instead of serving it with toast and a side of bananas, slice a rustic loaf of bread and serve a crisp green salad. ○ *Serves 6*

CASSEROLE DISH: 9 × 13-inch baking dish
BAKE TIME: 30 minutes

One 16-ounce bag frozen chopped spinach
2 teaspoons salt
1 tablespoon olive oil
1 medium onion, diced
2 cloves garlic, minced
6 large eggs
1½ cups milk
¼ teaspoon ground nutmeg
1 cup grated Gruyère cheese

1. Preheat the oven to 350°F. Lightly grease the baking dish with nonstick cooking spray or olive oil.

2. Dump the frozen spinach out of the bag into a colander set in the sink. Rinse for a moment with cold water to help the spinach begin to thaw. When it is coated with water, toss with 1 teaspoon of the salt and place a heavy bowl on top to weigh it down. Let thaw and drain while cooking the onion.

3. Heat the olive oil in a large skillet over medium heat. Cook the onion and garlic for 5 to 7 minutes, or until soft and fragrant.

4. Press the spinach down hard and drain off as much excess water as you can. Press lightly with paper towels to remove a bit more water, then add the spinach to the onions and cook, stirring frequently, for another 3 to 4 minutes. The spinach should be wilted and the onion and garlic fully mixed in. Turn off the heat, drain any excess liquid out of the skillet, and set aside to cool.

5. Thoroughly beat the eggs in a large bowl and whisk in the milk. Beat in the remaining 1 teaspoon salt and the nutmeg. Stir in the spinach mixture and cheese. Pour into the baking dish and bake for 30 minutes, or until just barely set. Let cool for 5 minutes, then serve.

Wonderful Gruyère

Gruyère is a hard cheese from Switzerland with a slightly sweet/salty taste; it's pungent, but in a good way. It's one of my favorite cheeses to pair with eggs. Its mellow, savory taste really enhances them, and the underlying nutty flavors round out egg dishes well. If you want or need to substitute another cheese, then Swiss Emmenthaler will also do, although it's really quite different. The supermarket cheese labeled "Swiss" imitates Emmenthaler, and that will also serve in a pinch. But the Gruyère is really worth finding; in a rather inexpensive casserole it elevates all the flavors around it,

Smoky Baked Hash Browns

HASH BROWNS are classic home-style diner food. But it takes an astonishing amount of butter to create those pan-fried cakes of shredded potatoes! This recipe lightens up the classic hash browns a little by baking them in the oven instead of frying them. They are crispy on the outside and light and creamy inside, with notes of smoke and spice from the smoked paprika—also known as *pimentón* or Spanish paprika. When they come out of the oven they're flipped upside down, revealing a smoky, crispy, crunchy plateful of oven-fried potatoes. Delicious!

○ *Serves 4*

CASSEROLE DISH: 10-inch cast-iron skillet
BAKE TIME: 45 minutes

One 15-ounce bag frozen hash browns
2 teaspoons smoked paprika (or 1½ teaspoons paprika plus ½ teaspoon chili powder)
1½ teaspoons kosher salt
1 teaspoon freshly ground black pepper
4 scallions (white and green parts), chopped
¼ cup olive oil
1 large egg, lightly beaten
2 tablespoons unsalted butter

1. Preheat the oven to 425°F. Take the frozen hash browns out of the bag and spread them out between 2 layers of paper towels or clean kitchen towels to absorb any excess moisture.

2. Put the hash browns in a large bowl and toss with the smoked paprika, salt, pepper, scallions, and olive oil. Stir in the beaten egg.

3. Place the cast-iron skillet over high heat. When the skillet is quite hot, melt the butter. When the butter foams up, add the hash brown mixture. Immediately put the skillet in the oven. Bake for 45 minutes, or until the top is golden brown and the potatoes are crispy around the edges.

4. Have a large platter ready. Remove the cast iron pan from the oven and flip the hash browns out upside down onto the platter. Serve immediately.

Herbed Egg White, Zucchini, and Potato Skillet

MANY CASSEROLES are heavy with cheese, milk, and lots of eggs. This one lightens things up a bit with egg whites, but it's still big on flavor. There's the delicate flavor of the herbs and the sweet summer taste of the zucchini, with thinly sliced potatoes between layers of egg white to hold everything together. Light, refreshing, and still quite filling! ❍ *Serves 4*

CASSEROLE DISH: 10-inch cast-iron skillet
BAKE TIME: 20 minutes

1 medium-size zucchini or yellow summer squash, sliced into very thin rounds
1 teaspoon salt
Several sprigs fresh thyme (leaves only)
One 4-inch sprig fresh rosemary (leaves only)
1½ pounds small red potatoes, sliced very thin
8 scallions (white and green parts), sliced
Olive oil
Small handful (about ¼ cup) fresh flat-leaf parsley, finely chopped
8 egg whites
2 large eggs
1¼ cups shredded Swiss cheese
½ teaspoon dry mustard
Freshly ground black pepper

1. Preheat the oven to 350°F. Prepare the cast-iron skillet by rubbing it lightly with olive oil.

2. Put the sliced zucchini in a colander and sprinkle with the salt. Set the colander in the sink to drain. (This draws some of the excess moisture out of the zucchini, and it will also remove some of its natural bitterness.)

3. Mince the leaves of the thyme and rosemary. Set the cast-iron pan over medium heat and add the potatoes, scallions, thyme, and rosemary, with a little extra drizzle of olive oil. Cook, stirring occasionally, for about 20 minutes, or until the potatoes are tender.

4. When the potatoes are quite soft, turn the heat to high and cook the potatoes until golden brown. Add the zucchini and chopped parsley and cook for another few minutes, or until the zucchini is just beginning to soften. Take the pan off the heat.

5. Whisk the egg whites with the eggs in a large bowl, and stir in 1 cup of the cheese, the dry mustard, and black pepper to taste. Pour over the zucchini and potatoes in the skillet and sprinkle with the remaining ¼ cup of cheese.

6. Put the skillet in the oven and bake for 20 minutes. When set and slightly puffed on top, remove from the oven and let stand for several minutes. Cut into wedges and serve hot.

Basic Oven Omelet

LIGHT AND FLUFFY OMELETS, brimming with delicious fillings, are a staple of breakfasts all over the United States. There are simple omelets, complicated omelets, heavy cheesy omelets, and light and airy omelets. This particular version is an easy omelet. It's baked in the oven instead of cooked and flipped in a skillet, and it bakes into that fluffy, light texture that we all love in a good morning omelet. ❍ *Serves 6*

CASSEROLE DISH: 9 × 13-inch baking dish
BAKE TIME: 45 minutes

10 large eggs
2 cups milk
1 cup grated Parmesan cheese
1 cup diced cooked ham
¼ cup finely chopped fresh flat-leaf parsley
1 teaspoon salt
Freshly ground black pepper

1. Preheat the oven to 375°F. Lightly grease the baking dish with olive oil or non-stick cooking spray.

2. Beat the eggs in a large bowl and whisk in the milk. Stir in the cheese, diced ham, and parsley. Season with 1 teaspoon of the salt and pepper to taste, and pour into the prepared pan. (At this point the casserole can be covered and refrigerated for up to 24 hours.)

3. Bake, uncovered, for 45 minutes, or until the top is slightly golden and a knife inserted in the middle comes out clean. Let cool for 5 minutes before slicing. Serve hot.

Oven Omelet with Caramelized Onions and Mushrooms

ONCE YOU'VE MASTERED the basic oven omelet, the sky's the limit! Try it with all your favorite omelet mix-ins and variations. Here's a popular version—mushrooms are always a good winter option. ● *Serves 6*

CASSEROLE DISH: 9 × 13-inch baking dish
BAKE TIME: 45 minutes

2 tablespoons unsalted butter
1 large onion, thinly sliced
1 pound white mushrooms, sliced
1 small sprig fresh rosemary (leaves only)
Salt and freshly ground black pepper
10 large eggs
2 cups milk
1 cup grated Asiago or Gruyère cheese

1. Preheat the oven to 375°F. Lightly grease the baking dish with olive oil or non-stick cooking spray.

2. In a large skillet, melt 1 tablespoon of the butter over medium-high heat. When it foams, add the onion slices. Cook, stirring frequently, for 10 to 15 minutes, or until the onions are deeply brown. Transfer the onions to a bowl and set aside.

3. Melt the remaining 1 tablespoon of butter in the skillet and add the mushrooms in an even layer. Let them cook for 5 minutes without flipping or stirring them. When their bottoms get golden and crusty, add the rosemary, stir, and cook for another 5 minutes. Sprinkle with a little salt and pepper. Remove from the heat and stir the mushrooms into the caramelized onions.

4. Beat the eggs in a large bowl and whisk in the milk. Stir in the cheese and the mushroom-onion mixture. Season with salt and pepper and pour into the prepared pan. (At this point the casserole can be covered and refrigerated for up to 24 hours.)

5. Bake, uncovered, for 45 minutes, or until the top is slightly golden and a knife inserted in the middle comes out clean. Let cool for 5 minutes before slicing. Serve hot.

Baked Denver Omelet

HERE'S ONE MORE POPULAR OVEN OMELET: the Denver, or Western, omelet. It's full of good vegetables and country ham, and it's a great dish to serve on a sunny summer morning. It's colorful and cheery, with red and green peppers and white onion, and it makes a lovely presentation with slices of bright oranges and brown toast. o *Serves 6*

CASSEROLE DISH: 9 × 13-inch baking dish
BAKE TIME: 45 minutes

Olive oil
1 large white onion, diced
1 green bell pepper, cored and diced
1 red bell pepper, cored and diced
8 ounces (8 thick slices) country-style ham, diced
10 large eggs
2 cups milk
1 teaspoon salt
Freshly ground black pepper

1. Preheat the oven to 375°F. Lightly grease the baking dish with olive oil or nonstick cooking spray.

2. In a large skillet, heat a drizzle of olive oil over medium heat. When the oil is hot, add the diced onion, bell peppers, and ham. Cook, stirring frequently, for about 5 minutes, or until the onion turns translucent and the peppers are soft and fragrant. Turn off the heat and set aside to cool.

3. Beat the eggs in a large bowl and whisk in the milk. Whisk in the salt and several grinds of fresh black pepper. Pour into the prepared dish. (At this point the casserole can be covered and refrigerated for up to 24 hours.)

4. Bake, uncovered, for 45 minutes, or until the top is slightly golden and a knife inserted in the middle comes out clean. Let cool for 5 minutes before slicing. Serve hot.

Leek and Lemon Frittata

LEMONS COOKED INTO EGGS make a dynamite combination. Eggs are sweet and mellow, while lemon is tangy and sharp. The two belong together, and if you don't believe me, try this easy frittata. This doesn't spend much time in the oven at all—it's mostly cooked on the stovetop. This is also a great breakfast to make ahead of time, since the frittata develops even more flavor as it sits in the fridge. It's good eaten cold, lukewarm, or hot. To reheat, place in a low oven (about 300°F) for about 15 minutes. ○ *Serves 4 to 6*

CASSEROLE DISH: 10-inch cast-iron or other ovenproof skillet
BAKE TIME: 3 to 5 minutes

7 large eggs
Zest of 1 lemon
4 ounces goat cheese
1 tablespoon olive oil, plus more if needed
2 large leeks, cut lengthwise, rinsed, trimmed, and sliced into half-moons
¼ cup fresh flat-leaf parsley, chopped
Salt and freshly ground black pepper

1. Preheat the broiler. In a large bowl, whisk the eggs until slightly bubbly and well mixed, then stir in the lemon zest. Crumble in the goat cheese. Set aside.

2. Heat the olive oil in the skillet over medium heat. Cook the leeks in the hot skillet for 10 minutes, or until they are fragrant and softened. Stir in the parsley and cook just until wilted.

3. Remove the pan from the heat and add salt and pepper to taste. Let cool slightly, then scrape all of the cooked leeks and parsley into the beaten egg mixture.

4. Put the skillet back on the heat and film lightly with a little more olive oil if necessary. Pour the egg and leek mixture in and cook over medium-low heat for 10 to 15 minutes, or until the frittata has set on the bottom. Use a spatula to lift up the edges and make sure it's cooking evenly, letting the uncooked eggs run down into the bottom of the pan.

5. When the bottom of the frittata has set, put the skillet under the broiler for 3 to 5 minutes, or until the top is golden brown and slightly puffy. Remove from the oven and let rest for 5 minutes. Flip the frittata out onto a platter and serve immediately in big wedges.

Basic Baked Eggs

BAKED EGGS ARE ONE OF THE EASIEST, prettiest ways to cook eggs, but they don't get much respect or attention compared to the almighty omelet and quick scrambled eggs. That's a shame, because they are just so unbelievably easy. They're also called shirred eggs or *oeufs en cocotte*, both old-fashioned names for a classic dish. Their ease and style make them very modern and chic, and they're the perfect egg dish for a brunch crowd. **o** *Serves 6*

CASSEROLE DISH: 9-inch pie dish or twelve 6-ounce ramekins
BAKE TIME: 10 to 20 minutes

12 large eggs
¼ cup finely grated Parmesan cheese (optional)
Salt and freshly ground black pepper

1. Preheat the oven to 375°F. Lightly grease the pie dish or ramekins with olive oil.

2. Crack 1 egg into each ramekin, or crack all the eggs into the pie dish. (The whites will run together in the dish, but the yolks will remain distinct and separate.) If using Parmesan, lightly sprinkle the eggs with a bit of cheese. Season generously with salt and pepper.

3. Bake for 10 to 20 minutes. The baking time will depend on the type of dish you use and how set you prefer your eggs. The whites should be opaque, at least, and the tops of the yolks shouldn't be liquid. You may enjoy your eggs runny; if so, bake for just 10 to 12 minutes and this recipe will give you beautifully jammy and runny egg yolks! Serve immediately.

Water Baths

Some instructions for baked eggs call for placing the ramekins in a larger pan half-filled with water, known as a water bath or bain-marie. This helps the eggs cook more evenly and can result in a creamier texture. Personally, I find it a little fussy and not worth the extra work and hot water slopping around in the oven. You may feel otherwise, however, and if you often find your eggs overcooked, try baking them in a water bath. You will need to add a few minutes to the cook time.

Eggs en Cocotte with Cream, Thyme, and Prosciutto

THE BASIC BAKED-EGG RECIPE is just a template for all sorts of delicious baked-egg goodness. I love to bake eggs in a little milk or cream with herbs or pepper for a custardy treat that's perfect for dipping toast. Here's one favorite combination of flavors, inspired by the breakfast menu at the chic French bistro Balthazar in New York City. ○ *Serves 6*

CASSEROLE DISH: Twelve 6-ounce ramekins
BAKE TIME: 15 to 20 minutes

¾ cup heavy cream
½ teaspoon salt, plus more as needed

Freshly ground black pepper

4 sprigs fresh thyme (leaves only)

6 thin slices prosciutto, chopped

12 large eggs

⅓ cup finely grated Grana Padano cheese

1. Preheat the oven to 375°F. Lightly grease the ramekins with olive oil.

2. Whisk the heavy cream in a bowl with the ½ teaspoon salt, a few grinds of black pepper, and the thyme leaves. Spoon 2 tablespoons of the cream mixture into each ramekin, and evenly divide the chopped prosciutto among the ramekins.

3. Crack 1 egg into each ramekin. Season lightly with salt and pepper. Bake for 15 to 20 minutes. The final baking time will depend on how set you prefer your eggs. The whites should be opaque, at least, and the tops of the yolks shouldn't be liquid. You may enjoy your eggs runny; if so, this recipe will give you beautifully jammy and runny egg yolks!

4. Immediately top with pinches of Grana Padano cheese and serve hot.

Baked Scrambled Eggs for a Crowd

GOOD SCRAMBLED EGGS are a labor-intensive dish. The best scrambled eggs are cooked on the stovetop over the barest whisper of a flame, stirred constantly and attended to lovingly. That's just not very practical, though, when you have other things to manage in the morning. This recipe for baked scrambled eggs makes enough to serve a full breakfast table, but it's nearly hands-off.

Serves 6

CASSEROLE DISH: 8-inch square glass baking dish

BAKE TIME: 20 to 25 minutes

12 large eggs

3 tablespoons unsalted butter, melted

1 cup milk

1 teaspoon salt

½ teaspoon freshly ground black pepper

1. Preheat the oven to 325°F. Lightly grease the baking dish with nonstick cooking spray or olive oil.

2. Beat the eggs thoroughly in a large bowl. Whisk in the butter, milk, salt, and pepper. Pour into the prepared baking dish and bake for 20 to 25 minutes. Stir at least once while the eggs are baking. The more frequently you stir them, the more they will look like stovetop scrambled eggs. The eggs are done when set and no longer runny. Serve immediately.

Baked Scrambled Eggs

Baked scrambled eggs are one of the best-kept secrets of the oven. They are creamy, fast, and so easy! Just keep an eye on them as they bake, since near the end of their baking time they go very quickly from creamy deliciousness to rubbery unpleasantness. Stir them halfway through the baking process (at about the 10-minute mark), then again at about 18 minutes, checking every minute or so after that until they are done to your liking.

Bacon and Lentils with Egg

HAVE YOU EVER EATEN LENTILS FOR BREAKFAST? This is one of those breakfast dishes that is really just as good for lunch or dinner. It's flexible; after you make up a batch of soft, mashed lentils with spices, you can serve them for any meal of the day. Serve this with Indian lime pickle or a spicy chutney.

o *Serves 6*

CASSEROLE DISH: Six 6-ounce ramekins
BAKE TIME: 15 to 20 minutes

4 slices bacon, cut into 1-inch pieces
4 shallots or ½ red onion, minced
2 cloves garlic, minced
2 teaspoons garam masala
2 cups red or yellow lentils, rinsed and drained
½ cup fresh cilantro leaves, chopped

4 cups water
Salt and freshly ground black pepper
6 eggs

1. Place the bacon in a 2-quart (or larger) saucepan and place over medium-low heat. Cook the bacon slowly, stirring occasionally, for about 10 minutes, or until it is crisp.

2. Turn the heat to medium and add the shallots and garlic. Cook, stirring, for about 5 minutes, then add the garam masala and lentils. Stir so the lentils are coated with the oil and garlic, then add the cilantro and cook until it is wilted.

3. Add the water and turn the heat to high. Bring to a boil, then cover and lower to a simmer. Cook for about 20 minutes. If the lentils are too watery at the end, leave the lid off for a few minutes until the liquid is reduced and the lentils are nearly dry. Turn off the heat and taste. Season the lentils with salt and pepper, then lightly mash them with a fork.

4. Preheat the oven to 350°F. Lightly grease the ramekins with baking spray or olive oil. Mound a few spoonfuls of the lentils in each (you may have some lentils left over), then make a hollow in the center of the lentils with the back of a spoon and crack in an egg. Sprinkle with salt and pepper. Bake for 15 to 20 minutes, or until the whites are just set. Serve immediately.

Sweet Potato Hash with Eggs, Turkey Bacon, and Red Peppers

S WEET POTATOES AND EGGS make a robust morning combination, with vibrant colors for a bright breakfast table and a healthy helping of vitamins in those tender orange potatoes. This particular version of breakfast hash is an homage to my favorite local restaurant, which serves sweet potatoes well seasoned with spicy peppers and with a beautiful egg cracked on top. ○ *Serves 6*

CASSEROLE DISH: 9 × 13-inch baking dish
BAKE TIME: 45 to 50 minutes

3 medium-size sweet potatoes, scrubbed and chopped into 1-inch chunks

1 medium onion, diced

4 slices turkey bacon, diced

1 large red bell pepper, cored and diced

2 large cloves garlic, minced

¼ teaspoon red pepper flakes (optional)

4 to 6 sprigs fresh thyme (leaves only)

¼ cup olive oil

1 teaspoon salt

Freshly cracked black pepper

6 to 12 eggs (1 or 2 per person)

1. Preheat the oven to 450°F. Lightly grease the baking dish with olive oil.

2. In large mixing bowl, toss the sweet potato chunks, diced onion, bacon, bell pepper, garlic, red pepper flakes (if using), and thyme. Add the olive oil, salt, and pepper and toss. Spread evenly in the baking dish and roast on the top oven rack for about 30 minutes, or until the vegetables are soft and beginning to brown.

3. Turn the oven down to 375°F. Slide the pan out of the oven, and crack 6 to 12 eggs on top of the sweet potatoes. (Adjust the quantity of eggs to fit the diners' appetites.) Season lightly with salt and pepper and return to the oven. Bake for another 15 to 20 minutes, or until the egg whites are set. Serve immediately.

Herbed Egg and Bacon Quiche

N**O DISCUSSION OF BREAKFAST** from the oven would be complete without quiche. Here is just one basic recipe for quiche; you can easily adapt this egg pie to your own taste. It's very simple: Follow the basic template below, then add and subtract mix-ins until you find your favorite combination. This version is one of my favorites. ○ *Serves 6*

CASSEROLE DISH: 9-inch pie plate
BAKE TIME: 10 to 12 minutes for the crust; 35 to 40 minutes for the quiche

One 9-inch pre-made pie crust, unbaked

4 slices bacon, chopped

¼ cup mixed fresh herbs, such as sage, rosemary, chives, and thyme

3 large eggs

1½ cups half-and-half

½ teaspoon salt

½ teaspoon freshly ground black pepper

1 cup grated Swiss cheese

1. Preheat the oven to 450°F. Fit the pie dough into your pie plate, or place the foil pie plate with crust inside a ceramic plate of your own. Lightly prick the dough all over with a fork. Bake according to package directions, and put the baked pie crust on a rack to cool. Lower the oven temperature to 350°F.

2. Cook the bacon in a cast-iron or other heavy skillet over moderately high heat for 10 minutes or until crisp, stirring occasionally. While the bacon cooks, finely chop the herbs. As the bacon is beginning to get crisp, stir in the herbs and cook until they wilt and the bacon becomes quite crisp. Remove from the heat and lift out the cooked bacon and herbs with a slotted spoon, placing them on a small plate lined with paper towels.

3. Whisk the eggs thoroughly in a large bowl, then whisk in the half-and-half, salt, and pepper. Stir in the bacon and herbs and the Swiss cheese.

4. Pour the mixture into the pie crust. Bake until the filling is just set, 35 to 40 minutes. Let the quiche cool for at least 20 minutes before serving.

Egg and Tortilla Casserole

THIS IS A MEATLESS BRUNCH DISH that is extremely fast and easy to put together. It makes use of some easy convenience ingredients, too, like canned chile peppers, shredded cheese, and jarred salsa. Of course, if you make your own salsa, use that instead! If you want to use fresh chiles, too, go for it. And if you'd like to include a little meat, add some cooked crumbled Mexican chorizo or other sausage to the filling. ○ *Serves 4*

CASSEROLE DISH: 9-inch square baking dish
BAKE TIME: 35 minutes

Twelve 6-inch corn tortillas
1 bunch scallions (white and green parts), chopped
1 cup tomato salsa, plus more for serving
One 4-ounce can diced green chiles, drained
1 cup shredded Monterey Jack cheese
1½ cups shredded cheddar cheese
5 large eggs
1 teaspoon salt
1 teaspoon ground cumin
¼ teaspoon freshly ground black pepper
Avocado slices, for serving
Sour cream, for serving

1. Preheat the oven to 350°F. Lightly grease the baking dish with olive oil.

2. Lay 4 tortillas in the dish, overlapping slightly so they cover the bottom of the dish.

3. Mix the scallions, salsa, chiles, Monterey Jack cheese, and 1 cup of the cheddar cheese in a bowl. Spread half of the mixture over the tortillas in the dish. Layer another 4 tortillas on top, then spread with the rest of the salsa-cheese mixture. Lay the 4 remaining tortillas on top.

4. Whisk the eggs in a bowl with the salt, cumin, and black pepper. Pour over the tortilla stack in the dish. Sprinkle the top with the remaining ½ cup of cheddar cheese. (At this point the casserole can be covered and refrigerated overnight. If you refrigerate it, let it come to room temperature for at least 15 minutes before baking.)

5. Bake, uncovered, for 35 minutes, or until the tortilla stack is firm and cooked through. Let cool for 5 minutes, then cut into squares or wedges and serve with avocado, sour cream, and extra salsa.

Baked Huevos Rancheros

HUEVOS RANCHEROS is a rustic Mexican dish that has spread all over the world. It's especially common to see big plates of huevos rancheros served in restaurants in California and the American Southwest. It's a simple home-style breakfast—corn tortillas topped with a zesty, chunky tomato sauce and an egg—that's easily made in the oven. ○ *Serves 6*

CASSEROLE DISH: Large rimmed baking sheet or two 9 × 13-inch baking dishes
BAKE TIME: 25 to 30 minutes

1 tablespoon olive oil
1 large onion, diced
1 clove garlic, minced
1 large green bell pepper, cored and diced
½ teaspoon ground cumin
¼ teaspoon salt
2 medium tomatoes, chopped
One 4-ounce can chopped green chiles (optional)
Six 6-inch corn tortillas
6 large eggs
1 cup shredded cheddar cheese

Sour cream
Black beans
Chopped black olives
Salsa
Avocado slices

1. Preheat the oven to 425°F.

2. Heat the olive oil in a large skillet over medium-high heat. When the oil is hot, add the onion, garlic, and bell pepper, and cook for 5 to 6 minutes, or until the vegetables are soft. Season with the cumin and salt, and then add the tomatoes and chiles, if using. Lower the heat to medium and cook for another 8 to 10 minutes, or until the tomatoes are hot and somewhat broken down. Turn off the heat. (This sauce can be made up to 3 days ahead of time and stored in the refrigerator.)

3. Lay the tortillas out in 2 rows on the baking sheet or in a single row in the baking dishes. Top each tortilla with a spoonful of the tomato sauce and crack an egg on top. Sprinkle evenly with the cheese. Bake for 25 to 30 minutes, or until the eggs are set.

4. Serve immediately with sour cream, black beans, olives, salsa, and avocado.

Oven Breakfast Burritos with Chorizo and Beans

BREAKFAST BURRITOS are my husband's specialty. He used to work in a co-op at college where he would help serve breakfast to hundreds of hungry graduate students. He would fill, roll, and wrap dozens of made-to-order breakfast burritos every morning, and you can eat one of his burritos down to the very end without it falling apart in your hands. These burritos are a little easier to prep; you don't have to put them together on the fly for each person at the table, and they'll arrive hot all at once. So practice your rolling and wrapping skills, and serve up burritos for breakfast! ○ *Serves 6*

CASSEROLE DISH: 9 × 13-inch baking dish
BAKE TIME: 20 minutes

1 tablespoon olive oil
1 teaspoon whole cumin seeds
¾ pound fresh chorizo sausage, casings removed, crumbled
1 small onion, diced
1 fresh green chile, seeded and diced
½ teaspoon salt
¼ teaspoon freshly ground black pepper
6 large eggs
One 12-ounce can black beans, rinsed and drained
½ cup shredded Monterey Jack cheese
6 large flour tortillas, at least 8 inches across

½ cup shredded cheddar cheese
Salsa, for serving
Sour cream, for serving

1. Preheat the oven to 375°F. Lightly grease the baking dish with olive oil.

2. Add the 1 tablespoon olive oil to a large skillet. Heat over medium-high heat, then add the cumin seeds. Cook, shaking the pan vigorously, for about 1 minute, or until the seeds start to smell toasty. Scoop the seeds out of the pan with a spoon and put them on a small plate to cool.

3. Return the pan to medium-high heat, and cook the crumbled chorizo for several minutes, or until well browned. Add the onion and chile, and cook until the onion is tender and translucent, about 6 minutes. Take off the heat and stir in the cumin seeds, salt, and pepper.

4. Beat the eggs in a large bowl. Stir in the black beans, Jack cheese, and the chorizo mixture. The mixture will be very chunky, with the egg just binding it together. Spoon a big spoonful into a tortilla and wrap it up like a burrito, folding in one side, then the ends, and then the other side over everything. Keep it as tight as you can, and put the finished burrito seam-side down in the prepared baking pan. Repeat with all the tortillas and filling. Sprinkle the cheddar cheese over the top of the burritos. (At this point the casserole can be covered and refrigerated for up to 24 hours.)

5. Bake the burritos, uncovered, for 20 minutes, or until the cheese inside is gooey and the eggs are cooked. Serve immediately with salsa and sour cream.

Hot Starters and Spreads from the Oven

I love starting dinner parties with a hot bite or appetizer. It's fun, hospitable, and a great way to welcome people to the table. Some of my favorite appetizers are super-simple, like little wedges of cheese with jam and crackers, or a bowlful of fresh grapes. But I also

love hors d'oeuvres that are baked in the oven. Think about Double-Baked Mini Potatoes with Bacon (page 79) or cubes of sourdough bread tossed with cheese and quickly roasted for hot, crispy, chewy Cheesy Bread Bites (page 83).

This chapter has a small selection of fresh and classic recipes for oven-baked appetizers and starters. Some of them, like the Roasted Red Onion Jam (page 82) and the Slow-Roasted Tomatoes with Garlicky Bread Crumb Topping (page 77) are easy, hands-off ways to make really versatile staples. These jammy spreads can be eaten on crackers and bread or tossed with pasta for an easy meal.

Other appetizers in this chapter are true crowd-pleasers and great for a football party or a casual weekend gathering. The Baked White Bean Dip with Rosemary and Parmesan (page 70) is elegant, delicious, and fairly healthy, too, while the Fresh Spinach and Asiago Dip in a Bread Boule (page 71) is surprisingly easy to make.

These are good recipes and templates to start you playing around with your own cupboard staples and favorite ingredients; try creating your own style of bean dip, tailored to your tastes, or roasting your favorite vegetables in tiny, skewerable bites.

Fresh Tex-Mex 8-Layer Dip

SEVEN-LAYER DIP is an absolutely classic party dish. It's very rich and creamy, a special treat for a summer party or movie night. This dip adds an extra layer of cheese for even more hot, gooey goodness from the oven. ○ *Serves 10*

CASSEROLE DISH: 9-inch glass pie dish or 9-inch square baking dish
BAKE TIME: 30 minutes

One 15-ounce can refried beans
½ teaspoon chili powder or chipotle chile powder
1 teaspoon ground cumin
¼ cup water
2 tablespoons olive oil
1½ cups shredded cheddar cheese
1 cup tomato salsa, plus more for serving
1½ cups shredded Monterey Jack cheese
1 avocado, peeled and cut into small pieces
⅓ cup sour cream
4 scallions, minced
½ cup sliced black olives
Tortilla chips, for serving

1. Preheat the oven to 375°F. Lightly grease the baking dish with nonstick cooking spray.

2. In a medium-size bowl, mix the refried beans, chili powder, cumin, water, and olive oil. Stir until the mixture is creamy and spreadable. Spread in an even layer in the bottom of the baking dish. Top with a layer of cheddar cheese. Cover with the salsa, then a layer of Monterey Jack cheese. Cover with pieces of avocado, then the sour cream, then the scallions and olives. (At this point the casserole can be covered and refrigerated for up to 24 hours.)

3. Cover with aluminum foil and bake for 20 minutes. Remove the foil and bake for an additional 10 minutes, or until the cheese is gooey and melted, and the dip is hot all the way through. Serve immediately with extra salsa and tortilla chips.

Baked White Bean Dip with Rosemary and Parmesan

BEANS ARE A MUCH-NEGLECTED INGREDIENT in cooking today. They can be rich, creamy, and unctuous without the addition of too much fat. A hot swirl of beans like this one is just as creamy and delicious as a baked appetizer with lots of cheese, but much healthier. Don't eat this just because it's nutritious, though; eat it because it's delicious! ○ *Serves 4*

CASSEROLE DISH: 1-quart gratin dish
BAKE TIME: 18 to 20 minutes

One 15-ounce can cannellini or Great Northern beans, rinsed and drained
1 clove garlic, minced
One 3-inch sprig fresh rosemary (leaves only)
2 shallots or ¼ small red onion, chopped
¼ cup whole-milk yogurt
3 tablespoons olive oil
¼ teaspoon salt
¼ teaspoon freshly ground black pepper
¼ cup dry bread crumbs
¼ cup grated Parmesan cheese
Pita chips, small rye toasts, or fresh cucumber slices, for serving

1. Preheat the oven to 350°F. Lightly grease the gratin dish with olive oil.

2. Put the beans into a food processor along with the garlic, rosemary leaves, and shallot. Blend in pulses until well pureed.

3. Add the yogurt, 1 tablespoon of the olive oil, and the salt and pepper, and blend until creamy. Pour into the prepared baking dish.

4. Combine the bread crumbs, Parmesan, and remaining 2 tablespoons of olive oil. Sprinkle evenly over the pureed white beans. (At this point the casserole can be covered and refrigerated for up to 24 hours.) Bake, uncovered, for 18 to 20 minutes, or until the topping is golden brown and the dip is hot. Serve immediately with pita chips, small rye toasts, or cucumber slices.

Fresh Spinach and Asiago Dip in a Bread Boule

SPINACH DIP in a hollowed-out loaf of bread is comfort food, party-style. You've probably had some version of it at a party; people always seem to gather around this creamy, savory dip. It's actually quite simple to make, and you don't need to be dependent on the deli or the grocery store to supply your spinach dip. Try this one instead; hot from the oven, it's rich with fresh spinach and savory cheese. ○ *Serves 10*

CASSEROLE DISH: Large baking sheet
BAKE TIME: 45 to 55 minutes

One 16-ounce round loaf whole-grain or sourdough bread
Two 8-ounce packages cream cheese, softened
1 cup whole-milk yogurt
1 pound fresh baby spinach (about 6 cups)
1 cup shredded Asiago cheese
⅓ cup minced fresh chives
1 tablespoon minced fresh dill
Kosher salt
Freshly ground black pepper
Olive oil

1. Preheat the oven to 350°F. Cut a round, thin slice off the top of the bread, leaving a flat top. Using a serrated bread knife, carefully cut into the bread, stopping about 1 inch from the bottom. Cut a wide cylinder and remove it. Widen the bottom of the cavity, still leaving at least 2 inches of bread walls all around. Set aside the extra bread you removed from the loaf.

2. In a large bowl, whip the cream cheese until light. Whip in the yogurt until all is creamy and well mixed. Chop the spinach into fine ribbons, then mix it into the cream cheese mixture, along with the Asiago cheese, chives, and dill. Taste, then season to taste with salt and pepper.

3. Fill the hollowed-out bread with the dip, then cover the bread completely with foil. (At this point the filled loaf can be refrigerated for up to 24 hours.) Place on the large baking sheet and bake for 45 to 55 minutes, or until the dip is heated through. (If it's been refrigerated, this dish may need about 15 extra minutes of bake time to get hot enough to serve.) Remove the bread boule from the oven, cover with foil to keep warm, and turn up the oven to broil.

4. Cut the reserved bread into 2-inch cubes and toss with olive oil, salt, and pepper until lightly coated. Spread out on a large baking sheet and toast under the broiler for 1 to 2 minutes, shaking the pan and flipping the cubes halfway so they toast evenly.

5. Serve the dip in the bread bowl with the toasted cubes of bread for dipping.

Roasted Artichoke Hearts with Parmesan and Oregano

THIS IS PERHAPS MY FAVORITE APPETIZER of all time. It's easy and convenient (you can always keep a bag of frozen artichoke hearts in the freezer) and takes very little time. It's also incredibly delicious: tangy, herbed, and tender. I serve these little morsels either on their own, speared with toothpicks, or more often as a topping for baguette slices spread with cream cheese. This is also wonderful tossed with hot cooked pasta. ○ *Serves 4*

> **CASSEROLE DISH:** 9-inch square baking dish
> **BAKE TIME:** 40 minutes

One 10-ounce package frozen artichoke hearts

Juice and zest of 1 lemon

¼ cup plus 3 tablespoons olive oil, plus additional for drizzling

2 cloves garlic, minced

Small handful (about ¼ cup loosely packed) fresh oregano sprigs

½ cup dry bread crumbs

¼ cup grated Parmesan cheese

½ teaspoon kosher salt

Freshly ground black pepper

1. Preheat the oven to 325°F. Lightly grease the bottom of the baking dish with olive oil.

2. Rinse the frozen artichoke hearts and pat dry. (If the hearts are not already sliced into quarters, as frozen artichoke hearts tend to be, then slice each into 3 or 4 pieces.) Whisk the lemon zest, juice, ¼ cup olive oil, and garlic together in a medium-size bowl. Add the artichoke hearts and toss. Spread the artichokes and dressing in one even layer in the baking dish.

3. Strip the oregano stalks of their leaves, and discard the stalks. Mix the oregano leaves in a separate bowl with the bread crumbs, Parmesan cheese, and remaining 3 tablespoons of olive oil. Season with the ½ teaspoon salt, plus pepper to taste. Spread the bread crumb mixture evenly over the artichoke hearts. Drizzle lightly with olive oil. (At this point the casserole can be covered and refrigerated for up to 24 hours.)

4. Cover the dish with foil. Bake for 25 minutes, then raise the heat to 400°F and remove the foil. Bake for an additional 15 minutes, or until the bread crumb topping is crispy and golden brown. Serve hot, at room temperature, or cold.

Creamy Brie with Cranberry Sauce

A RE YOU LOOKING FOR a sweet-and-savory appetizer for a holiday party or special meal? This is the one. It's always a hit, and it's a good way to use up leftover cranberry sauce from Thanksgiving. My friend Collette introduced me to this treat. She showed up at a potluck and popped it into the oven, and

10 minutes later there was a cluster of hungry people around a dish of molten cheese with sweet and bubbly cranberry sauce on top. Serve with small crackers, since this rich hors d'oeuvre is best eaten in small bites. ○ *Serves 8*

CASSEROLE DISH: 9-inch pie dish or small gratin dish
BAKE TIME: 8 minutes

One 4- to 7-ounce round Brie cheese
⅓ cup homemade or store-bought whole-berry cranberry sauce
2 tablespoons packed brown sugar (light or dark)
1 teaspoon vanilla extract
1 teaspoon rum (optional)
¼ teaspoon ground nutmeg
1 teaspoon orange zest
¼ cup chopped pecans or walnuts
Assorted crackers, for serving

1. Preheat the oven to 450°F. Using a sharp knife, shave off the top rind of the Brie cheese, exposing the cheese underneath. Place the cheese in the pie dish with the exposed side facing up.

2. Mix the cranberry sauce, brown sugar, vanilla, rum (if using), nutmeg, and orange zest in a small bowl. Spread this on top of the Brie. Layer the nuts on top.

3. Bake for about 8 minutes, or until the fruit is bubbling and the cheese is gooey. Serve immediately, with crackers to dip into the cheese and cranberry sauce.

Pesto and Goat Cheese Baked Rounds

FRESH BASIL PESTO is a wonderful thing in the late summer, especially when it's made with basil leaves from your own plants. Basil is famously productive at the end of the summer, as it invariably skyrockets and shoots out cups and cups' worth of vibrant leaves. Whiz those together with some pine nuts, Parmesan cheese, garlic, and olive oil for a zesty pesto, and then use it in this easy appetizer.

Think of these rounds as mini, self-contained casseroles. They are easy and fresh, but still warm and homey. ○ *Serves 6*

CASSEROLE DISH: Large baking sheet
BAKE TIME: 12 to 14 minutes

¼ cup olive oil, plus more for brushing the bread
One 6-inch French baguette, sliced into twelve ½-inch-thick rounds
⅓ cup sun-dried tomatoes (dry or oil-packed)
⅓ cup homemade or store-bought basil pesto
½ cup dry bread crumbs
One 6-ounce log goat cheese

1. Preheat the broiler. Put the baguette slices on the baking sheet and brush them with olive oil. Put the slices under the broiler to toast. Leave them in for only a minute or two; they should be just lightly golden brown and not completely dried out. Remove the baking sheet from the broiler and turn the oven down to 375°F.

2. In a food processor, blend the sun-dried tomatoes, pesto, the ¼ cup olive oil, and bread crumbs into a fine paste.

3. Slice the log of goat cheese into twelve ¼-inch-thick rounds. Top each baguette slice with a round of goat cheese, then spread a small spoonful of the pesto crumb mixture on top of the cheese. (At this point the prepared baguette rounds can be covered and refrigerated for up to 24 hours.)

4. Bake, uncovered, for 12 to 14 minutes, or until the cheese has softened and the topping is golden brown. Let cool for a few minutes, then serve.

Baked Baby Onions in Parmesan

NOTHING SAYS "COCKTAIL PARTY" like baby onions on toothpicks. This is a bit of a retro treat: baked baby onions in a savory mustard sauce. They are juicy and rather kicky. Serve them hot with chilled white wine or martinis. ○ *Serves 6*

CASSEROLE DISH: 9 × 13-inch baking dish
BAKE TIME: 18 to 20 minutes

One 12-ounce bag frozen boiling onions
¼ cup olive oil
¼ cup white wine
2 tablespoons Dijon mustard
4 cloves garlic, minced
¼ teaspoon chili powder
¼ teaspoon salt
Freshly ground black pepper
2 tablespoons minced fresh flat-leaf parsley
⅓ cup grated Parmesan cheese

1. Preheat the oven to 375°F. Lightly grease the baking dish with olive oil. Put the onions in a colander and rinse for a couple of minutes to partially defrost them. Drain well and pat dry.

2. Whisk together the olive oil, white wine, mustard, garlic, chili powder, salt, and pepper to taste. Add the onions and stir to coat. Pour into the baking dish and sprinkle with the parsley and Parmesan.

3. Bake for 18 to 20 minutes, or until well browned. Spear each onion with a toothpick and serve warm.

Roasted Shrimp and Tomatoes with Herbs

TOMATOES ROASTED WITH OLIVE OIL and black pepper, mixed with shrimp and fresh herbs and baked until bubbly: This is a really easy and impressive starter. Sop up the tomatoes with bread or scoop everything up with pita chips. Of course, like most good appetizers, this also makes a perfectly delicious dinner for two. ○ *Serves 6*

CASSEROLE DISH: 9-inch square baking dish
BAKE TIME: 35 minutes

1 pound small shrimp, peeled and deveined
5 ripe yet firm tomatoes, or one 28-ounce can plum tomatoes, drained
¼ cup olive oil
2 cloves garlic, minced
¼ teaspoon salt
¼ teaspoon freshly ground black pepper
Small handful (about ¼ cup) fresh flat-leaf parsley, minced
1 cup crumbled goat cheese
Pita chips or baguette slices, for serving

1. Preheat the oven to 450°F. Lightly grease the baking dish with olive oil. Cut each shrimp in half lengthwise. Set aside.

2. Chop the tomatoes into small pieces and toss in a large bowl with the olive oil, garlic, salt, and black pepper. Transfer to the baking dish and roast for 20 minutes, or until the tomatoes are soft and bubbly.

3. Stir the shrimp and parsley into the dish, and top evenly with the crumbled goat cheese. Bake for an additional 15 minutes, or until the shrimp are pink and fully cooked. Serve hot with pita chips or baguette slices.

Slow-Roasted Tomatoes with Garlicky Bread Crumb Topping

THE OVEN IS VERY HELPFUL when it comes to preparing jams, spreads, and condiments. Slow-roasting vegetables like tomatoes softens them into jammy, spreadable goodness. It also intensifies their flavor; even mealy, out-of-season tomatoes can be transformed into something really gorgeous by a long, slow roast in the oven. ● *Serves 6*

CASSEROLE DISH: 9 × 13-inch baking dish
BAKE TIME: About 2½ hours

One 28-ounce can plum tomatoes or 4 or 5 ripe tomatoes
2 cloves garlic, minced
½ teaspoon kosher salt
Freshly ground black pepper
¼ cup olive oil

FOR THE BREAD CRUMB TOPPING:
1 cup fresh bread crumbs
¼ cup olive oil
¼ cup mixed fresh herbs, such as sage, oregano, basil, thyme, and/or chives
4 cloves garlic, minced

Crackers, for serving

1. Preheat the oven to 325°F. Line the baking dish with aluminum foil and grease the foil lightly with olive oil or nonstick cooking spray.

2. If using canned tomatoes, cut or mash into small bits. Pour off about half the juices and then spread the tomatoes and remaining juice evenly in the baking dish. If using fresh tomatoes, chop into quarters and spread in the dish. Mix in the garlic, salt, and pepper, and pour the olive oil over the top. (At this point the casserole can be covered and refrigerated for up to 24 hours.)

3. Bake, uncovered, for about 2 hours, or until the tomatoes are very soft. (Canned tomatoes will need less time, about 1½ hours.)

4. To make the topping, whiz the bread crumbs in a food processor with the olive oil, herbs, and garlic until fully combined. The bread crumbs should be a light green color. Spread the mixture evenly over the tomatoes. Increase the oven temperature to 450°F and roast for an additional 20 to 30 minutes, checking every 10 minutes to make sure the topping does not burn.

5. Let cool for 10 minutes before serving. Serve with crackers.

Make-Ahead Hors d'Oeuvres

When my husband and I have guests over to dinner, I like to put out a few things for them to nibble on while we chat and I finish up cooking. (Despite my good intentions, dinner is never ready on time in my household! I get too distracted talking with guests.) These pre-dinner nibbles shouldn't make meal preparation any more taxing, though. There are many easy ways to have something homemade on hand when guests show up, and an oven-baked spread like Slow-Roasted Tomatoes with Garlicky Bread Crumb Topping is one of them (the Roasted Red Onion Jam on page 82 is another). It keeps well in the refrigerator and can be frozen, too, so when guests come I can just pull it out, heat it up, and put it on a big wooden board with some crackers and soft cheese.

Double-Baked Mini Potatoes with Bacon

DOUBLE-BAKED POTATOES ARE a little more labor-intensive than most of the recipes in this chapter. These creamy little potatoes are roasted once, then hollowed out, refilled, and baked again. But let me tell you, these creamy bites of deeply roasted potato, cream cheese, and bacon are worth it. This recipe is not for dieters, but it's great for a hungry crowd. Don't blink; they'll disappear. o *Serves 6 to 10*

CASSEROLE DISH: Large baking sheet
BAKE TIME: 50 to 55 minutes

2 pounds new red potatoes or thin-skinned fingerling potatoes (the smaller, the better)
Olive oil
Kosher salt and freshly ground black pepper
4 slices bacon
8 ounces cream cheese, softened
¼ cup whole-milk yogurt
¼ cup minced fresh chives

1. Preheat the oven to 450°F. In a large bowl, toss the potatoes with a drizzle of olive oil and a few shakes of salt and pepper. Spread on the baking sheet and roast for 35 to 40 minutes, or until easily pierced with a fork. Let cool.

2. While the potatoes are roasting, lay the bacon slices in a cold skillet and turn the heat to low. Cook for about 15 minutes, turning the bacon frequently. When the bacon is very crisp, remove it from the pan and place on a plate lined with paper towels. Blot the bacon with another paper towel to remove excess grease.

3. In a large bowl or in a food processor, whip the cream cheese until very soft and creamy. Whip in the yogurt and chives, along with a pinch of salt and a few grinds of black pepper. Crumble the bacon into very small bits, and whip them into the cream cheese as well.

4. When the potatoes have cooled, cut about ¼ inch off their tops. Roughly chop these tops and whip them into the cream cheese filling. Then use a teaspoon to scoop out the center of each potato. Mash this into the filling.

5. Refill the center of each potato with a spoonful of the creamy filling. Place the filled potatoes on the baking sheet. (At this point the potatoes can be covered and refrigerated for up to 24 hours.) Return the baking sheet to the oven and bake the potatoes, uncovered, for 15 minutes, or until lightly browned. Let cool for 5 minutes, then serve.

Roasted Garlic with Herbs

ONE OF MY FAVORITE APPETIZERS is a little dish of roasted garlic with good bread and butter. Serving whole cloves of garlic to your guests may seem a little startling, but roasted garlic has a mellow sweetness that's wonderful as a spread or topping for bread or pizza. ○ *Serves 6*

CASEROLE DISH: 9-inch pie dish or small gratin dish
BAKE TIME: 50 minutes

2 whole heads garlic
2 sprigs fresh thyme
2 sprigs fresh rosemary
2 small sprigs fresh sage
3 tablespoons olive oil
1 teaspoon kosher salt
½ teaspoon freshly ground black pepper
Baguette slices, for serving

1. Preheat the oven to 350°F. Put a square of aluminum foil inside the baking dish, and lightly grease the center of the foil with olive oil.

2. Cut the top off the garlic heads, exposing the cloves inside. Then break the heads apart into separate cloves, discarding the bottom of the base. Do not peel the cloves; just pull the head apart. Put the cloves in a small bowl and toss with the thyme, rosemary, sage, olive oil, salt, and pepper.

3. Spread the cloves and the herbs on the foil in the prepared baking dish. Fold the foil over them and seal like a small packet. Bake for 50 minutes, or until the cloves are very soft.

4. Serve immediately while hot, squeezing out the garlic over fresh slices of baguette.

Baked Avocados with Tomato and Crab

THE FIRST TIME I MADE THIS DISH my dinner guests were skeptical. "Baked avocados? Are you sure?" But the result was a smashing success; they ate every bite of the warm, silky avocados with their savory filling. The avocado is actually wonderful when baked. It gets even creamier and softer, with a luscious texture and an even more buttery taste. ○ *Serves 4*

CASSEROLE DISH: 9-inch square baking dish
BAKE TIME: 15 minutes

1 tablespoon olive oil
1 small white onion, diced
1 medium-size tomato, diced
¼ pound lump crabmeat, picked over to remove any bits of shell and cartilage
4 ounces cream cheese, softened
Salt and freshly ground black pepper
Juice and zest of 1 lime
2 large ripe avocados
Small handful (about ¼ cup) fresh cilantro, minced

1. Preheat the oven to 400°F.

2. Heat the olive oil in a skillet and cook the onion over medium heat for about 10 minutes, or until translucent. Add the tomato and cook for another 5 minutes, or until the tomato is bubbling. Turn off the heat.

3. Mash the crabmeat with the cream cheese in a medium-size bowl until thoroughly combined. Season with a pinch of salt and pepper. Stir in the cooked tomato and onion, lime zest, and cilantro. (At this point the crab mixture can be covered and refrigerated for up to 24 hours.)

4. Cut the avocados in half and remove the pits. Sprinkle the cut sides immediately with the lime juice. Fill the cavities with the cream cheese mixture. Place the filled avocado halves in the baking dish and bake for 15 minutes, or until the avocados are heated through. Serve immediately.

Roasted Red Onion Jam

RED ONION JAM is a versatile condiment. It's fabulous on burgers, great as a topping for toast slices spread with cream cheese, and elegant served on roasted pork loin. I like to keep a container of it in the fridge for impromptu dinner parties and appetizer platters. I put it out with a few crackers, some soft goat cheese, a handful of walnuts, some dried figs, and sliced pears or apples. And it's so easy to make in the oven! You don't even have to keep an eye on it.

o *Makes about 1½ cups*

CASEROLE DISH: 5- to 6-quart Dutch oven or
    other stovetop-to-oven pot with lid
BAKE TIME: 2 to 2½ hours

3 large red onions (2 pounds), very thinly sliced
¼ cup olive oil
¼ cup balsamic vinegar
1 teaspoon kosher salt
1 teaspoon freshly ground black pepper

1 teaspoon sugar
2 sprigs fresh rosemary
Crostini or crackers, for serving

1. Preheat the oven to 350°F. Lightly grease the Dutch oven with olive oil.

2. In a large bowl, toss the onions with the olive oil, vinegar, salt, pepper, and sugar. Spread evenly in the Dutch oven and tuck the rosemary sprigs in among the onions. Cover the dish and bake for 1 hour.

3. Stir the onions, cover, return them to the oven, and bake for 1 more hour. Check again and stir; if the onions have reduced and caramelized to a deep golden brown, take them out. If they are still pale golden, take off the lid and bake for an additional 30 minutes, stirring halfway through.

4. Serve the onion jam with crostini or crackers.

Cheesy Bread Bites

HOT CRISPY BREAD, GOOEY CHEESE, and savory scallions pretty much sum up this easy, crowd-pleasing hors d'oeuvre. It's always a total hit.

o *Serves 8 to 12*

CASSEROLE DISH: Large baking sheet
BAKE TIME: 6 minutes

One 16-ounce loaf rustic white bread or French baguette
1 cup sour cream
4 scallions, minced
1 cup shredded sharp cheddar cheese
1 cup shredded mozzarella cheese

1. Preheat the broiler. Cut the bread into 1-inch cubes.

2. Mix the sour cream, scallions, and the cheeses in a very large bowl. It will be a loose, sticky mixture. Add the bread cubes and mix with your hands until the bread is fully coated with the mixture.

3. Spread the cheesy bread cubes on the baking sheet in one even layer. Cook under the broiler for 4 minutes, or until the bread cubes are golden and the cheese is bubbly. Toss the bread with a spoon or spatula, then put the sheet back under the broiler for 2 more minutes.

4. Remove and serve while hot. Set out on a platter with a cup of toothpicks so guests can pick up hot cubes of bread without burning their fingers, or do it yourself and spear the cubes on toothpicks before serving.

Eggplant and Caper Caponata with Tahini Dressing

THIS IS A CHOPPED APPETIZER, a mix of summer vegetables roasted with a light dressing of sesame tahini and olive oil. While it draws its initial inspiration from baba ghanoush, the classic smoky eggplant dip from the Middle East, it also incorporates elements of caponata, the Italian roasted eggplant dish. This is delicious served on toasts or baguette slices spread with goat cheese. Or turn it into a meal by tossing it with pasta. **o** *Serves 12*

CASSEROLE DISH: 9 × 13-inch baking dish
BAKE TIME: 30 minutes

1 medium eggplant, cut into 1-inch cubes
1 medium zucchini, diced
2 teaspoons salt
1 medium red onion, diced
1 red bell pepper, cored and diced
One 2.25-ounce can sliced black olives, drained
¼ cup brine-packed capers, drained
4 cloves garlic, cut in half
½ cup olive oil
2 tablespoons tahini (sesame paste)
Juice of 1 lemon

Freshly ground black pepper
Toasts or small bread slices, for serving

1. Preheat the oven to 400°F. Lightly grease the baking dish with olive oil.

2. Toss the diced eggplant and zucchini with the salt and place them in a colander with a plate on top to weigh them down. Put the colander in the sink and let them drain for 20 minutes.

3. Toss the red onion and the red bell pepper in a large bowl with the olives, capers, and halved garlic cloves.

4. Whisk the olive oil, tahini, and lemon juice together in a small bowl until blended. Stir into the onion and bell pepper mixture. Toss the eggplant and zucchini in the colander to shake off any additional liquid, and then toss with the onion mixture. Season with pepper. Spread the mixture in the prepared dish. (At this point the casserole can be covered and refrigerated for up to 24 hours.)

5. Bake, uncovered, for 30 minutes, or until the vegetables are tender. Let cool slightly before serving as a topping on toasts or bread slices.

Vegetable Tians, Gratins, and Braises

I adore vegetables.

That's a broad statement, I know—but I really just love nearly every vegetable on the face of the earth. There's such a variety and range of tastes, textures, and colors, from crunchy orange carrots to crisp, pale fennel to juicy scarlet tomatoes. I love chopped salads and sautéed vegetables, but my favorite way to prepare most vegetables is in the oven.

The oven's dry, all-encompassing heat can transform crunchy vegetables into tender, melting morsels or silky, flavorful bites. In the oven you can infuse vegetables with the rich flavors of spices and herbs, and cover them in thin layers of melting cheese.

In this chapter, I've tried to give you recipes that are not too labor-intensive, although of course all vegetables require a certain amount of peeling, chopping, and preparation before baking. But most of these dishes don't require the vegetables to be precooked or pureed; the Simple Butternut Squash Bake with Sage (page 101), for instance, is a quick oven hash of squash cubes held together loosely with a layer of cheese and herbs. It's rich enough for a vegetarian dinner and quick enough for a side dish.

One of my personal favorites in this chapter is the Spinach, Broccoli, and Goat Cheese Casserole (page 93)—an easy, filling dish that makes a great vegetarian meal and that will surprise any guests who think they don't like broccoli. The Root Vegetable Cobbler with Whole-Grain Biscuit Topping (page 118) is similarly hearty and can also be served as a vegetarian meal. One more favorite is the Baked Eggplant Parmesan (page 90), which has a few shortcuts to lighten up and speed up the classic eggplant-and-cheese dish. It's fresh, full of garlicky flavor, and much faster than a more traditional recipe.

Baked Eggplant Parmesan

EGGPLANT PARMESAN is a classic Italian dish of fried eggplant, tomato sauce, and cheese. It's traditionally rather greasy (deliciously so!) and also rather involved to prepare. This version, on the other hand, radically cuts down on the time required to bring the dish to the table and makes it fresher and lighter, too. Chunky tomatoes, handfuls of fresh herbs, and crunchy bread crumbs make up a vivid, deliciously chewy, and saucy vegetarian meal that sacrifices no flavor!

○ Serves 4 to 6

CASSEROLE DISH: 3-quart round baking dish
BAKE TIME: 45 to 50 minutes, plus 6 minutes broiling time for the eggplant

2 medium-large eggplants
Salt
½ cup olive oil
2 tablespoons balsamic vinegar
1 large onion, diced
4 cloves garlic, minced
One 28-ounce can plum tomatoes, with their juice
½ cup loosely packed fresh basil leaves, coarsely chopped
½ teaspoon salt
1 teaspoon freshly ground black pepper
1 tablespoon sugar
2 cups grated Parmesan cheese

FOR THE BREAD CRUMB TOPPING:
¾ cup fresh bread crumbs
4 sprigs fresh thyme (leaves only)
1 small sprig fresh rosemary (leaves only)
2 sprigs fresh sage (leaves only)
¼ cup fresh flat-leaf parsley
¼ teaspoon salt
¼ teaspoon freshly ground black pepper
½ cup grated Parmesan cheese
¼ cup olive oil

1. Lightly grease the baking dish with olive oil. Cut the eggplants in half lengthwise, then crosswise into ½-inch-thick slices. Toss with a few pinches of salt. Let sit in a colander in the sink to drain for about 30 minutes. Rinse under cold water and pat dry. Preheat the broiler.

2. Spread the eggplant slices on a large baking sheet and lightly brush them with ¼ cup of the olive oil. (Make sure to spread them in a single layer; do this broiling in batches, if necessary.) Broil for 6 minutes, or until they are golden brown on top. Remove from the oven and turn the oven to 350°F.

3. In a large bowl, mix the remaining ¼ cup of olive oil, the vinegar, onion, garlic, and tomatoes. Lightly crush the tomatoes as you stir the mixture together. Stir in the basil, salt, pepper, and sugar. Taste and adjust the seasonings if necessary.

4. Layer one-third of the eggplant slices in the bottom of the baking dish. Spread half the tomatoes over the eggplant and sprinkle with half the Parmesan. Add another layer of half of the remaining eggplant, all of the remaining tomato sauce, and the remaining Parmesan; finish with a final layer of the remaining eggplant.

5. To make the bread crumb topping: In a small food processor, whiz the bread crumbs with the thyme, rosemary, sage, and parsley. Whiz in the salt, pepper, Parmesan, and olive oil. The bread crumbs should be a greenish gold color. Sprinkle the topping in a thick layer over the eggplant and drizzle with the olive oil. (At this point the casserole can be covered and refrigerated for up to 24 hours.)

6. Bake, uncovered, for 45 to 50 minutes, or until the bread crumbs are golden brown and the tomatoes are bubbling. Let cool for 10 minutes before serving.

Eggplant Rolls with Sun-Dried Tomato and Cream Cheese Filling

EGGPLANT, TOMATO, AND BASIL are quintessential summer eating. Their rich, ripe flavors meld in a remembrance of sunshine, and this dish packs them all in! Fresh, colorful, and very pretty, it makes a wonderful summer appetizer or vegetable side dish. This has a few separate steps, but they are all quite easy. Serve this with crusty bread and a green salad. ○ *Serves 4*

CASSEROLE DISH: 9-inch square baking dish
BAKE TIME: 30 minutes

2 large eggplants
1 tablespoon plus 1 teaspoon salt
½ cup dry-packed sun-dried tomatoes, coarsely chopped
Two 8-ounce packages cream cheese, softened
1 large egg
½ cup loosely packed fresh basil leaves, chopped
¼ teaspoon freshly ground black pepper
4 cups baby spinach
1 cup grated Parmesan cheese
¼ cup olive oil
2 cloves garlic, finely minced
4 sprigs fresh thyme (leaves only)

1. Preheat the oven to 350°F. Lightly grease the bottom of the baking dish with olive oil.

2. Trim off the top of each eggplant and slice the eggplants into thin lengthwise slices. You should have at least 8 slices from each eggplant. Lay the slices on paper towels on a large baking sheet and sprinkle them liberally with the 1 tablespoon salt. Let them sit for at least 30 minutes. Rinse the slices in cold water and pat dry.

3. While the eggplant is sitting in the salt, put the sun-dried tomatoes in a medium-size bowl and add boiling water to cover. Let them sit for at least 10 minutes.

4. Put the cream cheese in the bowl of a stand mixer and whip until soft and creamy. Beat in the egg, basil, remaining 1 teaspoon of salt, and pepper. Drain the tomatoes and mix them in as well.

5. To assemble the eggplant rolls, take a slice of eggplant that has been patted dry and spread it with a thin layer of the cream cheese mixture. Create a second layer by laying a few leaves of baby spinach on top. Sprinkle with a thin layer of Parmesan, then roll up and place seam-side down in the prepared baking dish. Repeat with the rest of the eggplant slices.

6. Whisk the olive oil in a small bowl with the garlic and thyme leaves. Pour over the eggplant rolls. Bake for 30 minutes. Serve immediately.

Spinach, Broccoli, and Goat Cheese Casserole

THIS RECIPE WAS CREATED after I made a double batch of a raw, marinated broccoli salad that uses only the broccoli florets. I love the stems of broccoli too, and it seemed a pity to waste them. So they went into a big green casserole with plenty of goat cheese for tangy creaminess. Serve this hearty dish with fresh bread for a great vegetarian meal. o *Serves 6*

CASSEROLE DISH: 9 × 13-inch baking dish
BAKE TIME: 45 minutes

1 pound broccoli stems or a mix of stems and florets,
    chopped into 1-inch pieces (about 5 cups)
⅓ cup short-grain rice
12 ounces baby spinach, coarsely chopped
1 tablespoon olive oil
4 ounces goat cheese
3 large eggs
1½ teaspoons salt
½ teaspoon freshly ground black pepper
½ teaspoon ground nutmeg
½ cup heavy cream
1 cup dry bread crumbs
½ cup fresh flat-leaf parsley, chopped
4 sprigs fresh thyme (leaves only)
Olive oil

1. In a large covered pot with a steamer basket, bring 1 inch of water to a boil. When the water is boiling, fill the basket with the broccoli. Cover, turn the heat to low, and steam for 5 minutes, or until the broccoli is just barely tender.

2. Preheat the oven to 375°F. Grease the bottom of the baking dish with olive oil.

3. Bring 2 cups of water to a boil in a small saucepan. Add the rice and boil for 10 minutes. Drain and set aside.

4. Mix the steamed broccoli, baby spinach, olive oil, and rice in a large bowl. Crumble in the goat cheese and mix. In a separate small bowl, beat the eggs with the salt, pepper, and nutmeg. Mix the eggs into the spinach and broccoli, and stir in the cream. Spread in the prepared baking dish.

5. Whiz the bread crumbs with the parsley and thyme in a blender or food processor. Drizzle in a little olive oil and whiz again until light green in color. Sprinkle over the broccoli and spinach, and drizzle the whole casserole with more olive oil. (At this point the casserole can be covered and refrigerated for up to 24 hours.)

6. Bake, uncovered, for 45 minutes, or until set and firm. Let cool for 5 minutes before serving.

Roasted Cauliflower with Lemon, Garlic, and Capers

WAS NOT A HUGE FAN OF CAULIFLOWER until I learned to roast it, and for this I owe Elise of the marvelous food blog Simply Recipes. This recipe is based on her family's favorite roasted cauliflower, with my own addition of capers, whose salty-sour bite complements the more relaxed, mellow taste of cauliflower drenched with olive oil. Using a baking dish so that the cauliflower pieces are clustered closely together and half-roast, half-steam makes it a casserole in my book. I could eat a pan of this all by myself. **o** *Serves 6*

CASSEROLE DISH: 9 × 13-inch baking dish
BAKE TIME: 20 minutes

1 head cauliflower
4 cloves garlic, minced
3 tablespoons capers in brine, drained
Juice and zest of 1 lemon
2 teaspoons coarse salt
Freshly ground black pepper
⅓ cup olive oil
1 cup grated Parmesan cheese

1. Preheat the oven to 400°F. Lightly grease the baking dish with olive oil.

¼ teaspoon red pepper flakes (optional)

2 cups low-sodium chicken broth

1½ teaspoons salt, if needed

Freshly ground black pepper

1. Preheat the oven to 325°F. Trim the collard greens away from their rib stems by folding each large leaf in half and, with one long motion of the knife, slitting the center rib away. Layer these leaves in stacks of 5 or 6, and roll them tightly. Slice each roll crosswise into ribbons about 1 inch wide. Rinse thoroughly in a colander and set aside to drain.

2. Cook the bacon in the Dutch oven over medium-low heat for 10 minutes, or until the fat has rendered out of the bacon and the bacon is becoming crisp. Add the garlic and onion and turn the heat to medium. Add the red pepper flakes, if using. Cook the onion and garlic, stirring frequently, until the onion is translucent, about 10 minutes.

3. Add the collard greens to the Dutch oven a handful at a time and cook over medium heat for about 8 minutes, or until the greens are slightly wilted. (You may need to let a few handfuls wilt down before adding the rest, so they all fit in your pot. They will reduce quite a bit as they cook, so don't worry if the pot is initially full to the brim!)

4. Pour in the broth, taste, and, if necessary, stir in the salt. Bring to a simmer, and then cover and put in the oven. Bake for 60 minutes, or until the greens are very soft. Taste and season with additional salt and pepper if necessary. Serve hot.

Variation: This recipe can be made vegetarian by omitting the bacon, cooking the greens in butter or olive oil instead of the bacon fat, and substituting vegetable broth for the chicken stock. In this case, however, I would suggest mixing 1 or more teaspoons of smoked paprika into the greens before putting the dish in the oven to help create that smoky flavor. If you like it spicy, you can also add ½ teaspoon or more of chipotle chile powder, which will give the greens even more smokiness and spice.

Wash Those Collards

Collard greens tend to be quite dirty and sandy. Make sure you wash the leaves very well. If you find it easier, they can also be washed in a salad spinner.

Oven Bubble and Squeak

IF YOU READ ENGLISH LITERATURE, you're bound to have encountered intriguing references to "bubble and squeak." What is this mysterious dish? Why, nothing more than leftover cabbage and potatoes fried up into a crispy, frugal weeknight supper. This version saves a bit of time (and calories) by oven-baking instead of frying on the stovetop. ○ *Serves 8*

CASSEROLE DISH: 9 × 13-inch baking dish
BAKE TIME: 35 minutes

1 small head cabbage
1 tablespoon unsalted butter
1 small onion, diced
3 russet potatoes, peeled, cooked, and mashed, or 2 to 3 cups mashed potatoes
1 teaspoon salt
½ teaspoon freshly ground black pepper

1. Preheat the oven to 350°F and lightly grease the baking dish with nonstick cooking spray or butter.

2. Cut the cabbage in quarters from top to bottom, and cut the stem at an angle to remove the hard inner core. Finely slice each quarter into thin ribbons. Bring about an inch of water to a boil in a deep pot, and add the cabbage. Cover the pot tightly and cook the cabbage for 7 minutes, or until very tender. Drain and set aside to cool.

3. Heat the butter in a heavy skillet over medium heat. When the butter foams and then subsides, add the onion and cook, stirring frequently, for about 10 minutes.

4. In a large bowl, mix the cooked onion, mashed potatoes, and cabbage with the salt and pepper. Press the mixture into the prepared baking dish and sprinkle the top with a little extra salt and pepper. Bake for 35 minutes, or until golden brown on top. Serve hot.

Creamy Cabbage Casserole

CABBAGE CASSEROLE is one of *those* classic casseroles—a potluck dish that usually calls for great quantities of shredded cheese and canned soup. My version is much lighter, and it's held together by a simple white sauce instead of the dreaded canned soup. I substitute Parmesan cheese for the traditional cheddar, too, as an homage to my favorite stovetop version of braised cabbage.

○ Serves 6 to 8

CASSEROLE DISH: 9 × 13-inch baking dish
BAKE TIME: 45 minutes

2 tablespoons unsalted butter
2 cloves garlic, minced
3 tablespoons all-purpose flour
1 teaspoon salt
¼ teaspoon ground nutmeg
1½ cups milk
1 large head Savoy or green cabbage
1 bunch scallions
2 cups grated Parmesan cheese
1 cup toasted bread crumbs
Freshly ground black pepper
Olive oil

1. Preheat the oven to 350°F. Lightly grease the baking dish with butter.

2. In a medium saucepan, heat the 2 tablespoons butter over medium heat. When it foams, add the garlic and cook slowly until it is fragrant and golden. Add the flour, salt, and nutmeg, turn the heat to low, and cook, stirring constantly, for about 3 minutes. Whisk in the milk and cook, whisking vigorously, for 3 to 4 minutes, or until the mixture is slightly thickened.

3. Cut the cabbage in quarters from top to bottom, and cut the stem at an angle to remove the hard inner core. Finely slice each quarter into thin ribbons. Chop the scallions. Place them in a large bowl and toss with the sauce and 1 cup of the Parmesan cheese. Spread the mixture in the prepared baking dish.

4. Mix the bread crumbs with the remaining 1 cup of Parmesan and season to taste with salt and pepper. Sprinkle evenly over the cabbage casserole. Drizzle generously with olive oil. (At this point the casserole can be covered and refrigerated for up to 24 hours.) Cover the baking dish tightly with foil and bake for 30 minutes. Uncover and bake for an additional 15 minutes, or until the top is browned and crisp. Serve hot.

Red Cabbage Bake with Cumin and Caraway

OH, CABBAGE! It has such an unfortunate reputation. But it is truly one of the greatest vegetables—readily available and inexpensive nearly all year long, so versatile and sweet when cooked right. This is one of the right ways: A long, slow simmer in wine, butter, and toasty spices turns simple red cabbage into a mellow vegetable with a warm, sweet broth that is good on just about anything. Serve as a side dish for pork or beef or with rice or egg noodles for a vegetarian meal. ○ *Serves 6 to 8*

CASSEROLE DISH: 2- to 4-quart stovetop-to-oven casserole dish with lid
BAKE TIME: 20 minutes

1 head red cabbage
3 tablespoons unsalted butter
1 teaspoon caraway seeds
1 teaspoon cumin seeds
4 cloves garlic, smashed
½ cup white wine
1 teaspoon salt
½ teaspoon freshly ground black pepper
1 cup grated Parmesan cheese

1. Preheat the oven to 325°F.

2. Remove the outer leaves from the cabbage. Cut the head into quarters and slice away the hard central core at the bottom with one angled stroke. Then slice each quarter in half, and shred the cabbage into thick ribbons.

3. Heat the butter in the casserole dish over medium heat. When it has melted and foamed up, add the caraway and cumin seeds and cook, stirring constantly, for about 1 minute, or until they start to smell toasty. Add the garlic, turn the heat to low, and cook slowly for about 5 minutes, until the garlic is golden and soft.

4. Add the cabbage and stir until the cabbage is coated with butter. Stir in the wine, salt, and pepper and bring to a simmer. Stir in the cheese. Cover the dish with a lid and put in the oven.

5. Bake for 20 minutes, or until the cabbage is very tender. Serve warm.

Note: This casserole keeps very well after cooking and even improves in flavor after a few days in the fridge.

Simple Butternut Squash Bake with Sage

MOST SQUASH CASSEROLES call for cooking the squash first. You have to boil, steam, or roast your squash before you even start putting the casserole together! While I do love many of the casseroles that call for this sort of preparation, it's much easier to prepare squash in this way: mixed and baked all at once, and only once. ● *Serves 6*

CASSEROLE DISH: 9 × 13-inch metal baking pan
BAKE TIME: 35 to 40 minutes

One 3- to 4-pound butternut squash
Two 3-inch sprigs fresh sage
4 cloves garlic, minced
¼ cup olive oil
1 teaspoon salt
½ teaspoon freshly ground black pepper
1¾ cups grated Gruyère cheese

1. Preheat the oven to 375°F. Lightly grease the baking dish with olive oil.

2. To peel the squash, first cut it in half crosswise through the middle. Stand up one half of the cut squash on the cutting board, cut side down, and with a sharp chef's knife slice off the outer peel in long, shallow strips. Repeat with the second half of the squash. Cut each half again in half lengthwise and scoop out and discard any seeds. Cut each quarter into evenly sized cubes about 1 inch square.

3. Pinch the top of the sage stalk between finger and thumb and run your pinched fingers down the stalk to remove the leaves. Discard the stalks. Chop the leaves finely; you should end up with about a tablespoon of sage.

4. Toss the sage, cubed squash, garlic, olive oil, salt, pepper, and 1 cup of the cheese in a large bowl, then spread the mixture in the prepared baking dish. Bake for 35 to 40 minutes, or until the squash is soft and cooked through.

5. Turn the oven up to broil. Sprinkle the top of the casserole with the remaining ¾ cup of cheese and broil for 2 to 3 minutes, or until the cheese is melted and bubbly. Serve hot.

Variation: If you like, fry several slices of bacon until crisp, then crumble and mix into the casserole mixture in step 4.

Spicy Butternut Squash Strata with Bacon

THIS IS ONE MORE no-need-to-cook-the-squash-ahead recipe. As I said in the previous recipe, I love some of those squash casseroles that call for pureed or pre-steamed squash, but in the end I usually opt for a recipe that lets me bang the whole thing into the oven in as little time as possible. This one ratchets up the time just a little, with the addition of cooked bacon and onions, but you can cut up the squash while the onions cook. ○ *Serves 6*

CASSEROLE DISH: 2-quart round or oval baking dish
BAKE TIME: 40 minutes

4 slices bacon, diced
1 medium onion, diced
4 cloves garlic, minced

One 2- to 3-pound butternut squash

½ teaspoon chipotle chile powder, cayenne pepper, or smoked paprika

1 teaspoon salt

½ teaspoon freshly ground black pepper

1 cup heavy cream

½ cup milk

½ cup grated Parmesan cheese

½ cup dry bread crumbs

2 tablespoons olive oil

2 short sprigs fresh thyme (leaves only)

1. Preheat the oven to 375°F. Grease the baking dish with olive oil or butter.

2. Put the bacon in a large skillet. Turn the heat to low and slowly cook the bacon for 10 minutes, or until the fat renders out and the bacon pieces curl up at the sides and begin to look crisp. Add the onion and cook over medium heat for another 10 minutes, or until the onion is translucent. Add the garlic and cook for 5 more minutes.

3. Meanwhile, peel the squash. First cut it in half crosswise through the middle. Stand up one half of the cut squash on the cutting board, cut side down, and with a sharp chef's knife slice off the outer peel in long, shallow strips. Repeat with the second half of the squash. Cut each half again in half lengthwise and scoop out and discard any seeds. Cut each quarter into half-moons about ¼ inch thick. Layer one-third of the squash half-moons in the bottom of the prepared dish, overlapping slices to make a solid layer.

4. As the garlic turns golden and fragrant in the skillet, stir in the chipotle powder, salt, and pepper. Stir in the cream and milk and bring to a light simmer, then remove from the heat.

5. Using a slotted spoon, remove half the onions from the pan and spread them on the squash in the dish. Sprinkle ¼ cup Parmesan cheese over the onions. Layer half of the remaining squash on top, then top with the remaining onions and Parmesan cheese. Layer the rest of the squash on top and pour all the liquid from the pan over the top.

6. Mix the bread crumbs, olive oil, and thyme leaves in a small bowl and sprinkle evenly over the casserole. (At this point the casserole can be covered and refrigerated for up to 24 hours.) Bake, uncovered, for 40 minutes, or until the squash is tender and the liquid is bubbling. Let stand for 10 minutes before serving.

Creamy Spaghetti Squash Casserole

SPAGHETTI DOESN'T GROW ON TREES, the classic April Fool's joke notwithstanding (you know, the Italian town that cultivates spaghetti bushes?), but spaghetti squash has always seemed like a little joke from Mother Nature, with its long, pasta-like strings hidden inside an innocuous yellow squash. Baked like this, with touches of indulgently creamy dairy, you'll swear you were eating a pasta casserole. The calorie (and carb) count says otherwise. ● *Serves 4 to 6*

CASSEROLE DISH: 9 × 13-inch baking dish
BAKE TIME: 45 minutes for the squash; 45 minutes for the casserole

One 3-pound spaghetti squash
1 tablespoon olive oil, plus extra for drizzling
1 medium onion, diced
1 small sprig fresh rosemary (leaves only)
2 cloves garlic, minced
1 teaspoon salt
½ teaspoon freshly ground black pepper
2 large eggs, beaten
1 cup sour cream
1 cup ricotta cheese, drained in a colander
1 cup grated Parmesan cheese
½ teaspoon ground nutmeg
¾ cup dry bread crumbs

1. To roast the squash, preheat the oven to 350°F. Cut the squash in half lengthwise with a sharp chef's knife. Scrape out the seeds with a spoon and discard. Pour ½ cup water into a 9 × 13-inch baking dish and place the squash halves, cut sides down, in the water. Roast for 45 minutes.

2. Meanwhile, in a heavy skillet, heat the 1 tablespoon of olive oil over medium heat. Cook the onions for 8 to 10 minutes, or until translucent. Mince the rosemary leaves and add to the onions, along with the garlic. Cook for an additional 5 minutes. Remove from the heat and stir in the salt and pepper.

3. Remove the roasted squash from the oven and turn the oven up to 375°F. Remove the squash from the baking dish and let it cool slightly. Dump out any water remaining in the baking dish. Wipe it dry and then grease it lightly with nonstick cooking spray.

4. Shred the inside of the squash with a fork into spaghetti-like strings and remove from the outer shell. Drain briefly in a sieve or colander to get rid of any excess moisture.

5. Mix the drained squash strings in a large bowl with the onion mixture. Stir in the eggs, sour cream, ricotta cheese, Parmesan, and nutmeg. Spread in the baking dish and top with the bread crumbs and a drizzle of olive oil. (At this point the casserole can be covered and refrigerated for up to 24 hours.)

6. Bake, uncovered, for 45 minutes, or until firm and golden on top. Let stand for 10 minutes before serving.

Simple Leek Bake

THIS RECIPE IS ADAPTED FROM Jamie Oliver's lovely braised leeks with wine. His recipe is intended as a pasta sauce, with plenty of liquid to pour over something else. But I found myself frequently standing over the hot pan eating it straight, so I adapted it to stand alone on its own merits. It is still good over pasta, though, if you can leave it alone long enough to get the pasta cooked. ● *Serves 8*

CASSEROLE DISH: 5- or 6-quart Dutch oven or other stovetop-to-oven pot
BAKE TIME: 25 minutes

6 large leeks
6 tablespoons unsalted butter
6 cloves garlic, minced
1 teaspoon salt
½ teaspoon freshly ground black pepper
2 cups dry white wine
1 cup low-sodium chicken or vegetable broth
½ lemon
1 cup grated Parmesan cheese

FOR THE BREAD CRUMB TOPPING:
4 cloves garlic
2 sprigs fresh thyme (leaves only)
¾ cup dry bread crumbs
¼ teaspoon salt
¼ teaspoon ground nutmeg
½ cup grated Parmesan cheese
Olive oil

1. Preheat the oven to 350°F. Trim off the ends of the leeks, then cut each leek in half lengthwise. Inspect them for any grit or dirt and wash out the centers, if necessary. Pat dry. Cut the leeks into half-moons about ½ inch wide, separating the chopped pieces of green tops from those of the white bulbs. Set the green tops aside.

2. In the Dutch oven, melt the butter over medium heat. Slowly cook the garlic in the butter until it is soft and golden. Do not let it burn. Stir in the white leek pieces. Let them cook slowly for 5 minutes, then add the chopped green tops, salt, and pepper. Cook for an additional 5 minutes, or until the green tops have softened slightly.

3. Add the wine and broth and bring to a light simmer. Turn off the heat and squeeze in the juice from the lemon half, then toss in the squeezed lemon half. Stir in the Parmesan.

4. To make the bread crumb topping, in a small food processor, whiz the garlic, thyme leaves, bread crumbs, salt, nutmeg, and Parmesan until combined. Sprinkle evenly over the hot leeks and drizzle with olive oil.

5. Bake for 25 minutes, or until the sauce has grown slightly shiny and emulsified. The leeks should be tender and very fragrant, and the bread crumb topping will be golden brown. Serve immediately.

Spinach and Artichoke Tian with Garlic Bread Crumbs

TOGETHER, SPINACH AND ARTICHOKES make up one of the most popular hot dips ever created, but it has always seemed a pity to me to waste this splendid combination on the appetizer table. I'd prefer to make them the stars! In this dish, they can play a leading role at a light supper. They both contain a great deal of water, so I use partially cooked rice to soak up a bit of that extra moisture—a technique you'll probably notice in several casseroles in this chapter.

○ *Serves 6 to 8*

CASSEROLE DISH: 9 × 13-inch baking dish
BAKE TIME: 45 minutes

½ cup short-grain white rice
1 tablespoon unsalted butter
1 large onion, chopped
4 cloves garlic, minced
1 teaspoon salt
½ teaspoon freshly ground black pepper
One 16-ounce package frozen chopped spinach, thawed and squeezed dry
Two 12-ounce packages frozen artichoke hearts, thawed and drained
One 15-ounce container ricotta cheese
1 cup shredded mozzarella cheese
1 cup grated Parmesan cheese
4 large eggs, beaten
½ teaspoon ground nutmeg

FOR THE BREAD CRUMB TOPPING:
2 cloves garlic, minced
¼ teaspoon salt
¼ teaspoon freshly ground black pepper
¾ cup fresh bread crumbs
¼ cup grated Parmesan cheese
Olive oil

1. Preheat the oven to 350°F. Lightly grease the baking dish with butter or non-stick cooking spray.

2. Bring 2 cups of water to a boil in a small saucepan and add the rice. Cook for 10 minutes, then drain into a sieve. Set aside.

3. In a large skillet, melt the butter over medium heat. Add the onion and cook, stirring frequently, until it is golden and translucent, about 5 minutes. Add the garlic, salt, and pepper and cook for another few minutes, or until the garlic is golden and translucent.

4. Pat the spinach and artichokes dry with a paper towel. Combine in a large bowl with the ricotta, mozzarella, and Parmesan cheeses. Fold in the drained rice and cooked onions and garlic, and then the eggs and nutmeg. Spread in the prepared baking dish.

5. To make the bread crumb topping, whiz the garlic, salt, pepper, bread crumbs, and Parmesan in a food processor until well combined. Sprinkle evenly over the casserole and drizzle with olive oil. (At this point the casserole can be covered and refrigerated for up to 24 hours.)

6. Bake, uncovered, for 45 minutes, or until firm and golden. Let stand for 10 minutes before serving.

Creamed Baby Onions with Grana Padano

"CREAMED" IMPLIES CREAM, OF COURSE, and this dish has plenty of it. It's no one's idea of low-calorie eating, but oh, how good it is served alongside a Christmas roast or Thanksgiving turkey. It's also a remarkably tasty topping for pasta. Fresh pearl onions are the best choice here, but you can use frozen onions for convenience, if you prefer. ❂ *Serves 6*

CASSEROLE DISH: 9 × 13-inch baking dish
BAKE TIME: 30 minutes

2 pounds boiling or pearl onions, root and stem ends trimmed, or

2 pounds frozen pearl onions, thawed and drained

2 tablespoons unsalted butter

2 tablespoons all-purpose flour

½ cup milk

1½ cups heavy cream

1 cup frozen green peas

1 teaspoon salt

2 tablespoons finely chopped fresh flat-leaf parsley

4 ounces Grana Padano cheese, shaved

Freshly ground black pepper

1. Preheat the oven to 400°F. Lightly grease the 9 × 13-inch baking dish with olive oil or nonstick cooking spray. If using fresh onions, bring a large pot of water to a boil on the stove.

2. When the water boils, add the onions and immediately turn off the heat. Let them sit for 8 to 10 minutes, then drain and rinse them under cool water. Squeeze each onion to pop it out of its skin; they should peel easily at this point. Discard the skins. Set the peeled onions aside.

3. In a large skillet capable of holding all the onions plus a little more, heat the butter over medium heat. Add the peeled or thawed onions and cook over medium heat for about 10 minutes, or until they start to soften. Remove the onions to a plate.

4. Keep the skillet over medium heat. Whisk the flour into the leftover butter and juices from the onions and cook, stirring, for 2 to 3 minutes. Whisk in the milk and cook, stirring, until the mixture thickens. Whisk in the cream and cook until the cream begins to simmer.

5. Add the onions, peas, salt, and parsley and stir to combine. Turn off the heat and pour the onion mixture into the prepared dish. Top with shavings of Grana Padano cheese and a few grinds of pepper. (At this point the casserole can be covered and refrigerated for up to 24 hours.)

6. Bake, uncovered, for 30 minutes, or until the cream is thickened and bubbling and the onions are tender. Serve hot.

Luscious Oven Creamed Corn

C REAMED CORN with just a touch of onion and the sweetness of cornbread— this casserole is halfway between traditional stovetop creamed corn and the absolutely classic cornbread casserole of the South. It lets the corn shine more than a bread usually does, but it also won't run all over your plate. Serve with something light, like chicken and steamed broccoli, so you can really enjoy this indulgent treat. ● *Serves 6 to 8*

CASSEROLE DISH: 9 × 13-inch baking dish
BAKE TIME: 45 minutes

2 tablespoons unsalted butter
1 small onion, diced
4½ cups frozen corn kernels (about 26 ounces), thawed
1 teaspoon salt
1 tablespoon sugar
½ teaspoon freshly ground black pepper
1 cup milk
½ cup heavy cream
2 tablespoons all-purpose flour
¼ cup minced fresh chives
½ cup coarse yellow cornmeal
½ cup grated Parmesan cheese

1. Preheat the oven to 350°F. Lightly grease the baking dish with nonstick cooking spray or butter.

2. In a large skillet, heat the butter over medium heat. When it foams, add the onion and cook for 5 minutes, stirring frequently. Stir in the corn and cook just until the corn is hot. Stir in the salt, sugar, and pepper.

3. Stir in the milk and cream and bring to a simmer. Whisk in the flour and cook, stirring constantly, until the mixture thickens slightly, about 5 minutes. Remove from the heat and stir in the chives and cornmeal. Spread in the prepared dish and sprinkle with the Parmesan. (At this point the casserole can be covered and refrigerated for up to 24 hours.)

4. Bake, uncovered, for 45 minutes, or until the top is golden. Let stand for 10 minutes before serving.

Frozen Versus Fresh

Like many recipes in this book, this corn casserole calls for frozen vegetables. For much of the year, frozen corn is the best option available to most shoppers (in terms of both economics and taste). But if it's high summer and you have fresh ears of corn, by all means use them instead!

Winter Vegetable and Comté Gratin

ONE OF THE BEST WAYS to use seasonal vegetables is to mix them with a bit of cheese and bake. This recipe and the four that follow adhere to this principle and are designed to help you make the most of whatever is on hand, whatever season it might happen to be. In winter it often seems that nothing is in season except turnips, rutabagas, and potatoes. But a dish that tosses them all together revives both the root vegetables and the table that's weary of winter produce. Experiment with the vegetables suggested below; if you don't like one, leave it out, or, if you love rutabaga, try making this with just that alone. ○ *Serves 6*

CASSEROLE DISH: 9 × 13-inch baking dish
BAKE TIME: 45 to 50 minutes

¼ cup short-grain white rice
1 large onion, diced
2 cloves garlic, minced
1½ cups grated Comté cheese
1 small bunch fresh flat-leaf parsley, finely chopped
3 pounds mixed winter root vegetables, such as carrots, turnips, rutabagas, parsnips,
  white potatoes, and sweet potatoes, peeled
2 teaspoons kosher salt
Freshly ground black pepper
Olive oil

1. Preheat the oven to 400°F. Lightly grease the baking dish with olive oil. Bring a small saucepan of water to a boil and add the rice. Cook, uncovered, for 10 minutes, then drain and set aside.

2. Mix the onion, garlic, cheese, and parsley in a medium bowl. Stir in the parboiled rice.

3. Slice all of the vegetables to an even thickness of about ¼ inch. A mandoline or slicer is extremely helpful for doing this quickly! Toss the vegetables in a large bowl with the kosher salt, a generous amount of black pepper, and enough olive oil to lightly coat the slices. Layer one-third of the sliced vegetables in the baking dish; you can make each layer a different vegetable or overlap slices from different vegetables in each layer. This dish should be beautiful as well as delicious, so do what looks good to you.

4. Spread half of the onion mixture over the layer. Repeat, using half of the remaining vegetables and all of the remaining onion mixture, then finish with a final layer of vegetables. Drizzle with olive oil.

5. Cover tightly with aluminum foil and bake for 25 minutes. Uncover and bake for an additional 20 to 25 minutes, or until all the vegetables are soft and tender. Serve hot.

Roasted Autumn Vegetables
with Parmesan and Sage

AUTUMN VEGETABLES MEAN SQUASH! Butternut squash and two kinds of potatoes make up this savory orange side dish, roasted into deep flavor with Parmesan cheese to hold it all together. ○ *Serves 8*

CASSEROLE DISH: 9 × 13-inch baking dish
BAKE TIME: 60 to 75 minutes

One 2½-pound butternut squash
1 pound sweet potatoes, unpeeled, cut into 1-inch cubes
1 pound Yukon gold potatoes, unpeeled, cut into ½-inch cubes

1 small red onion, diced

3 cloves garlic, minced

¼ cup olive oil

2 teaspoons kosher salt

1 teaspoon freshly ground black pepper

4 sprigs fresh sage (leaves only), minced

1½ cups grated Parmesan cheese

1. Preheat the oven to 350°F. Lightly grease the baking dish with nonstick cooking spray.

2. To peel the squash, first cut it in half crosswise through the middle. Stand up one half of the cut squash on the cutting board, cut side down, and with a sharp chef's knife slice off the outer peel in long, shallow strips. Repeat with the second half of the squash. Cut each half again in half lengthwise and scoop out and discard any seeds. Cut each quarter into evenly sized cubes about 1 inch square.

3. Toss the cubed squash, sweet potatoes, and white potatoes in a very large bowl with the red onion, garlic, and olive oil. Add the salt, pepper, sage, and 1 cup Parmesan cheese and mix well.

4. Spread in the prepared baking dish and roast, stirring occasionally, for 60 to 75 minutes, until the vegetables are tender and lightly browned. In the final 15 minutes of cooking, sprinkle with the remaining ½ cup of Parmesan cheese and bake until the cheese is sizzling. Serve hot.

Cut Veggies Evenly

What size are you cutting your vegetables? The baking times for many casseroles hinge on how large (or small) you've chopped your vegetables or other ingredients. Big chunks of potato will take longer to roast than tiny cubes. It's okay if you cut your squash a little bigger than 1 inch to a side, for instance; no need to pull out the tape measure. The most crucial thing, in the end, is that you cut vegetables to a uniform size, so that everything is cooking at the same rate. Be flexible with your cooking times when roasting vegetables. Keep an eye on them and test before pulling them out of the oven.

Summer Vegetable and Fresh Mozzarella Gratin

SUMMERTIME IS THE BEST TIME to make quick and easy casseroles out of fresh vegetables. Late-summer squash, ripe tomatoes, olive oil, and cheese are all you need for a quick dinner. This gratin can be a main dish or a side; I particularly like it paired with the Smoked Sausage and Sage Pasta Casserole (page 188). Look for good fresh mozzarella at the deli counter. If you can't find it there, then use the fullest-fat mozzarella you can find in the dairy case. Make sure you're buying fresh mozzarella (usually sold in brine), not the low-moisture kind that's available pre-shredded. ● *Serves 6*

CASSEROLE DISH: 9 × 13-inch baking dish
BAKE TIME: 45 minutes

2 small yellow summer squash
2 small zucchini
4 small tomatoes
1 large red bell pepper, cored
2 cloves garlic, minced
3 tablespoons olive oil
1½ teaspoons salt
1 teaspoon freshly ground black pepper
6 ounces fresh whole-milk mozzarella cheese
½ cup grated Parmesan cheese
½ cup dry bread crumbs

1. Preheat the oven to 375°F. Lightly grease the baking dish with olive oil.

2. Slice the yellow squash and zucchini into half-moons, and coarsely chop the tomatoes and bell pepper. Stir all the vegetables and garlic together in a large bowl and toss with the olive oil, salt, and pepper. Spread in the casserole dish.

3. Chop the mozzarella into evenly sized cubes and tuck between the vegetables. Mix the Parmesan and bread crumbs in a small bowl and sprinkle evenly over the top of the vegetables and cheese.

4. Bake for 45 minutes, or until the top is well browned. Let rest for 10 minutes before serving.

The Useful Mandoline

I am not a big proponent of owning a lot of fancy kitchen equipment. Most recipes in this book can be made with a good knife, a few spoons, a bowl, and a peeler (and a casserole dish, of course). But I do think that a mandoline or Japanese slicer is a huge help in preparing some of these casseroles—especially ones like this vegetable gratin, which calls for very thin, even slices of vegetables. You can find a Benriner Japanese mandoline for about $25 online. It will massively speed up your slicing. After I got one, I wondered what I ever did without it!

Creamy Spring Vegetable Gratin with Grana Padano

THE IDEA OF SPRING VEGETABLES is a bit deceptive. Although vegetable gardens are sprouting and the trees are turning green, there is actually very little ready to eat yet! So a spring vegetable gratin turns to those lovely over-wintered vegetables that are still so fresh and appealing in the early springtime, like leeks and crisp fennel. ○ *Serves 6*

CASSEROLE DISH: 9 × 13-inch baking dish
BAKE TIME: 1 hour

2 small fennel bulbs, trimmed
2 large leeks
2 large russet potatoes (¾ pound), peeled
1 large onion, thinly sliced
4 cloves garlic, minced
1 cup sour cream
1 teaspoon salt
½ teaspoon ground nutmeg
¼ teaspoon freshly ground black pepper
1 cup grated Grana Padano cheese

1. Preheat the oven to 400°F. Lightly grease the baking dish with olive oil.

2. Using a mandoline or very sharp knife, cut the fennel bulb into thin slices. Cut each leek in half lengthwise and rinse to remove any grit; pat dry. Slice the leek halves into 1-inch-wide half moons and separate each layer. Slice the potatoes about as thin as the fennel, and toss all these vegetables in a large bowl with the onion and garlic.

3. Stir in the sour cream, salt, nutmeg, pepper, and cheese. Scrape into the prepared baking dish and cover tightly with foil. Bake for 30 minutes, then remove the foil and bake for an additional 30 minutes to let the top brown. Serve hot.

Creamy Celery Root Gratin

MOST OF THE RECIPES IN THIS BOOK don't call for great quantities of cream or butter; you can find those sorts of recipes elsewhere easily enough. But there are a few exceptions, and this celery root gratin is one of them. Celery root, or celeriac, is a delicately flavored root vegetable that is often overlooked because of its intimidatingly knobbly appearance, but it deserves the rich, luxurious treatment it gets in this dish. More flavorful than potatoes and much more subtle than its sister, celery, it deserves a starring role at the winter table. ○ *Serves 4 to 6*

CASSEROLE DISH: 9-inch square baking dish or 2-quart gratin dish
BAKE TIME: 50 minutes

2 tablespoons unsalted butter
1 large onion, finely diced
1½ cups heavy cream
1½ teaspoons salt
½ teaspoon freshly ground black pepper
½ teaspoon ground nutmeg
2 medium heads celery root (about 3 pounds), peeled
2 cups grated Parmesan cheese
¼ cup fresh bread crumbs

1. Preheat the oven to 400°F. Lightly grease the baking dish with nonstick cooking spray or butter.

2. Melt the 2 tablespoons butter in a large skillet over medium heat. When it foams, add the onion and cook for 10 minutes, or until the onion is translucent, golden, and fragrant. Add the cream and cook just until the cream is warmed through. Turn off the heat and add the salt, pepper, and nutmeg.

3. Cut each celery root in half. With a mandoline or very sharp knife, cut each half into ¼-inch-thick slices. Place the slices in the cream mixture as you cut them to keep them from discoloring; celery root turns brown when exposed to the air.

4. Stir the celery root into the cream mixture, along with 1½ cups of the Parmesan. Pour the whole mixture into the prepared baking dish and spread it evenly.

5. Mix the remaining ½ cup of Parmesan with the bread crumbs in a small bowl and sprinkle evenly over the top. (At this point the casserole can be covered and refrigerated for up to 24 hours.) Bake, uncovered, for 50 minutes, or until the top is browned and the vegetables are tender. Let the gratin set for 15 minutes before serving.

Working with Celeriac

Peeling celery root is similar to peeling butternut squash. Cut off the ends so it can stand upright without wobbling; cut it in half crosswise into two more accessible halves if necessary. Then take a sharp chef's knife and carefully slice away the outer skin with long, shallow cuts. You'll lose a little of the celeriac's flesh as you do this, but it is much, much faster than attempting to peel it with a paring knife or vegetable peeler.

Root Vegetable Cobbler with Whole-Grain Biscuit Topping

USUALLY A COBBLER IS A SWEET DISH (blueberry cobbler, anyone?). But cobblers aren't only for fruit; potatoes, carrots, and rutabagas should get their turn, too. This creamy, wholesome casserole is an all-in-one supper for a cold winter's night, rich with herbs and vegetable flavor and topped with a savory Parmesan biscuit. ◦ *Serves 8*

CASSEROLE DISH: 9 × 13-inch baking dish
BAKE TIME: 45 minutes

2 tablespoons unsalted butter

1 large yellow onion, diced

2 large carrots, peeled and diced into ½-inch cubes

2 stalks celery, diced

4 cloves garlic, minced

¼ teaspoon red pepper flakes (optional)

1 rutabaga (about 2½ pounds), peeled and diced into 1-inch cubes

2 small turnips (about ½ pound), peeled and diced into 1-inch cubes

1½ pounds small red potatoes, diced into 1-inch cubes

2 sprigs rosemary (leaves only)

2 sprigs sage (leaves only)

Small handful (about ¼ cup) fresh flat-leaf parsley, chopped

1 cup low-sodium beef or vegetable broth

1 cup grated Parmesan or Asiago cheese

1 cup heavy cream

1¼ teaspoon salt

1 teaspoon freshly ground black pepper

2 tablespoons all-purpose flour

FOR THE BISCUIT TOPPING:

1½ cups whole wheat flour

½ cup rolled oats

¼ cup grated Parmesan or Asiago cheese

2½ teaspoons baking powder

½ teaspoon salt
¼ cup (½ stick) unsalted butter, cut into small chunks
1¼ cups milk

1. Preheat the oven to 325°F. Lightly grease the baking dish with olive oil.

2. Heat the butter in a Dutch oven or wide pot with high sides over medium heat. When the butter foams, add the onion, carrot, and celery and cook over medium heat, stirring frequently, until the onion is golden and fragrant and the vegetables are soft, about 8 minutes. Add the garlic and red pepper flakes, if using, and cook for another 4 to 5 minutes, or until the garlic is golden and fragrant.

3. Add the rutabaga, turnips, and potatoes and stir to mix well with the onion and butter mixture. Add the rosemary, sage, and parsley, and cook, stirring, for 2 to 3 minutes.

4. Add the broth and bring to a simmer. Cover partially and cook for 15 minutes. Turn off the heat.

5. Using a slotted spoon, transfer the vegetables to the prepared baking dish. Add the cheese and toss to combine. Stir the cream, salt, and pepper into the broth remaining in the pot. Whisk in the flour and cook over low heat until the sauce thickens slightly. Pour over the vegetables in the baking dish. (At this point the casserole can be covered and refrigerated for up to 24 hours.)

6. For the biscuit topping, in a large bowl mix the flour, oats, cheese, baking powder, and salt. Using a pastry blender or your fingers, blend the butter into the flour until it is incorporated and the flour-and-butter chunks are the size of small peas. (You can also do this in the food processor: Pulse the flour mixture with the butter in 3 to 5 short bursts until coarsely mixed.)

7. Stir in the milk just until the dough comes together roughly; do not overmix. Drop by spoonfuls on top of the vegetables, flattening each spoonful until it is no more than ½ inch thick.

8. Bake for 45 minutes, or until the biscuit crust is browned and golden, the vegetables are tender, and the filling is hot and bubbly. Let stand for 10 minutes before serving.

Sweet and Spicy Parsnip Bake

PARSNIPS, LIKE SWEET POTATOES, are one of those naturally sweet vegetables that are often cooked and served in ways that enhance their sweetness. You often see parsnips glazed with brown sugar or baked with other sweeteners, but I prefer to play against their sweetness with a little spice. This very quick vegetable bake tosses sweet, mellow parsnips with spicy, smoky chipotle powder. Substitute the more mellow smoked paprika if you prefer your side dishes less spicy.

○ Serves 4 to 6

CASSEROLE DISH: 9-inch square baking dish or 2-quart gratin dish
BAKE TIME: 30 minutes

2½ pounds parsnips, peeled
⅓ cup olive oil
1 teaspoon chipotle chile powder or smoked paprika
1 teaspoon salt
½ teaspoon freshly ground black pepper
1 cup grated Swiss or Gruyère cheese

1. Preheat the oven to 375°F. Lightly grease the baking dish with olive oil.

2. Shred the parsnips into coarse shreds using a food processor. (This can also be done using a box grater, but it takes longer. You can also shred the parsnips into thin matchsticks using the appropriate mandoline attachment.)

3. Toss the shredded parsnips in a large bowl with the olive oil, chipotle powder, salt, pepper, and ½ cup of the cheese. Spread evenly in the prepared baking dish. Sprinkle with the remaining ½ cup of cheese.

4. Bake for 30 minutes, or until tender. Serve immediately.

Baked Summer Ratatouille

RATATOUILLE IS THE QUINTESSENTIAL French harvest dish. It is tradition-ally a lightly cooked stew of eggplant, zucchini, summer squash, tomatoes, and herbs—the best parts of a summer's garden bounty. But ever since Pixar's delightful animated film *Ratatouille*, this dish has been re-created all over the Internet and in restaurants as a deconstructed and even more colorful version, in imitation of the film's signature dish (and climactic moment). It just so happens that this version is baked, so here is ratatouille, *Ratatouille*-style. ○ *Serves 6*

CASSEROLE DISH: 9 × 13-inch baking dish
BAKE TIME: 40 minutes

1 large eggplant, cut in half lengthwise
Salt
Olive oil
2 large onions, diced
6 cloves garlic, minced
¼ teaspoon red pepper flakes (optional)
One 3-inch sprig fresh rosemary
One 28-ounce can crushed tomatoes, drained, or 2 pounds fresh tomatoes, finely chopped
½ cup dry white wine
1 red bell pepper
1 green bell pepper
1 medium-size zucchini
1 medium-size yellow summer squash
½ teaspoon freshly ground black pepper
½ cup loosely packed fresh basil leaves, chopped
½ cup loosely packed fresh flat-leaf parsley, chopped

FOR THE BREAD CRUMB TOPPING:
1½ cup bread crumbs
2 cloves garlic, peeled
½ cup loosely packed fresh flat-leaf parsley
2 sprigs thyme (leaves only)
¼ teaspoon salt
¼ cup olive oil

1. Preheat the oven to 350°F. Grease the baking dish with olive oil. Set aside.

2. Line 2 plates with paper towels. Using a mandoline or chef's knife, slice the eggplant into very thin slices—about ⅛ inch thick. Place the eggplant on the plates and sprinkle lightly with salt. Let these slices sit while you prepare the sauce and the rest of the vegetables.

3. In a deep skillet or wide saucepan, heat a drizzle of olive oil over medium heat. Add the onions and cook over medium heat until golden, about 10 minutes. Add the garlic, red pepper flakes, if using, and the rosemary sprig. Cook, stirring frequently, until the garlic is softened and golden.

4. Add the tomatoes and cook over medium heat for 10 minutes, or until broken down and bubbling. Stir in the wine, bring to a simmer, and turn the heat to low. Let the sauce simmer for another 15 minutes while you prepare the vegetables.

5. Cut the bell peppers in half crosswise and remove the seeds and core. Slice them into rounds, as thin as possible. Slice the zucchini and summer squash into thin slices as well; they should be about the same thickness as the eggplant. Rinse the eggplant of salt and any liquid that has seeped out, and pat dry.

6. Turn off the heat under the sauce, and stir in 1 teaspoon salt, the black pepper, and the basil and parsley. Spread half the sauce in the prepared dish.

7. Layer half of the vegetables in overlapping rows in the dish on top of the sauce, alternating eggplant, zucchini, summer squash, and bell peppers evenly. Pour the rest of the sauce over the top. Layer the rest of the vegetables on top.

8. For the bread crumb topping, whiz the bread crumbs, garlic, parsley, thyme, salt, and olive oil in a food processor until well combined. Sprinkle evenly over the casserole.

9. Bake for 40 minutes, or until the vegetables are tender and just releasing their juices. Serve immediately.

Summer Squash and Tomato Casserole with Crunchy Topping

THE IDEA FOR THIS RECIPE comes from Vanessa Barrington, a wonderful chef and author out in the San Francisco Bay Area. We co-wrote a weblog together for a while, and I was always so inspired by her fresh, practical, and simple approach to seasonal food. ○ *Serves 6 to 8*

CASSEROLE DISH: 9 × 13-inch baking dish
BAKE TIME: 35 minutes

3 medium-size zucchini, sliced crosswise into ¼-inch-thick coins
3 medium-size summer squash, sliced crosswise into ¼-inch-thick coins
⅓ cup olive oil, plus more for drizzling
½ cup loosely packed fresh basil leaves, finely chopped
4 sprigs fresh oregano (leaves only)
1 teaspoon salt
½ teaspoon freshly ground black pepper
3 large tomatoes, thinly sliced
½ cup grated Parmesan cheese

FOR THE BREAD CRUMB TOPPING:
1 cup dry bread crumbs
⅓ cup grated Parmesan cheese
½ teaspoon salt
½ teaspoon freshly ground black pepper

1. Preheat the oven to 400°F. Lightly grease the bottom of the baking dish with olive oil.

2. Toss the zucchini and squash in a large bowl with the olive oil, basil, oregano, salt, and pepper.

3. Lay half the sliced zucchini and squash in the bottom of the baking dish, overlapping the slices. Top with an overlapping layer of half of the tomatoes, drizzle lightly with olive oil, and cover with the Parmesan. Add a layer of the remaining zucchini and squash and one more of the remaining tomatoes.

4. For the bread crumb topping, mix the bread crumbs, Parmesan, salt, and pepper in a small bowl, and sprinkle thickly on top of the casserole. Drizzle with olive oil and bake for 35 minutes, or until the casserole is bubbly and the bread crumbs are browned. Let stand for 10 minutes before serving.

Greek Braised Green Beans

GREEN BEANS ARE OFTEN TREATED DELICATELY—sautéed or quickly blanched to preserve their color and snap. But only the thinnest, freshest baby green beans really benefit from such quick cooking. Mature green beans have fibers that are broken down, and flavors that are released, only after long, slow cooking. You can see this slow braising employed in many green bean recipes from around the world, but my favorite is the Greek style, with touches of lemon, cinnamon, and tomato. ○ *Serves 8*

CASSEROLE DISH: 4-quart Dutch oven or heavy ovenproof sauté pan with lid
BAKE TIME: 45 to 60 minutes

2 pounds fresh or frozen green beans
Olive oil
1 large onion, finely chopped
4 cloves garlic, minced
½ teaspoon red pepper flakes (optional)
One 14.5-ounce can diced tomatoes, drained
1 cup white wine
1 teaspoon salt
1 teaspoon ground cinnamon
½ teaspoon freshly ground black pepper
1 lemon, cut into wedges

1. Preheat the oven to 325°F. Wash and snap the green beans, if using fresh beans. If using frozen, thaw them a little by rinsing with cold water; let them drain in a colander in the sink.

2. Heat a drizzle of olive oil in the Dutch oven or sauté pan over medium heat. Add the onion, garlic, and red pepper flakes, if using, and cook, stirring frequently, for 10 minutes, or until the onions and garlic are soft and fragrant. Add the green beans, tomatoes, and wine. Stir in the salt, cinnamon, and black pepper and bring to a simmer.

3. Bake, covered, for 45 to 60 minutes, or until the beans are very tender. Serve immediately, with the lemon wedges on the side.

Green Bean and Wild Mushroom Casserole with Shallot Topping

GREEN BEAN CASSEROLE— is there a more classic casserole dish? The typical green bean casserole calls for several processed ingredients, like cream of mushroom soup and canned fried onions. This version echoes that old favorite quite closely, but it uses all-natural ingredients and a few special touches like wild mushrooms and delicate, savory shallots for a topping. ❍ *Serves 6*

CASSEROLE DISH: 9 × 13-inch baking dish
BAKE TIME: 55 to 65 minutes

1½ pounds fresh or frozen green beans
½ ounce dried wild mushrooms
½ cup boiling water
3 tablespoons unsalted butter
½ pound white mushrooms, diced
¼ cup all-purpose flour
½ cup low-sodium chicken broth
¾ cup milk
¾ teaspoon salt
½ teaspoon freshly ground black pepper
10 large shallots
Vegetable oil

1. Preheat the oven to 350°F. Lightly grease the baking dish with butter or non-stick cooking spray. If using fresh green beans, trim them of their stems. If using frozen, thaw them and drain off any excess water.

2. Place the dried mushrooms in a small bowl and pour the boiling water over them; let steep to rehydrate.

3. In a large skillet or sauté pan, melt the butter over medium-high heat. When it foams, add the white mushrooms, spreading them in an even layer. Do not stir or move the mushrooms for 3 to 4 minutes; let them brown. Then toss the mushrooms and cook thoroughly on the other side.

4. Drain the wild mushrooms, reserving the steeping liquid in the bowl. Add the wild mushrooms to the skillet with the other mushrooms and cook, stirring, for 2 to 3 more minutes.

5. Add the flour to the mushrooms and stir to coat the mushrooms. Add the mushroom steeping liquid and chicken broth and whisk the liquid to break up any clumps. Stir in the milk and cook, stirring and whisking alternately, until the liquid is slightly thickened.

6. Take the mushrooms off the heat and stir in the salt, pepper, and green beans. Spread in the prepared casserole dish. (At this point the casserole can be covered and refrigerated for up to 24 hours.)

7. Peel and finely slice the shallots. Thoroughly wipe out or wash the skillet and heat about ½ inch of vegetable oil in it over high heat. When it is quite hot but not yet smoking, add the shallots in a thin, even layer. Turn the heat to medium-low and cook for 10 minutes, or until light golden brown. Stir occasionally if necessary to keep the shallots from burning or sticking together.

8. Remove the shallots from the oil with a slotted spoon and stir half of them into the green bean casserole. Cover with aluminum foil and bake for 50 to 60 minutes.

9. Spread the remaining fried shallots on top of the green bean casserole. Bake, uncovered, for 5 minutes, or until the topping is crispy. Let stand for 5 minutes, then serve.

Fresh Versus Frozen

Frozen beans will need less cooking time than fresh beans. Check them after 45 minutes, and keep checking every few minutes after that. Frozen beans have a tendency to get mushy when overcooked, whereas fresh beans will keep their texture for much longer into the cooking process.

Tomato, Arugula, and Mushroom Casserole

TOMATOES AND MUSHROOMS are an unlikely pair. One is bright and juicy and loves the sunshine, and the other is savory and spongy and grows in the dark. But they really are so delicious when served together. This is a very simple vegetable gratin with big handfuls of cheese and fresh herbs, too.

○ Serves 4 to 6

CASEROLE DISH: 9-inch square baking dish or 2-quart gratin dish
BAKE TIME: 30 minutes

3 large tomatoes, sliced
Salt
½ cup short-grain rice
2 tablespoons unsalted butter
1 pound white mushrooms, sliced
4 sprigs fresh thyme (leaves only)
4 cloves garlic, minced
3 large eggs, well beaten
1 teaspoon salt
½ teaspoon freshly ground black pepper
5 ounces arugula, coarsely shredded
2 cups grated Asiago cheese

1. Preheat the oven to 350°F. Grease the baking dish with olive oil. Layer half of the sliced tomatoes in the bottom of the dish in overlapping rows. Sprinkle the tomatoes lightly with salt.

2. Bring a small saucepan of water to a boil and add the rice. Cook for 10 minutes, then drain the rice into a sieve and set aside.

3. In a large skillet, heat the butter over medium-high heat until it foams. Add the mushrooms and cook without moving them for 4 minutes. Flip and stir and cook for another 4 minutes. Add the thyme leaves and garlic and cook for 5 minutes, stirring frequently. Pour the mixture into a large bowl, add the rice, eggs, salt, and pepper, and mix. Stir in the shredded arugula and 1 cup of the Asiago.

4. Spread the mushroom mixture over the tomatoes in the dish. Layer the rest of the tomatoes on top in overlapping rows and sprinkle with the remaining 1 cup of Asiago. (At this point the casserole can be covered and refrigerated for up to 24 hours.) Bake, uncovered, for 30 minutes, or until set and bubbly. Serve hot.

Mediterranean Tomato-Stuffed Tomatoes

RIPE, RED, JUICY SUMMER TOMATOES just beg to be stuffed with good things (like cheese) and roasted until soft and sweet. Many stuffed-tomato recipes discard all that luscious tomato pulp or have you save it for later uses; this particular version doesn't waste it. All that juicy tomato goodness is mashed together with Mediterranean delicacies like capers and pine nuts and stuffed back into the tomato with not one but two kinds of cheese. Happy summer!

○ *Serves 6*

CASSEROLE DISH: 9 × 13-inch baking dish
BAKE TIME: 20 minutes

6 large, ripe, firm tomatoes
Salt
Sugar
½ cup couscous
½ cup boiling water
¼ cup pine nuts
Olive oil
2 cloves garlic, minced
¼ cup brine-packed capers, drained
½ cup loosely packed fresh flat-leaf parsley, finely chopped
2 sprigs fresh oregano (leaves only)
4 ounces whole-milk mozzarella cheese, cut into small cubes
½ teaspoon salt
½ teaspoon freshly ground black pepper
½ cup grated Parmesan cheese

1. Preheat the oven to 350°F. Cut off the top of each tomato, remove and discard the hard core on top, and scoop out the insides, reserving the tomato pulp in a separate bowl. (If the tomatoes don't want to stand up, cut off their bottoms instead and stand them on their stem ends.) Place the tomatoes in the baking dish and sprinkle their insides lightly with a pinch of salt and sugar. Drain off any really juicy liquid from the bowl of tomato pulp, leaving flesh and seeds behind.

2. Put the couscous in a medium bowl and pour the boiling water over it. Cover and let stand for 5 minutes.

3. Heat a large, dry skillet over medium heat. When it is quite warm to the touch, add the pine nuts. Cook for about 3 minutes, stirring frequently. When the pine nuts are turning golden brown and fragrant, transfer them to a plate to cool.

4. Return the skillet to the stove and add a drizzle of olive oil; heat over medium heat. Add the garlic and cook slowly, stirring frequently, until golden and fragrant. Add the couscous, capers, parsley, oregano, pine nuts, and tomato pulp, and cook, stirring frequently, until hot.

5. Turn off the heat and stir in the mozzarella, salt, and pepper. Stuff each tomato with this mixture. Sprinkle with the Parmesan. (At this point the tomatoes can be covered and refrigerated for up to 24 hours. Bring to room temperature before baking.) Bake, uncovered, for 20 minutes, or until bubbling and hot. Serve immediately.

Beet Gratin with Goat Cheese and Greens

LOVE BEETS' SWEET EARTHINESS and their brilliant red hue. I also think that their flavor is best brought out by the oven. This recipe bakes beets with two of their classic accompaniments: their own green tops and soft, creamy goat cheese. It's quicker than most beet gratins, since it doesn't require the beets to be roasted ahead of time. You do need two extra pieces of equipment for this recipe: a mandoline to cut the tough beet root into even slices, and disposable kitchen gloves to prevent your fingers from being dyed hot pink. ○ *Serves 8*

CASSEROLE DISH: 9 × 13-inch baking dish
BAKE TIME: 1 hour

3 pounds red beets (about 6 medium beets), with greens attached
Salt and freshly ground black pepper
Olive oil
2 cloves garlic, minced
2 ounces goat cheese, finely crumbled
½ cup whole milk
1 cup dry bread crumbs
Zest of 1 lemon
4 sprigs fresh thyme (leaves only)

1. Preheat the oven to 350°F and lightly grease the baking dish with olive oil.

2. Put on disposable kitchen gloves and chop the stalks and green tops off the beets. Cut off the root and stem ends of each beet root so that each end is flat. Lightly rinse the beet roots in the sink and peel them with a vegetable peeler. Slice the peeled beets very thin with a mandoline—the slices should be about ⅛ inch thick. (This entire operation is best done in the sink, to avoid beet-juice splatters.) Line the prepared baking dish with half of the beet slices, overlapping them as necessary to form a thick layer. Sprinkle the slices lightly with salt and pepper.

3. Separate the green leaves from the lower, thicker stalks. Cut the stalks into ½-inch segments and rinse them well. Drain and set aside in a small bowl.

4. Cut each beet leaf in half, then into thin ribbons. Wash very well and drain thoroughly.

5. Set a deep 10-inch sauté pan over medium heat and add a generous drizzle of olive oil. When the oil is shimmering, add the minced garlic and cook for a moment, then add the chopped beet stalks. Cook, stirring occasionally, for about 5 minutes. Add the ribbons of beet greens and stir them in. Add a pinch of salt and pepper and cook, stirring frequently, for another 5 minutes, or until the greens are slightly wilted. Turn off the heat.

6. Use a slotted spoon to lift out the beet stalks and greens, leaving any extra liquid behind in the pan. Spread the greens and stalks evenly over the sliced beets in the baking dish. Sprinkle the crumbled goat cheese evenly over the greens. Top with the remaining beet slices, again overlapping them as needed to form a thick layer. Sprinkle them lightly with salt and pepper. Pour the milk evenly over the beets.

7. Mix the bread crumbs, lemon zest, and thyme leaves in a small bowl. Add a pinch of salt and pepper and a drizzle of olive oil. Mix until the bread crumbs

have the texture of wet sand, and then spread them evenly over the top layer of beets. Drizzle with olive oil.

8. Bake for 1 hour, or until the beets are tender when pierced with a fork and the bread crumbs are golden. Remove the dish from the oven and let it stand for 15 minutes before serving.

Shredded Beets Baked with Caramelized Onions and Orange Zest

THESE DOUBLE-BAKED BEETS are a treat, cooked with caramelized onions and orange zest to brighten them. They are very rich, with blue cheese and all the savory sweetness that beets have, so serve them in small quantities next to grilled pork chops or roasted chicken thighs. ○ *Serves 6*

CASSEROLE DISH: 9-inch square baking dish
BAKE TIME: 60 to 70 minutes for the beets; 30 minutes for the casserole

4 medium beets
4 cloves garlic, peeled
Olive oil
Salt and freshly ground black pepper
2 tablespoons unsalted butter
4 small onions, thinly sliced
2 oranges, zested and juiced
4 ounces blue cheese, crumbled

1. Preheat the oven to 375°F. Line the baking dish with aluminum foil and place the beets in the center, along with the garlic. Drizzle olive oil generously over the beets and season with salt and pepper. Seal the foil by gathering up the ends and folding them in the center. Bake for 60 to 70 minutes, or until the beets are quite tender when pierced with a fork. Remove the beets from the pan and open the foil packet to let them cool. Remove the roasted garlic cloves and discard, or save as a sandwich spread or bread topping. Use a paper towel to rub any olive oil that leaked out of the packet over the bottom of the baking dish, and set the dish aside.

2. While the beets are roasting, heat the butter in a large skillet over medium-high heat. When it foams, add the onions. Turn the heat to medium-low and cook the onions slowly, stirring every few minutes, until they are deep golden brown. Depending on the thickness of the onions and the size of the skillet, this will take anywhere from 25 to 35 minutes.

3. Let the roasted beets cool for 15 minutes before handling them. Then peel each beet by holding it in a paper towel and lightly rubbing it to remove the skin. It should peel right off. The paper towels should keep your fingers from getting too stained. Shred the beets using a box grater. (You may want to do this in the sink to minimize beet-juice splatter.) Place the shredded beets in a large bowl and toss with the orange juice and zest. Mix in the caramelized onions and the cheese, and then season with salt and pepper to taste.

4. Spread the mixture in the prepared baking dish. (At this point the casserole can be covered and refrigerated for up to 24 hours.) Bake, uncovered, for 30 minutes, or until the cheese crumbles have softened. Serve hot.

Oven-Braised Radishes with Balsamic Vinegar

HAVE YOU EVER COOKED A RADISH? Basic red radishes are almost never cooked; they're grated for salads and slaws, but rarely tossed in a hot pan. Well, this recipe is a favorite spring dish that demonstrates how yummy a radish can be when it's cooked. These braised radishes are warm and tender with a crisp bite, nearly bursting with flavorful juices. ○ *Serves 4*

CASSEROLE DISH: 10-inch cast-iron skillet
BAKE TIME: 15 minutes

3 large bunches radishes (about 2 pounds)
2 slices bacon, diced
1 small red onion, diced

¼ cup balsamic vinegar
⅔ cup water
½ cup loosely packed mint leaves, finely chopped
1 teaspoon kosher salt
Freshly ground black pepper

1. Preheat the oven to 350°F.

2. Trim away the tops and bottoms of the radishes (if they came with green tops, reserve them for soup or a peppery addition to a green salad). Slice each radish in half from top to bottom.

3. Place the bacon in the cast-iron skillet and turn the heat to medium. Slowly cook the bacon until the fat renders out. Add the red onion and cook for about 10 minutes, stirring frequently, until it is soft and nearly translucent.

4. Turn the heat to medium-high and add the radishes, cut side down. If they won't all fit into the skillet in one layer, layer some on top. Cook for 3 minutes.

5. Add the balsamic vinegar and the water and immediately place the skillet in the oven. Cook for 15 minutes, or until the sauce has reduced to a syrup and the radishes are tender. Toss with the mint leaves, salt, and pepper. Serve immediately.

Roasted Carrots with Lemon, Feta, and Mint

CARROTS ARE SO DELICIOUS WHEN ROASTED. It really brings out their innate sweetness. Here that sweetness is balanced by the tanginess of feta cheese and a touch of lemon. I love a healthy helping of spicy red pepper flakes, too. If you prefer a less spicy dish, use smoked paprika instead, or just a pinch of red pepper. ○ *Serves 4 to 6*

CASSEROLE DISH: 9 × 13-inch baking dish
BAKE TIME: 30 to 45 minutes

2 pounds carrots, peeled and sliced on the diagonal into ½-inch pieces

⅔ cup olive oil

Zest and juice of 2 lemons

½ teaspoon red pepper flakes

4 ounces feta cheese, crumbled

½ teaspoon salt

⅓ cup fresh mint leaves, coarsely chopped

1. Preheat the oven to 425°F. Toss the carrots in a large bowl with ⅓ cup of the olive oil, the lemon zest, and the red pepper flakes. Spread the mixture in the baking dish and crumble the feta cheese on top.

2. Roast for 30 to 45 minutes, or until the carrots are tender and slightly browned. Mix the remaining ⅓ cup of olive oil in a small bowl with the lemon juice, salt, and mint leaves. Toss with the carrots and serve immediately.

Mushroom Casserole with Cheese and Onions

ONE OF MY FAVORITE COMBINATIONS is mushrooms, onions, and cheese. It's homey, savory, and so comforting. This is that favorite combo in casserole form, with plenty of cheese, creamy filling, and mushroom flavor to satisfy. It is adapted from the mushroom casserole at Heidi Swanson's lovely blog, 101 Cookbooks. ○ *Serves 6*

CASSEROLE DISH: 9 × 13-inch baking dish

BAKE TIME: 45 minutes

1 cup short-grain rice

2 tablespoons all-purpose butter

½ pound white mushrooms, chopped

½ pound portobello mushrooms, chopped

1 large onion, diced

4 cloves garlic, minced

1 small sprig fresh rosemary (leaves only), finely chopped

1 teaspoon salt

½ teaspoon freshly ground black pepper

½ teaspoon ground nutmeg

½ cup dry white wine

4 large eggs, beaten

1½ cups ricotta cheese

½ cup sour cream

½ cup grated Gruyère cheese

1. Preheat the oven to 350°F. Lightly grease the baking dish with olive oil.

2. Heat several cups of salted water to boiling in a medium-size saucepan. Add the rice and cook for 12 minutes. Drain in a sieve and set aside.

3. In a large skillet over medium-high heat, melt the butter. When it foams, add the mushrooms in as thin a layer as possible. Let them cook undisturbed for 5 minutes, then flip them and cook for another 3 to 4 minutes.

4. Transfer all the mushrooms to a large bowl and set aside. Turn the heat to medium-high and add the onions and garlic to the skillet. Cook for 6 to 8 minutes, or until they are fragrant and soft. Stir in the rosemary, salt, pepper, and nutmeg. Cook for another minute, or until the herbs are fragrant.

5. Add the onion mixture to the mushrooms in the bowl. Turn the heat to high and add the white wine, scraping and stirring up any stuck bits from the pan. Add the wine and any scraped-up bits to the bowl with the mushrooms and onions. Add the drained rice, eggs, ricotta, sour cream, and Gruyère to the bowl with the mushrooms and onions and combine thoroughly.

6. Spread the mixture in the prepared baking dish. (At this point the casserole can be covered and refrigerated for up to 24 hours.) Cover with foil and bake for 30 minutes. Remove the foil and bake for an additional 15 minutes, or until set and the top is golden. Let stand for 10 minutes before serving.

Oven-Baked Rice, Potatoes, and Beans

When I think of casseroles, potatoes are one of the first ingredients that come to mind. My favorite casseroles when I was a kid were dishes like scalloped potatoes and my mom's cheesy potato bake (look for my adapted version on page 156). This chapter pays homage to the role of potatoes in classic casseroles, while also lightening things up

a bit. One of my favorite recipes is in this chapter, too: Potato and Tomato Gratin (page 160), an ultra-quick and easy gratin that is elevated beyond basic by a hint of garlic. It is one of my favorite quick suppers in the whole world.

If you have trouble cooking rice, then try one of the dependable oven-based methods here. I've included basic instructions for cooking white and brown rice in the oven, along with some favorite variations like Butter-Baked Rice with Herbs and Garlic (page 140) and Baked Coconut Rice with Spices (page 148). In fact, can I talk about that coconut rice for a moment? I could eat it every day, for dinner or for breakfast. I tested it many times to make sure it would come out exactly the way I like it—light, with dry and fluffy grains of rice; flavorful, with hints of cinnamon and pepper; and rich, with coconut milk and chewy flecks of dried coconut.

There are full one-dish rice meals here, too, like an adaptation of a classic Indian rice dish, Spiced Lamb Biryani (page 142), and the easy Baked Mushroom and Rosemary Risotto (page 150). My mushroom-loving husband would particularly like you to know that this risotto is "killer" (his words, not mine).

And then there are the beans. Beans are a nutritious and sometimes overlooked source of protein, but they are also a secret source of great flavor. There are recipes here for basic dried beans, baked in the oven, which cuts down their cooking time considerably. There are also recipes that call for convenient canned beans, like the Spicy Mexican Bean and Rice Bake (page 171) and the refreshing and satisfying Chickpea Casserole with Lemon, Herbs, and Shallots (page 164).

Basic Butter-Baked Rice

DID YOU KNOW THAT RICE CAN BE COOKED with no fuss in the oven? If you have trouble getting rice just right, try this method. The addition of butter makes this a richer version of rice, and it's good enough to eat all by itself. ○ *Serves 6*

CASSEROLE DISH: 9 × 13-inch baking dish or any 3-quart baking dish
BAKE TIME: 35 minutes

1½ cups long-grain or basmati rice
1½ teaspoons salt
¼ cup (½ stick) unsalted butter
3 cups boiling water

1. Preheat the oven to 350°F and lightly grease the baking dish with nonstick cooking spray.

2. Stir together the rice and salt in the prepared baking dish. Dot the rice with chunks of the butter, then pour the boiling water into the dish. Stir quickly to mix, then cover the dish with a lid or with a double layer of foil.

3. Bake for 35 minutes, or until the liquid is completely absorbed and the rice is tender. Let stand, covered, for an additional 5 minutes. Fluff with a fork and serve.

Variations: This is an easy way to make delicious rice, and it's also easy to change it up into a stand-alone dish. Substitute chicken or vegetable broth for the water, or toss the finished rice with a handful of currants, chopped almonds or other nuts, and fresh herbs.

Butter-Baked Rice with Herbs and Garlic

THIS VERSION OF BAKED RICE jazzes up the basic recipe just a little with sautéed garlic, herbs, and a dash of black pepper. ○ *Serves 6*

CASSEROLE DISH: 9 × 13-inch baking dish or any 3-quart baking dish
BAKE TIME: 35 minutes

1 small handful (about ¼ cup) fresh thyme sprigs, dill, or chives, or a mix of all three
¼ cup (½ stick) unsalted butter
4 cloves garlic, finely minced
1½ cups long-grain or basmati rice
1 teaspoon salt
Freshly ground black pepper
3 cups boiling water

1. Preheat the oven to 350°F and lightly grease the baking dish with nonstick cooking spray.

2. If using thyme or dill, strip the herbs off the stalk. Mince the herbs and set aside.

3. Melt the butter in a skillet over medium heat. When it foams up, add the garlic. Turn the heat to low and cook, stirring frequently, for about 5 minutes, or until the garlic is golden, soft, and fragrant.

4. Add the herbs, rice, salt, and pepper and sauté together for 2 to 3 minutes. Turn off the heat and transfer the rice mixture to the prepared baking dish. Pour the boiling water into the dish, stir quickly to mix, then cover the dish with a lid or with a double layer of foil.

5. Bake for 35 minutes, or until the liquid is completely absorbed and the rice is tender. Let stand for 5 minutes, then fluff with a fork and serve.

Basic Baked Brown Rice

BROWN RICE IS ALSO VERY EASY TO COOK in the oven; in fact, I prefer oven-baked brown rice to the stovetop version. One note of caution: Be sure to use short-grain or medium-grain brown rice. Long-grain brown rice takes longer to cook and will not absorb the liquid as reliably. Personally, I prefer the chewy, moist texture of short-grain rice to that of its longer-grained counterpart anyway. ○ *Serves 4 to 6*

CASSEROLE DISH: 9-inch square baking dish
BAKE TIME: 1 hour

1½ cups short- or medium-grain brown rice
½ teaspoon salt
1 tablespoon olive oil
2½ cups boiling water

1. Preheat the oven to 375°F. Lightly grease the baking dish with butter or non-stick cooking spray. Stir together the rice, salt, and olive oil and spread the mixture evenly in the pan.

2. Pour the boiling water over the rice. Cover the dish tightly with a lid or with a double layer of foil and bake for 1 hour.

3. Remove the dish from the oven and uncover carefully. It will be hot, with plenty of steam under the foil. Fluff the rice with a fork, and let it sit for 5 minutes before serving.

Spiced Lamb Biryani

LAMB BIRYANI IS A FAMOUS DISH in Indian cuisine. It's a party-worthy meal, traditionally taking hours to prepare, with an ingredient list that goes on for miles. This version is a less intensive preparation, but it still has masses of flavor and can be pulled together quickly! Serve this with cucumbers and yogurt.

Serves 6

CASSEROLE DISH: 9 × 13-inch baking dish or 3-quart round baking dish
BAKE TIME: 1 hour

FOR THE RICE:
2 cups basmati rice
1 tablespoon butter
2 green cardamom pods
2 black cardamom pods
2 cinnamon sticks
3½ cups water
2 teaspoons salt

FOR THE LAMB AND ONIONS:
3 tablespoons vegetable oil
1 pound lamb leg, cut into ½-inch cubes
2 cinnamon sticks
8 to 10 whole black peppercorns
3 medium onions, diced
One 2-inch piece fresh ginger, peeled and grated
10 cloves garlic, minced
One 14.5-ounce can diced tomatoes, drained
2 bay leaves
1 teaspoon chili powder (optional)
2 teaspoons ground cumin
2 tablespoons garam masala
1 teaspoon salt
1 cup plain yogurt
¼ cup unsalted cashew pieces
¼ cup golden raisins

Fresh cilantro leaves, for garnish

1. Preheat the oven to 300°F. Grease the baking dish with butter.

2. Put the rice in a sieve and rinse it thoroughly to remove extra starch. Set aside to drain.

3. Heat the butter over medium-high heat in a large, wide pot with a lid. When it foams up, add the green and black cardamom pods and the cinnamon sticks. Sauté the spices, stirring constantly, for a couple of minutes, or until they are fragrant. Add the drained rice and sauté it with the spices for another minute.

4. Add the water and salt and bring to a boil. Cover and cook for 6 minutes. Remove the lid and stir the rice. It will not be entirely cooked. Spread the rice in the prepared baking dish.

5. Wipe out the pot and return to medium heat. Heat the oil. When it is quite hot, add the lamb chunks and brown them well on all sides. This should take 5 to 8 minutes. Remove the browned lamb from the pan and set aside in a bowl.

6. Add the cinnamon sticks and peppercorns to the hot pan and sauté for a minute, or until fragrant. Watch out—the peppercorns can pop up right in your face! Add the onion, ginger, and garlic. Turn the heat to low and cook, stirring frequently, for 10 minutes, or until the onions are softened and very fragrant.

7. Return the lamb to the pan, along with the drained tomatoes, bay leaves, chili powder (if using), cumin, garam masala, salt, and yogurt. Cook for another 5 minutes, stirring frequently.

8. Turn off the heat and scrape the lamb and its sauce into the baking dish, on top of the rice. Mix it in a little, covering the lamb partially with rice. Sprinkle the top with the cashews and raisins.

9. Cover the dish tightly with foil and bake for 1 hour. Garnish with cilantro leaves and serve.

Buying Spices

Although some of the spices in this recipe may be unfamiliar, they are easy to find. But don't buy them at your local supermarket! Cardamom and cinnamon sticks are far too expensive when purchased in those little spice jars. Look for these whole spices in the bulk section of a Whole Foods Market or your local co-op. Better yet, go into an Indian grocery and buy them in larger bags.

Vegetable Curry Biryani

LIKE LAMB BIRYANI (page 142), vegetable biryani involves more preparation than most of the recipes in this book. But oh, the payoff—melting vegetables in a deliciously fragrant sauce with tender, gorgeous rice. This recipe knocks off a few steps from more traditional recipes, so it's still not *that* labor-intensive. Serve with sliced cucumbers, yogurt, and warm flatbread. ● *Serves 6*

CASSEROLE DISH: 9 × 13-inch baking dish or 3-quart round baking dish
BAKE TIME: 40 minutes

FOR THE RICE:
2 cups basmati rice
1 tablespoon unsalted butter
1 cinnamon stick
3 cups water
2 teaspoons salt

FOR THE FRIED POTATOES AND NUTS:
2 tablespoons unsalted butter
2 medium potatoes (about 1 pound), cut into ¼-inch cubes
½ cup sliced almonds
¼ cup golden raisins

FOR THE VEGETABLE CURRY:
5 cups frozen mixed vegetables, such as broccoli, cauliflower, and carrots
3 tablespoons vegetable oil
3 medium onions, diced
One 2-inch piece ginger, peeled and grated
5 cloves garlic, minced
1 teaspoon chili powder (optional)
1 teaspoon ground turmeric
1 tablespoon garam masala
1 cup plain yogurt
1½ teaspoons salt

Fresh cilantro leaves, for garnish

1. Preheat the oven to 400°F. Grease the baking dish with butter.

2. Put the rice in a sieve and rinse it thoroughly to remove extra starch. Set aside to drain. Heat the 1 tablespoon butter over medium-high heat in a large, wide pot with a lid. When it foams up, add the cinnamon stick and the rice. Fry, stirring constantly, for a couple of minutes, or until fragrant.

3. Add the water and salt and bring to a boil. Cover and cook for 6 minutes. Remove the lid and stir the rice. It will not be entirely cooked. Spread the rice in the prepared baking dish.

4. Heat the 2 tablespoons butter in a wide skillet over medium-high heat and fry the potatoes until they begin to turn golden and crispy on each side. Do this in batches, if necessary, to keep the potatoes from steaming instead of frying. Remove the browned potatoes from the pan and set aside in a bowl.

5. In the same skillet, fry the almonds and raisins in the leftover butter for about 5 minutes, or until hot. Remove them from the pan and mix in with the cooked potatoes.

6. Steam the frozen vegetables until just tender.

7. Heat the oil in the skillet over medium-high heat. Add the onions, ginger, and garlic, and turn the heat to medium-low. Cook, stirring frequently, for about 10 minutes, or until the onions are cooked down and the mixture is fragrant.

8. Stir in the chili powder, if using, the turmeric, and the garam masala. Cook, stirring frequently, for about a minute, then stir in the steamed vegetables and yogurt. Bring to a simmer, then take off the heat. Stir in the salt.

9. Create a well in the middle of the rice in the baking dish by pushing the rice out to the corners and sides of the dish. Spread half of the potato mixture in the bottom, then cover with the vegetable curry. Spread the rice over the curry so it is partially covered and pat the rest of the potatoes and nuts into the top of the dish.

10. Cover the pan tightly with a double layer of foil or a lid, and bake for 40 minutes. Let rest for 5 minutes, then garnish with cilantro leaves and serve.

Spanish Saffron Pilaf

SAFFRON IS A LUXURIOUS INGREDIENT that adds a delicately sweet yet musky flavor to dishes, while also giving them a brilliant yellow color. It's a special and expensive ingredient, but it needs to be used only in tiny quantities. Even a pinch can elevate basic baked rice into a centerpiece of a dish. This is good served with chicken and steamed vegetables. ● *Serves 6*

CASSEROLE DISH: 2-quart stovetop-to-oven casserole with lid
BAKE TIME: 25 minutes

1½ cups basmati rice
Pinch of saffron threads
¼ cup milk, warmed
2 tablespoons unsalted butter
½ medium onion, diced
2½ cups low-sodium chicken or vegetable broth
1 teaspoon salt
½ teaspoon freshly ground black pepper

1. Preheat the oven to 400°F. Rinse the rice in a sieve under running water to remove any extra starch. When the water coming from the rice runs clear, drain the rice thoroughly and set aside to dry. Crumble the saffron threads into the warm milk in a small cup and set aside.

2. Heat the butter in the casserole dish over medium heat. Add the onion and cook, stirring frequently, for about 5 minutes, or until the onion is golden, soft, and fragrant. Add the rice and cook for another 3 to 4 minutes, or until the rice is turning translucent and is fully coated with the butter and onion.

3. Add the broth to the rice and onion, and stir in the salt, pepper, and the milk with the steeped saffron. Bring to a simmer, then cover and put in the oven.

4. Bake for 25 minutes, then remove and let sit, covered, for 5 minutes before serving.

Lemon Pilaf with Salmon

THIS IS A LOVELY ONE-DISH MEAL: succulent salmon baked with tangy, fluffy rice, flavored with lemon, garlic, and olive oil. It doesn't get much better than that. This is also a true 60-minute meal; turn on the oven, and you'll be sitting down to eat in less than an hour. ○ *Serves 6*

CASSEROLE DISH: 3-quart (or larger) Dutch oven or other stovetop-to-oven pot with lid
BAKE TIME: 35 minutes

4½ cups low-sodium chicken broth
2 tablespoons unsalted butter
1 medium onion, diced
2 cloves garlic, minced
2½ cups long-grain white rice
Zest and juice of 2 lemons, plus an additional lemon, sliced, for serving
1 bay leaf
1 teaspoon salt
½ teaspoon freshly ground black pepper
Olive oil
1 pound salmon fillets
Small handful (about ¼ cup) fresh flat-leaf parsley, chopped

1. Preheat the oven to 350°F and lightly grease the Dutch oven with olive oil. In a medium-size saucepan, heat the chicken broth to boiling. Lower the heat and keep the broth at a light simmer.

2. Melt the butter in the Dutch oven over medium heat. When the butter foams, add the onion and garlic and cook, stirring frequently, for about 5 minutes, or until the onion is softened and fragrant. Add the rice and cook for another 2 minutes, stirring frequently.

3. Pour in the hot chicken broth and stir in the lemon juice, lemon zest, bay leaf, salt, and pepper. Bring to a boil. Drizzle the top of the dish with olive oil.

4. Cover the baking dish with a lid or a double layer of aluminum foil and bake for 20 minutes, or until all the liquid is absorbed and the rice is beginning to be tender.

5. Remove the lid or foil carefully, as there will be a great deal of hot steam in the dish. Lay the salmon across the top and bake, uncovered, for another 15 minutes, or until just done. Lift the salmon out onto a serving dish and fluff the rice with a fork. Garnish with lemon slices and chopped parsley. Serve immediately.

Baked Coconut Rice with Spices

HERE'S ANOTHER FAVORITE BAKED RICE DISH: savory coconut rice with just a hint of exotic cinnamon and a pinch of black pepper. This is addictively good! ○ *Serves 6*

CASSEROLE DISH: 9 × 13-inch baking dish or 3-quart casserole dish with a lid
BAKE TIME: 25 minutes

2 cups long-grain or basmati rice
1 tablespoon unsalted butter
One 14-ounce can coconut milk
2 cups water
1½ teaspoons salt
¼ teaspoon ground cinnamon
¼ teaspoon freshly ground black pepper
½ cup unsweetened grated coconut (see Note)

1. Preheat the oven to 350°F and lightly grease the baking dish with nonstick cooking spray.

2. Rinse the rice in a sieve to remove any excess starch. Set aside to drain thoroughly. In a large saucepan, melt the butter over medium-high heat and, when the butter foams up, add the rice. Sauté the rice for several minutes, until it is fragrant and hot.

3. Add the coconut milk and water and stir to combine. Turn the heat to high and bring to a boil.

4. Remove the pan from the heat and stir in the salt, cinnamon, pepper, and coconut. Pour into the prepared baking dish and cover with a lid or a double layer of foil. Bake for 25 minutes, or until the rice is tender. Halfway through the baking time, carefully lift the lid and stir the rice thoroughly. (This lets a little of the steam escape and creates a drier texture for the rice, which is desirable in this particular dish.) Cover again tightly and return to the oven. After 25 minutes of total baking time, remove the dish from the oven and let it stand covered for 5 minutes, then carefully remove the foil and fluff the rice. Serve immediately.

Note: Do not use sweetened flaked coconut in this recipe. Unsweetened coconut is not often found in the baking aisle at all. Head to the bulk bins or the health food store, where you should find bags of unsweetened grated coconut.

Baked Risotto with Pancetta and Caramelized Onions

HERE'S AN EASY BAKED RISOTTO that is oh-so-delicious and indulgent. It's a marvelous winter dish, with the smoky richness of crispy pancetta and a topping of sweet, dark caramelized onions. ○ *Serves 6*

CASSEROLE DISH: 3-quart Dutch oven or large ovenproof saucepan with lid
BAKE TIME: 20 to 25 minutes

¼ **pound pancetta, diced**
1 **tablespoon olive oil**
1 **medium white onion, finely diced**
4 **cloves garlic, minced**
¾ **cup Arborio rice**
¼ **cup dry white wine**
2½ **cups low-sodium chicken broth**
½ **teaspoon salt**
¼ **teaspoon freshly ground black pepper**
2 **tablespoons unsalted butter**
2 **medium yellow onions, sliced into thin half-moons**
½ **cup freshly grated Parmesan cheese**
2 **tablespoons finely chopped fresh flat-leaf parsley (optional)**

1. Preheat the oven to 425°F. In the Dutch oven or ovenproof saucepan, cook the pancetta over medium-high heat for about 5 minutes, or until crisp. Add the olive oil and finely diced onion and turn the heat to medium-low. Cook the onion slowly, stirring frequently, until translucent. This will take about 10 minutes.

2. Add the garlic and the rice and cook, stirring to coat the rice grains with oil. Cook for about 5 minutes, or until the garlic is fragrant and tender. Turn the heat up to high.

3. Stir in the wine and cook until it has completely evaporated, about 1 minute. Stir in the broth, salt, and pepper. Bring to a boil. Cover the pan with a tight-fitting lid, transfer to the oven, and bake for 20 to 25 minutes, or until most of the liquid has been absorbed by the rice.

4. While the risotto is baking, caramelize the onions. Heat the butter over medium heat in a heavy sauté pan, preferably a cast-iron skillet. When the butter foams up, add the sliced onions and stir to coat them with butter. Sprinkle them liberally with salt. Cook, stirring every 5 minutes or so, for at least 25 minutes, or until the onions have turned a rich mahogany brown.

5. When the risotto is finished, remove from the oven and stir in the Parmesan cheese. Serve immediately, topped with spoonfuls of caramelized onions and sprinkled with parsley, if using.

Baked Mushroom and Rosemary Risotto

MOST RISOTTO RECIPES call for more than 45 minutes of laborious attention, gradually ladling in wine and stock and stirring the rice without stopping until it is tender and creamy. This version of rich, creamy mushroom risotto is much simpler. The texture is a little softer than classic stovetop risotto, but the dish is every bit as delicious. ○ *Serves 4*

CASSEROLE DISH: 3-quart stovetop-to-oven covered casserole or Dutch oven
BAKE TIME: 35 minutes

½ ounce dried porcini mushrooms, chopped
½ ounce dried shiitake mushrooms, chopped
2 cups boiling water

2 tablespoons unsalted butter

1 small yellow onion, finely chopped

4 cloves garlic, minced

One 4-inch sprig fresh rosemary

1 cup Arborio or other short-grain white rice

½ cup dry white wine, such as Sauvignon Blanc

2 cups low-sodium chicken or vegetable broth

½ teaspoon salt, or to taste

¼ teaspoon freshly ground black pepper, or to taste

¼ teaspoon ground nutmeg

4 ounces mascarpone cheese

Parmesan cheese curls, for garnish

1. Preheat the oven to 300°F. Rinse the dried mushrooms lightly, to remove any dust or grit. Place the mushrooms in a ceramic bowl and pour the boiling water over them.

2. Heat the butter in the casserole or Dutch oven over medium heat. Add the onion and cook, stirring occasionally, for about 8 minutes, or until soft and golden.

3. Drain the mushrooms, reserving the liquid. Add the mushrooms, garlic, and rosemary sprig to the pan and sauté on low heat for about 10 minutes, or until the mushrooms have sweated out some moisture and the garlic is fragrant and golden.

4. Add the rice and cook, stirring once or twice, for about 4 minutes, or until the rice begins to turn transparent.

5. Turn the heat to high and add the white wine, broth, and reserved mushroom steeping liquid. Bring to a boil. Cover the pan with a tight-fitting lid and put it in the oven to bake for 20 minutes.

6. Remove and stir in the salt, pepper, nutmeg, and mascarpone cheese. Return the casserole to the oven for 15 minutes.

7. Remove and stir vigorously. Serve immediately, garnished with curls of Parmesan.

Parmesan Curls

Parmesan cheese curls are a lovely way to garnish dishes like risotto. To create curls of Parmesan, run a sharp vegetable peeler down the side of a block of Parmesan. You'll get little curls of hard cheese that can be mounded on top of a plate of risotto for an elegant finishing touch.

Brown Rice Casserole with Cheese and Onions

THIS IS ONE OF THE EASIEST one-dish suppers I know. It's absolutely fool-proof, blazingly fast, and inexpensive, too. Unlike the rice gratins that follow later in this chapter, this recipe does not require rice that has been cooked ahead of time. It all cooks together in the oven—a hands-off dish for you!

o *Serves 6*

CASSEROLE DISH: 9 × 13-inch baking dish
BAKE TIME: 1¼ hours

1 tablespoon olive oil
1 medium onion, finely diced
1 red bell pepper, cored and diced
2 cloves garlic, minced
1 cup short-grain brown rice
3 cups low-sodium chicken or vegetable broth
¾ teaspoon salt
½ teaspoon ground ginger
¼ teaspoon freshly ground black pepper, or to taste
1 cup shredded sharp cheddar cheese

1. Preheat the oven to 325°F and lightly grease the baking dish with olive oil. Coat a large skillet with the 1 tablespoon olive oil and heat over medium-high heat. Add the onion and red pepper and cook, stirring frequently, for about 8 minutes. Add the garlic and cook for another few minutes, or until the garlic is fragrant and golden.

2. Add the rice and cook for another minute or two, and then pour in the chicken broth and stir in the salt, ginger, and pepper. Bring to a simmer, then transfer the rice and broth mixture to the prepared dish.

3. Cover the dish tightly with a double layer of aluminum foil and bake for 1 hour. Carefully remove the foil (steam will billow up) and stir in the cheese. Return to the oven and bake, uncovered, for an additional 15 minutes. Let stand for 5 to 10 minutes before serving.

Variations: If you have fresh herbs around, stir in a tablespoon of minced sage with the red pepper, or add a handful of minced flat-leaf parsley with the cheese.

Baked Rice and Lentils (Mujadara)

MUJADARA IS A CLASSIC MIDDLE EASTERN DISH that is vegan and gluten-free. It's full of whole-grain goodness, and yet it's also incredibly rich and delicious in a way that belies its simple, minimalist ingredients. This recipe takes some of the work out of cooking the rice and lentils separately, and calls for baking them together with caramelized onions for an even tastier dish.

○ *Serves 6*

CASSEROLE DISH: 9 × 13-inch baking dish
BAKE TIME: 60 to 70 minutes

2 tablespoons olive oil
2 tablespoons unsalted butter
2 large onions, sliced into thin half-moons
1 teaspoon salt
4 cups low-sodium vegetable or chicken broth
¾ cup brown or green lentils
½ cup medium-grain brown rice
½ teaspoon freshly ground black pepper, or to taste
½ teaspoon ground cinnamon
½ teaspoon ground cumin
Fresh flat-leaf parsley, minced, for garnish

1. Preheat the oven to 325°F and lightly grease the baking dish with olive oil.

2. Coat a large skillet with the 2 tablespoons olive oil and melt the butter in the skillet over medium-high heat. When the butter foams up, turn the heat to medium and add the onions. Sprinkle the onions with the salt. Cook, stirring occasionally, for about 30 minutes. When the onions are a deep mahogany brown, take them off the heat.

3. While the onions are cooking, heat the broth to boiling in a small saucepan. After it comes to a boil, turn down the heat and keep it just under a simmer.

4. Scrape the caramelized onions into the prepared dish and stir in the lentils and rice. Stir in the pepper, cinnamon, and cumin, then add the hot broth and stir.

5. Cover the dish tightly with a double layer of aluminum foil and bake for 60 to 70 minutes, or until the rice and lentils are tender and have absorbed the liquid. Serve sprinkled with parsley.

Brown Rice Gratin with Lemon, Pine Nuts, and Chicken

THIS IS A QUICK AND EASY CASSEROLE that is a great way to resurrect leftovers. It uses cooked shredded chicken (from your fridge or from a deli rotisserie chicken) and pre-cooked or leftover brown rice. If you're making brown rice for a meal one night, make a double batch and put it away to make this later in the week. ○ *Serves 6*

CASSEROLE DISH: 3-quart baking dish
BAKE TIME: 45 minutes

5 cups cooked brown rice
2 cups shredded cooked chicken
Zest and juice of 2 lemons
½ cup toasted pine nuts
Salt and freshly ground black pepper
1 tablespoon olive oil
1 large onion, diced
4 cloves garlic, finely minced
½ cup white wine or low-sodium chicken broth
1 small bunch scallions, trimmed and chopped into ¼-inch pieces
1 cup shredded Parmesan cheese, plus extra for serving

1. Preheat the oven to 375°F. Lightly grease the baking dish with olive oil. In a large bowl toss the cooked brown rice, shredded chicken, lemon zest, pine nuts, and salt and pepper to taste.

2. Heat the olive oil in large, deep skillet over medium heat. Add the onion and cook, stirring frequently, until golden and translucent, about 7 minutes. Add the garlic and continue cooking until it is fragrant and golden.

3. Add the lemon juice and white wine and bring to a simmer. Simmer for 5 minutes, then pour over the rice and chicken mixture and mix well. Stir in the scallions and Parmesan and spread in the prepared baking dish. (At this point the casserole can be covered and refrigerated for up to 24 hours. Let come to room temperature before baking.)

4. Bake, covered, for 25 minutes, then uncover and bake for an additional 20 minutes, or until a slightly golden crust forms on top. Serve with extra Parmesan cheese.

Quick and Easy Ham and Potato Casserole

HAM AND POTATO CASSEROLE is one of those totally classic casserole recipes that always seem to call for copious quantities of heavy cream or condensed cream-of-something soup. Well, here's a recipe for a comforting ham and potato dish that achieves a lighter, fresher taste without sacrificing quickness and convenience. ○ *Serves 6*

CASSEROLE DISH: 9 × 13-inch baking dish
BAKE TIME: About 1 hour

¼ cup (½ stick) unsalted butter
2 cloves garlic, minced
2 tablespoons minced fresh rosemary (leaves only)
¼ cup all-purpose flour
2 cups milk
3 tablespoons Dijon mustard
Salt and freshly ground black pepper
1 pound cooked ham, chopped into small cubes
One 32-ounce bag frozen cubed potatoes
1 medium onion, diced
1½ cups shredded Monterey Jack cheese

1. Preheat the oven to 350°F and lightly grease the baking dish with olive oil or nonstick cooking spray.

2. In a small saucepan, heat the butter over medium-high heat until it foams. Turn the heat down to low and add the garlic. Cook, stirring frequently, until the garlic is golden and fragrant, about 5 minutes. Add the rosemary and cook for another minute.

3. Turn the heat up to medium and add the flour. Cook for about 5 minutes, or until the flour and butter form a smooth paste. Whisk in the milk and cook, stirring frequently, until the mixture comes to a simmer and thickens slightly. Take off the heat, whisk in the mustard, and season with salt and pepper to taste.

4. In a large bowl, combine the white sauce, ham, frozen potatoes, onion, and Monterey Jack cheese. Spread the potato mixture in the prepared baking dish. (At this point the casserole can be covered and refrigerated for up to 24 hours.)

5. Bake, uncovered, for about 1 hour, or until bubbling and hot. Let stand for 10 minutes before serving.

Creamy Cheesy Potatoes

THIS WAS LITERALLY MY MOTHER'S RECIPE, and I stole it away, slashed out the cream of chicken soup, and tweaked a few things to my taste. It's still incredibly indulgent, and delicious in that bubbly, cheesy, decadent way that is permissible only when it is truly cold outside. So let it snow, and enjoy this casserole at least once a year. ○ *Serves 6*

CASSEROLE DISH: 9 × 13-inch baking dish
BAKE TIME: 30 minutes

6 medium white potatoes, diced
3 tablespoons unsalted butter
3 tablespoons all-purpose flour
½ cup low-sodium chicken broth
½ cup milk
½ cup low-fat sour cream
4 ounces low-fat cream cheese
¾ cup shredded extra-sharp cheddar cheese
¼ cup sliced scallions

3 tablespoons minced fresh flat-leaf parsley

3 cloves garlic, minced

1 teaspoon salt

½ teaspoon freshly ground black pepper

1. Preheat the oven to 350°F and lightly grease the baking dish with butter or non-stick cooking spray.

2. In a large saucepan, cook the potatoes in just enough boiling salted water to cover for 10 to 12 minutes, or until tender. Drain and rinse the potatoes with cold water, then transfer them to a large bowl.

3. Meanwhile, heat the butter in a small saucepan over medium heat and stir in the flour. Cook, stirring constantly, until the flour is fragrant and forms a smooth paste with the butter, about 3 minutes. Whisk in the broth and milk, and cook, whisking constantly, for several minutes, or until the mixture thickens slightly.

4. Add the sauce to the cooked potatoes, and stir in the sour cream, cream cheese, cheddar cheese, scallions, parsley, garlic, salt, and pepper. Transfer to the prepared casserole dish. (At this point the casserole can be covered and refrigerated for up to 24 hours.)

5. Bake, uncovered, for 30 minutes, or until heated through and bubbling. Serve hot.

Baked Sweet Potatoes with Smoky Chipotle and Onions

HAVE NEVER BEEN A BIG FAN of extra-sweet recipes for sweet potatoes. Their natural earthy sweetness doesn't need extra sugar; if anything, it needs a little spice to balance it out. This recipe is for a smoky, spicy sweet potato gratin that would be at home on the Thanksgiving table—without the marshmallow goo on top, thank you very much. ○ *Serves 6*

CASSEROLE DISH: 9 × 13-inch baking dish or 3-quart gratin dish

BAKE TIME: 45 minutes

Olive oil

4 large sweet potatoes (about 2½ pounds)

Salt and freshly ground black pepper

2 tablespoons unsalted butter

1 medium onion, sliced into thin half-moons

4 cloves garlic, minced

¼ cup fresh sage leaves, chopped

½ teaspoon chipotle chile powder

½ cup cream

FOR THE TOPPING:

1 tablespoon unsalted butter

½ cup dry bread crumbs

½ cup finely grated Parmesan cheese

1. Preheat the oven to 350°F and grease the dish with olive oil.

2. Peel and thinly slice the potatoes. Toss them in a bowl with a little olive oil and salt and pepper.

3. Heat the butter in a large heavy skillet over medium heat. When it foams up, add the onion slices and slowly caramelize them to a pale golden brown. This will take about 15 to 20 minutes. When the onions are golden brown, add the garlic and cook just until golden.

4. Add the sage, chipotle powder, and cream. Cook until the cream is slightly reduced, then remove from the heat.

5. Layer the potatoes in the prepared dish with the onions, lifting the onions out of the cream with a slotted spoon. Pour the cream over the top. (At this point the casserole can be covered and refrigerated for up to 24 hours.) Bake, uncovered, for about 30 minutes, or until the potatoes are barely tender.

6. While the gratin cooks, make the topping. Heat the butter in the skillet and toast the bread crumbs in the butter until golden and fragrant. Remove from heat and toss with the Parmesan. Sprinkle over the top of the hot gratin after it's baked for 30 minutes, then return it to the oven for about 15 minutes, or until brown and crispy.

Curried Potato Strudel (Samosa Roll)

POTATOES ARE INFINITELY ADAPTABLE and accommodating. Here they form the spiced filling for a quick rolled-up strudel, constructed from store-bought phyllo dough. ○ *Serves 24 as an appetizer*

CASSEROLE DISH: Baking sheet
BAKE TIME: 30 minutes

2 pounds russet potatoes, peeled and cut into quarters
2 tablespoons vegetable oil
1 medium onion, diced
2 cloves garlic, minced
2 tablespoons curry powder
1 cup plain yogurt
2 cups thawed frozen peas
1 teaspoon salt
Freshly ground black pepper
1 tablespoon unsalted butter
3 tablespoons olive oil
½ package (about 20 sheets) frozen phyllo dough,
    thawed overnight in the refrigerator

1. Preheat the oven to 400°F and lightly grease the baking sheet with nonstick cooking spray. Bring a large pot of well-salted water to a boil. Slip in the potato pieces, and boil until they are quite tender. This will take anywhere from 10 to 20 minutes, depending on how large the potato pieces are. Drain and return the potatoes to the cooking pot. Mash them thoroughly.

2. While the potatoes are cooking, heat the vegetable oil in a deep skillet over medium heat. Add the onion and cook for about 10 minutes, or until the onion is quite translucent and fragrant. Add the garlic and cook for an additional 5 minutes.

3. Turn the heat up to medium-high and add the curry powder. Fry the curry powder with the onion and garlic for a minute, then add the mashed potatoes. Fry, stirring, until the potatoes are coated with the oil and the onions have been fully incorporated. Turn off the heat and stir in the yogurt, peas, salt, and pepper.

4. Melt the butter in a small bowl and add the olive oil. On a large piece of waxed paper, lay out one sheet of phyllo dough. Brush it with the butter-oil mixture, then stack another sheet on top. Repeat until there are 10 layers stacked up.

5. Spread about half of the potato mixture over the phyllo, leaving an inch of room at the edges, then roll up from the long side, tucking the ends in as you go. Pick up the wax paper and carefully roll the strudel off the paper and onto the prepared baking sheet, turning it seam side down. Repeat to make another strudel.

6. Bake for about 30 minutes, or until the strudels are golden and crispy. Cut into slices and serve immediately. Or, if these have to be held before serving, you can re-crisp them for a few minutes in a 400°F oven.

Potato and Tomato Gratin

FRIED POTATOES WITH TOMATO SAUCE (*patatas bravas*) are a staple of Spanish tapas bars. This is a lighter, fresher version, with tomatoes and potatoes baked together in a gorgeous, colorful swirl. But there's still a Spanish warmth, thanks to the gentle heat of smoked paprika and a pinch of fresh thyme. ○ *Serves 6*

CASSEROLE DISH: 9 × 13-inch baking dish or 3-quart baking dish
BAKE TIME: 25 minutes

2 pounds Yukon Gold potatoes, sliced ¼ inch thick
¼ cup short-grain white rice
3 large tomatoes, sliced into ¼-inch-thick half-moons
Salt and freshly ground black pepper
4 sprigs fresh thyme
2 cloves garlic, minced
2 teaspoons smoked paprika
2 cups shredded mozzarella cheese
½ cup grated Parmesan cheese
Olive oil

1. Preheat the oven to 350°F and lightly grease the baking dish with olive oil.

2. Bring a large pot of well-salted water to a boil. Add the sliced potatoes and cook for just 5 minutes. Drain. In the same pot, or in a small saucepan, bring a few cups of salted water to a boil. Add the rice and cook for 10 minutes. It will not be fully cooked. Drain and set aside.

3. Lay the tomatoes out on a plate or baking sheet and sprinkle them lightly with salt and pepper.

4. Strip the leaves from the thyme stalks by pinching them and running a thumb and finger down the stalk. You should end up with about 2 teaspoons of thyme leaves. Toss the leaves in a bowl with the garlic, smoked paprika, and mozzarella cheese.

5. In the prepared baking dish, layer half the potatoes with half the tomatoes, overlapping the slices in straight lines down the length of the dish. Spread all of the rice on top. Top with half of the mozzarella mixture. Repeat with the remaining potato and tomato slices, spread the remaining mozzarella mixture on the top layer, and sprinkle the Parmesan on top of that. Drizzle with olive oil.

6. Bake for 25 minutes, or until the cheese is bubbly and the potatoes are tender. Let stand for 10 minutes before serving.

Twice-Baked Potatoes Stuffed with Ricotta and Ground Sausage

TWICE-BAKED POTATOES are a fabulously cozy and comforting dish: hot potatoes, stuffed with cheese and some snipped herbs, or perhaps some crispy savory sausage, as they are here. Try playing around with other fillings and toppings too. When sufficiently bulked out with filling ingredients, these are substantial enough to be a dinner entrée. ● *Serves 8*

CASSEROLE DISH: Large baking sheet
BAKE TIME: 70 to 90 minutes

4 extra-large russet potatoes
Olive oil
Salt and freshly ground black pepper
½ pound bulk pork, turkey, or chicken sausage (use your favorite)
1 small onion, diced
1 cup ricotta cheese
¼ cup chopped fresh chives
1 cup shredded cheddar cheese

1. Preheat the oven to 400°F. Pierce each potato with a fork several times and place on the baking sheet. Drizzle the potatoes with olive oil and sprinkle with salt and pepper. Bake for 50 to 60 minutes, or until they are tender when pierced with a fork.

2. Heat a deep skillet over medium-high heat. Add the sausage and cook, stirring frequently to break up the crumbles, until the sausage is fully cooked and crispy. Add the onion and turn the heat to medium. Cook for 10 minutes, or until the onion is soft and fragrant. Drain the grease and place the sausage and onion mixture in a large bowl.

3. When the potatoes are finished baking, cut each in half lengthwise. Scoop out the inner flesh of each half, leaving a thin shell behind, and crumble it into the bowl with the sausage and onion. Mix thoroughly, taking care to mash the potatoes as you mix.

4. Stir in the ricotta, chives, and about 1 teaspoon of salt, as well as pepper to taste. Stir in ½ cup of the cheddar cheese. Mound the potato filling back into each potato shell. (At this point the potatoes can be covered and refrigerated for up to 3 days.) Sprinkle the top of each potato with the remaining ½ cup of cheddar cheese.

5. Bake, uncovered, for 20 to 30 minutes, or until the potatoes are hot all the way through and the cheese is melted. Serve immediately.

Sweet Potato, Chard, and Coconut Milk Casserole

SWEET POTATOES AND COCONUT MILK were made for each other. They both have a smooth, creamy richness that is wonderful when layered together, especially with robust greens sandwiched between them. But this sweet, spicy casserole isn't too rich; in fact, it happens to be vegan. ◦ *Serves 8*

CASSEROLE DISH: 9 × 13-inch baking dish
BAKE TIME: 45 minutes

2 pounds (4 medium or 3 large) sweet potatoes, peeled and sliced into ⅛-inch-thick rounds
Salt and freshly ground black pepper
1 pound Swiss chard
2 tablespoons olive oil
1 medium onion, diced
4 cloves garlic, minced
One 3-inch piece fresh ginger, peeled and grated
Pinch of red pepper flakes
One 14-ounce can coconut milk, well stirred

1. Preheat the oven to 400°F. Lightly grease the baking dish with olive oil. Layer half of the sweet potato rounds in the bottom of the dish, overlapping them slightly. Sprinkle them lightly with salt and pepper.

2. Prepare the Swiss chard by folding each leaf in half and cutting away the rib. Slice the ribs into ½-inch pieces and set aside. Stack the leaves up in several piles, and roll each pile into a tight cigar. Slice in half lengthwise, then crosswise into thin ribbons.

3. In a very large, deep skillet or Dutch oven, heat the olive oil over medium heat and add the onion. Cook for 5 minutes, or until the onion is translucent. Add the garlic, ginger, and red pepper flakes and cook for an additional 5 minutes.

4. Add the sliced chard stems and cook for 5 minutes, or until the stems begin to soften. Turn up the heat, add the chard leaves, and cook, stirring frequently, until the leaves have wilted substantially. Remove from the heat and season with salt and pepper.

5. Spread half of the greens mixture over the sweet potatoes in the baking dish, then pour half of the coconut milk over the top. Top with the remaining potato slices, and sprinkle them lightly with salt and pepper. Top them with the remaining greens and coconut milk. Press down on the top layer to help submerge it below the coconut milk. (At this point the casserole can be covered and refrigerated for up to 24 hours.)

6. Bake, uncovered, for 45 minutes, or until the liquid is absorbed. Let stand for 10 minutes before serving.

Chickpea Casserole with Lemon, Herbs, and Shallots

COOKED CHICKPEAS form the toothsome base of this delicious dinner casserole. It's vegetarian and so very nice for a meatless supper. With its herbed and lemony creaminess, it also makes a great side dish for roasted chicken or grilled pork chops. ❍ *Serves 6 to 8*

CASSEROLE DISH: 9 × 13-inch baking dish or 3-quart gratin dish
BAKE TIME: 45 minutes

Three 15-ounce cans chickpeas, rinsed and drained, or 5 cups cooked chickpeas
1 cup cooked brown rice
4 large shallots, minced
2 cloves garlic, minced
Juice and zest of 1 lemon
Salt and freshly ground black pepper
2 large eggs, beaten
1 cup cottage cheese
½ cup plain yogurt
1 cup grated Parmesan cheese
½ cup fresh flat-leaf parsley
2 stalks fresh rosemary (leaves only)
⅔ cup dry bread crumbs
Olive oil

1. Preheat the oven to 375°F and lightly grease the baking dish with olive oil.

2. In a large bowl, mix the chickpeas with the rice, shallots, garlic, and lemon zest and juice. Season with salt and pepper.

3. Mix the beaten eggs in a medium bowl with the cottage cheese, yogurt, and ½ cup of the Parmesan cheese. Finely mince the parsley and fresh rosemary leaves. Stir the cottage cheese mixture and herbs into the chickpea mixture.

4. Spread the mixture in the prepared baking dish and top with the remaining ½ cup of Parmesan and the bread crumbs. (At this point the casserole can be covered and refrigerated for up to 24 hours.) Drizzle with olive oil. Bake, uncovered, for 45 minutes, or until bubbling and golden. Let stand for 10 minutes before serving.

Basic Potluck Baked Beans with Bacon

BAKED BEANS ARE A STAPLE OF POTLUCKS and winter gatherings. Here is a sweet and smoky recipe that uses dried beans instead of the canned mushy sort. It doesn't take any longer to bake, and the result is tender beans in a smoky glaze rich with bacon and hints of mustard. ● *Serves 10*

CASSEROLE DISH: 3-quart Dutch oven or other stovetop-to-oven pot with lid
BAKE TIME: 2½ hours

1 pound dried navy or kidney beans
8 slices bacon, cut into small pieces
1 medium onion, diced
1 green bell pepper, cored and diced
½ cup pure maple syrup
¼ cup cider vinegar
2 tablespoons Dijon mustard
3 teaspoons salt
Freshly ground black pepper

1. Preheat the oven to 325°F. Put the dried beans in a saucepan and cover with about 2 inches of water. Cover the pot, bring to a boil, and boil vigorously for 15 minutes, then turn off the heat.

2. Place the bacon pieces in the Dutch oven and turn the heat to medium-low. Cook the bacon slowly for about 15 minutes, or until it has released most of its fat. Add the onion and green pepper and cook until tender and fragrant, about 10 minutes.

Basic Instructions for Cooking Lentils and Beans in the Oven

Dried beans are a well-kept kitchen secret to many people. When we think of beans, we most often think of slightly mushy canned beans in conventional varieties like kidney, black, or white. Pebble-hard dried beans, with their desiccated appearance, look intimidating and not worth the trouble.

But dried beans can hold an incredible store of flavor and nutrition. If you cook ordinary black beans and kidney beans yourself, from dried beans, the result will be a revelation: They taste so much more complex and meaty than the canned varieties. And if you branch out into more unusual sorts of heirloom beans, widely available now from farmers and sources like Rancho Gordo beans (www.ranchogordo.com), you'll be shocked at the dizzying heights of flavor you will find in a humble pot of beans!

Cooking dried beans does take time. But your oven is a secret weapon for cooking beans in a quicker and more hands-off way. This method for cooking beans is becoming more popular, thanks to the efforts of Russ Parsons, an author and food correspondent for the *Los Angeles Times*.

How to Cook Dried Beans in the Oven

This will work for really any sort of dried bean. Soaking is not necessary, which cuts down the time from dried bean to cooked bean even more. The one exception is chickpeas, which are so tough they should be soaked overnight before cooking. This is a standard set of instructions for cooking 1 pound of dried beans.

CASSEROLE DISH: Clay, cast-iron, or other stovetop-to-oven cooking pot with a lid
BAKE TIME: 1 to 2 hours

3. Add the beans and all their liquid. Stir in the maple syrup, cider vinegar, mustard, salt, and pepper to taste. Bring back to a simmer, then cover with the lid and slide into the oven.

4. Bake for 1½ hours, then uncover and bake for 1 hour longer, or until the liquid has reduced to a thick syrup and the top is crusty and browned.

---

1. Preheat the oven to 350°F. Pour the dried beans into the cooking pot. Add enough water to cover the beans by about 1 inch. Place the uncovered pot on the stove and bring to a gentle boil. Stir in 2 teaspoons of salt, then put the lid on the pot and slide it into the oven.

2. Bake for 1 hour, then remove the lid and check for doneness. If the beans are not fully tender yet, return them to the oven, checking every 15 minutes after that. If they are looking quite dry, add boiling water in 1-cup increments. The cooking time will vary depending on the type of bean, but it shouldn't take longer than a total of 2 hours at the absolute most.

How to Cook Dried Lentils in the Oven

Lentils are even quicker to cook than beans, and once they've been cooked they're quick and easy to use in many recipes, including salads, dips, and other quick dinner dishes. You can substitute chicken, vegetable, or beef broth for the water in this method, which will produce silky and flavorful lentils worth eating on their own with a little yogurt and chopped steamed vegetables. This is a standard set of instructions for cooking 1 pound of dried lentils.

CASSEROLE DISH: Clay, cast-iron, or other stovetop-to-oven cooking pot with a lid
BAKE TIME: 1 hour

1. Preheat the oven to 350°F. Pour the dried lentils into the pot. Add enough water to cover them by 1 inch. Place the uncovered pot on the stove and bring it to a gentle boil. Stir in 1½ teaspoons of salt. Put the lid on the pot and slide it into the oven.

2. Bake for 1 hour, or until the lentils are tender.

White Bean Casserole with Herbs and Pork Sausage

THERE ARE MANY CLASSIC WHITE BEAN CASSEROLES, but none are more famous than the French cassoulet. Cassoulet is an elaborate preparation of beans, slow-cooked duck, and several kinds of meat. This recipe is nowhere as complex as that, but it nods in the direction of cassoulet with its fragrant herbs and cooked base of onions, celery, and carrot, which gives this a slow-cooked flavor.

Serves 6

CASSEROLE DISH: 9 × 13-inch baking dish
BAKE TIME: 40 minutes

1 pound uncooked Italian pork sausage, casings removed
1 medium onion, diced
2 medium carrots, diced
1 stalk celery, diced
4 cloves garlic, minced
One 12-ounce jar roasted red peppers, drained and coarsely chopped
½ cup fresh flat-leaf parsley, minced
2 sprigs fresh thyme (leaves only)
2 sprigs fresh rosemary (leaves only), minced
½ cup dry white wine
½ cup low-sodium chicken broth
1½ teaspoon salt
Freshly ground black pepper
Two 15-ounce cans Great Northern beans, rinsed and drained, or
    3 cups cooked white beans
¾ cup dry bread crumbs
¼ cup grated Parmesan cheese
Olive oil

1. Preheat the oven to 400°F and lightly grease the baking dish with olive oil. In a large deep skillet, cook the sausage over medium-high heat, stirring frequently to break it into crumbles. When the sausage is cooked and a little crispy, remove it with a slotted spoon and place it on a plate lined with paper towels.

2. Add the onion, carrots, and celery to the pork fat remaining in the pan. Cook, stirring occasionally, for about 15 minutes, or until the vegetables are very fragrant and tender. Add the garlic, red peppers, parsley, thyme, and rosemary and cook for an additional 10 minutes.

3. Pour in the wine and chicken broth and bring to a simmer. Remove from the heat and stir in the 1½ teaspoons salt and pepper to taste.

4. Puree ½ cup of the white beans in a food processor or mash them well in a bowl. Mix the pureed and whole beans with the cooked pork crumbles in the prepared baking dish. Pour the vegetable and broth mixture over the top and stir.

5. Mix the bread crumbs and Parmesan cheese in a small bowl and spread over the top of the beans. Drizzle with olive oil. Bake for 40 minutes, or until the top is golden brown and the beans are bubbling. Let stand for 5 minutes before serving.

Phyto-what?

Red kidney beans and cannellini beans contain a natural compound called phytohemagglutinin, which induces food-poisoning effects in humans. These beans need to be boiled for at least 15 minutes in order to negate these effects. Depending on how hot your oven is, and the size of your pot, this may occur in the oven. But to be really sure, when making those types of beans, boil them for a full 15 minutes on the stovetop before putting them in the oven.

Beans Baked with Caramelized Onions, Corn, and Cheese

WHILE DRIED BEANS really do provide superior flavor, canned beans are also a wonderful cupboard staple for quick meals. This protein-rich casserole comes together very quickly. Prep your other ingredients while the onions are caramelizing, and this should be ready to go in the oven in less than half an hour. It's cozy, flavorful, and satisfyingly gooey without being too heavy on the cheese. ● *Serves 8*

CASSEROLE DISH: 9 × 13-inch baking dish
BAKE TIME: 50 minutes

2 tablespoons unsalted butter
2 large onions, peeled and sliced into thin half-moons
Salt
Two 15-ounce cans kidney beans, rinsed and drained
One 15-ounce can black beans, rinsed and drained
One 16-ounce bag frozen corn, thawed and drained
1 bunch scallions, chopped into ¼-inch-thick rounds
Freshly ground black pepper
1½ cups ricotta cheese
2 large eggs, beaten
2 cups shredded cheddar cheese

1. Preheat the oven to 375°F and lightly grease the baking dish with olive oil.

2. Heat the butter over medium-low heat in a large, heavy sauté pan, preferably a cast-iron skillet. When the butter foams, add the onion slices. Sprinkle with salt. Cook slowly for about 25 minutes, stirring occasionally. When the onions are a rich golden brown, take the pan off the heat and set aside.

3. In a large bowl, mix the beans, corn, and scallions. Season with about 1½ teaspoons of salt and pepper to taste. In a small bowl, mix the ricotta cheese, eggs, and 1½ cups of the cheddar cheese.

4. Mix the ricotta mixture into the beans, and stir in the caramelized onions. Spread in the prepared baking dish and top with the remaining ½ cup of cheddar cheese. (At this point the casserole can be covered and refrigerated for up to 24 hours.) Bake, uncovered, for 50 minutes, or until the beans are hot and the cheese is melted. Serve hot.

Spicy Mexican Bean and Rice Bake

THIS CASSEROLE is another pantry dish; it calls mostly for ingredients found in the cupboard. With a handful of fresh herbs, cheese, and spices, it's a fast and easy supper dish. Serve with salsa and tortilla chips. ○ *Serves 6*

CASSEROLE DISH: 9 × 13-inch baking dish
BAKE TIME: 1 hour

Olive oil
1 large onion, diced
1 green bell pepper, cored and diced
4 cloves garlic, minced
Pinch of red pepper flakes (optional)
3 cups cooked white rice, from 1 cup rice steamed in 2 cups water
One 15-ounce can kidney beans, rinsed and drained
One 15-ounce can black beans, rinsed and drained
One 15-ounce can diced tomatoes, well drained
Small handful (about ¼ cup) fresh cilantro, chopped
2 cups shredded cheddar cheese
1 cup sour cream
2 large eggs, beaten
1 teaspoon mild chili powder or chipotle chile powder
2 teaspoons ground cumin
1 teaspoon salt
Freshly ground black pepper

1. Preheat the oven to 375°F and lightly grease the baking dish with olive oil.

2. Heat a drizzle of olive oil in a heavy skillet over medium heat and add the onion and green pepper. Cook for about 10 minutes, or until the vegetables are soft and fragrant. Add the garlic and red pepper flakes, if using, and cook for an additional 5 minutes.

3. In a large bowl, toss the cooked onion and pepper mixture with the rice, beans, and tomatoes. Stir in the cilantro and 1½ cups of the cheddar cheese.

4. In a separate bowl, mix the sour cream with the beaten eggs, chili powder, cumin, salt, and pepper to taste. Stir into the beans and then spread the mixture in the prepared baking dish. Sprinkle the remaining ½ cup of cheddar cheese on top and bake for 1 hour, or until hot and bubbly. Serve hot.

Baked Tofu Marinated in Soy, Sesame, and Ginger

UNTIL RECENTLY I only thought of tofu as an ingredient to be cooked in quick stir-fries. But my friend Emma, a food writer, taught me this method of baking tofu so that it turns into crispy, chewy squares full of flavor from the marinade. You can bake this for a short time, and keep that silken texture inside, or bake it longer and make it a chewy snack good for eating on the go! It's delicious either way. ◉ *Serves 2 to 4*

CASSEROLE DISH: 8-inch square baking dish
BAKE TIME: 20 to 40 minutes

1 pound firm or extra-firm tofu, rinsed
¼ cup reduced-sodium soy sauce
2 tablespoons sesame oil
1 tablespoon rice vinegar
1 tablespoon grated fresh ginger
¼ cup fine cornmeal

1. Cut the tofu into a few pieces, like long sticks or chunky squares. Set the pieces of tofu in a shallow pie plate and place in the sink, and then place a plate on top of the tofu. Put a weight on top, such as a can of beans or another heavy plate. Let the tofu drain for about 20 minutes.

2. Whisk together the soy sauce, sesame oil, rice vinegar, and ginger. When the tofu has expressed all of its excess liquid, drain it away from the plate and pat the tofu dry with paper towels. Pour the marinade over the top of the tofu. Let it sit for

15 to 30 minutes, flipping it over now and then so it absorbs the marinade on both sides.

3. Preheat the oven to 350°F and line the baking dish with aluminum foil. Grease lightly with nonstick cooking spray or vegetable oil.

4. Place the cornmeal on a plate. Take the tofu pieces out of their marinade and roll them in the cornmeal to lightly coat. Place them in the prepared baking dish and bake for about 30 minutes, flipping them over every 10 minutes. Cook for 10 minutes less if you want it to stay silken inside, and cook for 10 minutes longer if you want it extra-chewy. Serve warm.

Creamy Oven Stew with Tofu, Cauliflower, and White Beans

THIS OVEN STEW IS A HEALTHY ALTERNATIVE to rich, cream-based sauces and soups. It's packed full of cauliflower and silky tofu, with a crunchy topping of golden bread crumbs. This is great served over rice. **○** *Serves 6*

CASSEROLE DISH: 9 × 13-inch baking dish or 3-quart gratin dish
BAKE TIME: 45 minutes

1 pound firm tofu, rinsed
2 tablespoons reduced-sodium soy sauce
1 tablespoon rice vinegar
1 teaspoon paprika
Olive oil
4 cloves garlic, minced
1 small onion, diced
2 large stalks celery, diced
1 head cauliflower, cut into small florets
¼ cup all-purpose flour
1½ cups milk
One 15-ounce can white beans, such as Great Northern or cannellini, rinsed and drained
1½ teaspoons salt
Freshly ground black pepper
⅔ cup dry bread crumbs

1. Preheat the oven to 350°F and lightly grease the baking dish with olive oil.

2. Set the tofu in a shallow pie plate and place in the sink, and then place a plate on top of the tofu. Put a weight on top, such as a can of beans or another heavy plate. Let the tofu drain for about 20 minutes. Drain off the excess water and chop the block of tofu into 1-inch pieces. Whisk together the soy sauce, vinegar, and paprika, and pour it over the tofu to marinate.

3. Heat a drizzle of olive oil in a wide, heavy skillet over medium-low heat. When the oil is hot, add the garlic, onion, and celery and cook slowly until they are golden and fragrant. Turn the heat to medium-high, add the cauliflower, and cook, stirring frequently, for about 8 minutes, or until the cauliflower is toasted and golden.

4. Toss the flour with the vegetables in the skillet, cooking for another couple of minutes. Stir in the milk and bring to a simmer. Simmer for 5 minutes, or until the sauce just begins to thicken, then turn off the heat. Stir in the beans, salt, and pepper to taste. Add the tofu and its marinade and toss.

5. Pour the mixture into the prepared baking dish. Spread the bread crumbs on top and drizzle generously with olive oil. (At this point the casserole can be covered and refrigerated for up to 24 hours.) Bake, uncovered, for 45 minutes, or until it is bubbling and the bread crumbs are golden. Serve hot.

Sweet and Spicy Baked Tempeh

LIKE TOFU, tempeh is a vegetarian source of protein. It's also chewy, yummy, and rather meat-like in texture. It's wonderful in sandwiches or served sliced with roasted peppers and tomatoes or spooned over rice. Here's a recipe for baked tempeh in a sweet and spicy Asian-inspired sauce—good for dinner or lunch, or speared on toothpicks for cocktail snacking. The step of boiling the tempeh before marinating it is something I learned from *Veganomicon* (Da Capo Press, 2007), a marvelous vegan cookbook; this extra step really helps the marinade soak into the tempeh. ● *Serves 8*

CASSEROLE DISH: 9 × 13-inch baking dish
BAKE TIME: 25 minutes

1 pound tempeh

1 cup low-sodium vegetable broth

¼ cup cornstarch

4 cloves garlic, minced

One 2-inch piece fresh ginger, peeled and grated

3 tablespoons sugar

½ cup reduced-sodium soy sauce

¼ cup rice vinegar

2 tablespoons sriracha chili sauce (optional)

1. Bring a pot of water to a boil over high heat. Cut the tempeh into long strips and slip them into the boiling water. Boil for 10 minutes.

2. While the tempeh is boiling, make the sauce. In a food processor or blender, whiz all the remaining ingredients together. When the tempeh has finished boiling, drain and place in a bowl. Pour the sauce over the tempeh and marinate for at least 1 hour, or up to 2 days in the fridge.

3. Preheat the oven to 375°F and grease the baking dish with nonstick cooking spray. Lift the tempeh out of its marinade and spread the pieces out in the baking dish, leaving some space between them. Pour about ½ cup of the marinade over the pieces.

4. Bake for 15 minutes, then flip the tempeh pieces over. Bake for an additional 10 minutes. Serve warm.

Oven-Baked Pastas and Grains

Some of the most famous casseroles in the world are pasta-based—lasagna, anyone? Pasta casseroles are also among the easiest, quickest casseroles and one-dish suppers. There's a simple formula: Cook a pound of pasta, toss with some vegetables, meat, and cheese, and bake for an hour. Done!

This chapter builds on that simple formula with a few of my personal favorites, and it adds some more complex recipes, too, like Butternut Squash and Sage Lasagna (page 179) and Hearty Lasagna with Sausage (page 181). There are extremely quick recipes, such as Baked Ravioli with Chunky Tomatoes (page 184); there are more elaborate recipes, too, like my mother-in-law's breathtakingly delicious Pasta al Forno (page 183).

Most of the recipes here are fast and easy, yet full of interesting flavors. One of my favorite pasta casseroles is Baked Shells with Zucchini, Gouda, and Herbs (page 196). It mixes tiny pasta shells with shredded zucchini, aged Gouda, and handfuls of summery herbs. Another favorite is Baked Spaghetti Carbonara (page 205), which is creamy and fragrant with cheese and bacon.

This chapter also includes dishes based on grains, like the Hearty Barley Casserole with Lamb and Mushrooms (page 213) and Baked Quinoa with Sweet Potatoes and Almonds (page 209). And if you want a warm, nourishing dish on a cold winter's night, try the simple yet sublime Bread and Onion Panade with Spicy Greens (page 206). It's like Thanksgiving stuffing, but much easier and without the turkey!

Butternut Squash and Sage Lasagna

MY HUSBAND AND I had butternut squash pasta with sage served at our wedding; that's how much we like it. This lasagna recipe is a little different from our wedding recipe, but very similar in spirit. Serve this when the leaves turn red and the air starts getting nippy. It's warm, cozy, and, incidentally, vegetarian. ○ *Serves 8*

CASSEROLE DISH: 9 × 13-inch baking dish
BAKE TIME: 45 to 55 minutes for the squash; 1 hour for the lasagna

One 3- to 4-pound butternut squash
Olive oil
Salt and freshly ground black pepper
1 pound (about 20) dried lasagna noodles
2 tablespoons unsalted butter
⅔ cup loosely packed fresh sage leaves, coarsely chopped
8 cloves garlic, minced
1 pound ricotta cheese, drained of excess liquid
2 large eggs, beaten
½ cup heavy cream
1 cup low-sodium chicken or vegetable broth
¾ cup grated Parmesan cheese
Ground nutmeg
8 ounces fresh mozzarella cheese, chopped into ¼-inch cubes

1. Preheat the oven to 400°F. Lightly grease the baking dish with olive oil.

2. Cut the squash in half lengthwise and scoop out the seeds. Lightly brush with olive oil and sprinkle with salt and pepper. Place the squash halves, cut side up, on a large baking sheet and put in the oven to roast for 45 to 55 minutes, or until very soft inside. Remove from the oven and let cool. Reduce the oven temperature to 375°F.

3. Meanwhile, bring a large pot of water to a boil over high heat. Salt the water liberally, and add the dried lasagna noodles. Cook until al dente, drain the noodles, and lay them on clean kitchen towels to cool.

4. Melt the butter in a small frying pan over medium-high heat. As soon as it starts to sizzle, add the sage, and cook until light gold and slightly crisp at the edges, 2 to 3 minutes. Turn the heat down to low and add the garlic. Move the pan slightly off the heat so the garlic doesn't burn and continue cooking over low heat until the garlic is just golden. Set aside.

5. Stir together the ricotta, the beaten eggs, and ¼ cup of the heavy cream. Add the sage mixture and mix well. Season with 1 teaspoon of salt and pepper to taste.

6. Scoop the cooled roasted squash out of its skin, and place it in a bowl. Mash it with a fork and then stir in the remaining ¼ cup of cream and the chicken broth. Stir in ½ cup of the Parmesan cheese. Season with 1 teaspoon of nutmeg, 1 teaspoon of salt, and pepper to taste.

7. Spread a few spoonfuls of the ricotta mixture on the bottom of the prepared baking dish. On top of the ricotta, place 4 cooked lasagna noodles, overlapping them slightly. Spread half of the remaining ricotta mixture on top. Top with another 4 overlapping noodles. Spread half of the butternut squash mixture over the noodles, and dot with mozzarella. Repeat with the rest of the ricotta, noodles, and squash, ending with a fifth layer of noodles. Sprinkle the remaining ¼ cup of Parmesan on top, as well as a little extra pepper and nutmeg. (At this point the lasagna may be covered and refrigerated for up to 48 hours. It may also be securely wrapped and frozen for up to a month; see the sidebar below for tips on thawing and baking.)

8. Cover loosely with foil and bake for 45 minutes. Remove the foil and bake for an additional 15 minutes, or until the cheese is golden and bubbling. Let stand for 15 minutes before slicing and serving.

Adjusting Cook Times

Lasagna is one pasta dish that freezes well. I prefer to freeze it unbaked. When I want to serve it, I leave it in the refrigerator overnight to thaw, and then I bake it at its normally specified temperature but for about 30 minutes longer than it would usually take because it starts out cold. If you need to put it in the oven straight from the freezer, be prepared to bake it for about twice as long as usual.

Hearty Lasagna with Sausage

YOU CAN'T BEAT LASAGNA FOR COMFORT FOOD. It's an essential part of any casserole collection because it's the perfect casserole: hearty, wholesome, comforting, utterly delicious. Who would ever turn down homemade lasagna? This recipe produces a true, classic lasagna, with everything but the noodles made from scratch. But almost everything can be prepared ahead, with the lasagna itself coming together rather quickly. ❍ *Serves 8*

CASSEROLE DISH: 9 × 13-inch baking dish
BAKE TIME: 45 minutes

1 pound (about 20) dried lasagna noodles
1 pound ground beef
¾ pound spicy smoked sausage, chopped into small pieces
1 small onion, chopped
5 cloves garlic, minced
One 28-ounce can plum tomatoes, with their juices
One 6-ounce can tomato paste
One 28-ounce can tomato sauce
1 tablespoon balsamic vinegar
1 teaspoon sugar
½ teaspoon freshly ground black pepper
Large pinch of red pepper flakes (optional)
2 teaspoons salt
1½ pounds ricotta cheese
2 large eggs, beaten
½ cup grated Parmesan cheese
2 tablespoons olive oil
Small handful (about ¼ cup) fresh flat-leaf parsley, minced
3 cups shredded fresh mozzarella cheese

1. Preheat the oven to 350°F and lightly grease the baking dish with olive oil. Place a large pot of water over high heat and salt it generously. Bring to a boil, add the lasagna noodles, and return to a boil. Cook until the lasagna is al dente. Drain and lay the noodles out on clean kitchen towels to cool.

2. Place a large skillet over medium high heat and add the ground beef and sausage. Cook, stirring frequently, until the beef is very well browned. Add the chopped onion and garlic and turn the heat to medium. Cook, stirring frequently, for another 10 minutes. Turn off the heat and drain off most of the fat.

3. Stir the plum tomatoes, including their liquid, the tomato paste, and tomato sauce into the cooked meat. Crush the plum tomatoes with your hands or with a spoon. Stir in the vinegar, sugar, black pepper, red peppers, if using, and 1 teaspoon of salt. Turn the heat to medium and bring back up to a simmer. Simmer for about 10 minutes, while you make the ricotta mixture.

4. Stir together the ricotta, beaten eggs, Parmesan cheese, remaining 1 teaspoon of salt, olive oil, and minced parsley in a large bowl.

5. Line the bottom of the prepared baking dish with 4 cooked lasagna noodles, overlapping them. Spread one-quarter of the ricotta mixture on top. Spread about one-quarter of the meat sauce on top of that, and sprinkle with one-quarter of the grated mozzarella. Top with another 4 noodles. Repeat layering the ricotta, meat sauce, cheese, and noodles, finishing with 4 noodles as the top layer; you should have 4 layers of ricotta and meat sauce, and 5 layers of noodles. (If your package contains fewer than 20 noodles, or if some break during cooking, then use just 3 noodles in one or more of the middle layers, reserving your 4 best-looking noodles for the top layer.) Sprinkle any remaining mozzarella cheese on top of the noodles. (At this point the lasagna may be covered and refrigerated for up to 48 hours. It may also be securely wrapped and frozen for up to a month; see sidebar on page 180 for tips on thawing and baking.)

6. Bake, uncovered, until the cheese is golden and the sauce is bubbling, 45 minutes. Let stand for 15 minutes before slicing and serving.

Know Your Ground Beef

Ground beef is one ingredient to be very picky about. With recent outbreaks of *E. coli* and discomfiting stories in the news about ground beef's various health liabilities, it's important to be really sure that you are buying good beef. The best way to do this is to buy whole pieces of chuck or other beef cuts and grind them yourself in a food processor or meat grinder. Otherwise, buy your beef only from farmers who butcher and grind the beef themselves, or from a store where the beef is ground daily from only one or two cuts of meat. Always ask where the beef is from, which cuts went into it, and when it was ground.

Elaine's Pasta al Forno

THIS MAY NOT BE YOUR MOTHER'S casserole cookbook, but I'm not saying anything bad about *my* mother! In fact, there are some pretty great recipes that I owe completely to my mother and, in this case, my mother-in-law. This is my mother-in-law Elaine's famous pasta al forno, a creamy lasagna with spinach and four kinds of cheese. It's a dish for homecomings and family nights, and not to be missed. ○ *Serves 9*

CASSEROLE DISH: 9 × 13-inch baking dish
BAKE TIME: 1 hour

FOR THE WHITE SAUCE:
½ cup (1 stick) unsalted butter
¼ cup all-purpose flour
2 cups milk
½ teaspoon salt
¼ teaspoon ground nutmeg

FOR THE PASTA:
1 pound (about 20) dried lasagna noodles
One 16-ounce bag frozen spinach
¼ cup homemade or store-bought pesto
8 ounces cream cheese
1 cup shredded mozzarella cheese
1 cup shredded cheddar cheese
1 cup shredded Swiss or fontina cheese
1 cup homemade or store-bought tomato sauce
1 cup sour cream

1. To make the sauce, in a medium saucepan, melt the butter over medium-high heat. Add the flour, 1 tablespoon at a time, stirring constantly with a wooden spoon. Cook for another minute, still stirring, until the flour and butter paste pulls away from the bottom of the pan.

2. Slowly add the milk, whisking constantly. Whisk in the salt and nutmeg. Cook, stirring constantly, until the sauce thickens. This will take anywhere from 2 to 5 minutes. Remove from the heat and set aside.

3. Preheat the oven to 350°F. Lightly grease the baking dish with olive oil. Bring a large pot of water to a boil over high heat, and salt the water generously. Cook the lasagna noodles until al dente, then drain and lay out on clean kitchen towels to cool.

4. Thaw the frozen spinach, and squeeze it dry in paper towels or a clean kitchen towel. Place it in a medium bowl and mix thoroughly with the pesto. Cut the block of cream cheese into small cubes and set aside. Toss together the mozzarella, cheddar, and Swiss cheese.

5. Spread about ¾ cup of the tomato sauce on the bottom of the prepared baking dish. Place a layer of 4 overlapping lasagna noodles on top of the sauce.

6. Mentally divide the dish into 9 serving squares. In the center of each square, place a teaspoon of the spinach-pesto mixture. Top with a teaspoonful of white sauce, a cube of cream cheese, a sprinkling of the mixed cheeses, and a dab of sour cream.

7. Add another layer of 4 noodles, overlapping, and repeat the same layering of ingredients in each "square." Repeat one more time with the noodles and filling ingredients, then end with a top layer of noodles. Place a teaspoon of tomato sauce on top of each "square."

8. Using a sharp knife, carefully cut through the lasagna noodles to form 9 neat squares. Sprinkle any remaining mixed cheese over the top. (At this point the lasagna may be covered and refrigerated for up to 48 hours. It may also be securely wrapped and frozen for up to a month; see sidebar on page 180 for tips on thawing and baking.)

9. Bake, uncovered, for 1 hour. Let stand for 5 to 10 minutes before serving.

Baked Ravioli with Chunky Tomatoes

HERE'S AN EASY DISH for a fast supper! It takes advantage of the rather good frozen ravioli available in the grocery store, but covers it up with a quick homemade tomato sauce. Just bake until bubbling and toasty. You don't even have to defrost the ravioli. ○ *Serves 4*

CASSEROLE DISH: 8-inch square baking dish
BAKE TIME: 35 to 40 minutes

2 tablespoons olive oil
1 medium onion, chopped
4 cloves garlic, minced
Coarse salt and freshly ground black pepper
1 tablespoon tomato paste
1 teaspoon thyme leaves, minced
One 28-ounce can plum tomatoes, with their juices
1 teaspoon sugar
1 pound store-bought frozen cheese ravioli
1 cup shredded mozzarella cheese
¼ cup grated Parmesan cheese

1. Preheat the oven to 375°F. Lightly grease the baking dish with olive oil.

2. Heat the 2 tablespoons of olive oil in a deep skillet over medium heat. Add the onion and garlic and season with pinches of salt and pepper. Cook, stirring occasionally, until the onion is translucent and the garlic is golden and fragrant, about 10 minutes.

3. Turn the heat to medium-high and add the tomato paste. Cook, stirring constantly, until the tomato paste is softened and mixed in well with the onions. Add the thyme and tomatoes with their juices. Lightly crush the whole tomatoes as you add them to the onions. Add the sugar, 1 teaspoon of salt, and ½ teaspoon of pepper. Bring to a boil, reduce the heat, and simmer for about 15 minutes, or until somewhat reduced.

4. Spread half of the frozen ravioli in the prepared baking dish. Spread half of the sauce over the ravioli, and sprinkle with half of the mozzarella cheese. Spread the rest of the ravioli, sauce, and mozzarella in layers in the dish, and top with the Parmesan.

5. Cover the dish tightly with foil and bake for 30 minutes. Remove the foil and bake for an additional 5 to 10 minutes to let the top get golden and melted. Cool slightly before serving.

Baked Ravioli with Homemade White Sauce and Crunchy Herbed Topping

HERE'S ANOTHER DISH that can be made with prepared fresh or frozen ravioli. It calls for a simple but elegant white sauce that makes the final dish richly creamy and fragrant. ○ *Serves 6*

CASSEROLE DISH: 9 × 13-inch baking dish or 3-quart baking pan
BAKE TIME: 40 minutes

2 pounds fresh or frozen cheese or spinach ravioli
½ cup (1 stick) unsalted butter
4 cloves garlic, minced
½ cup all-purpose flour
4 cups whole milk
¼ teaspoon ground nutmeg
1 teaspoon salt
Freshly ground black pepper
1¼ cups Parmesan cheese
½ cup fresh or dry bread crumbs
1 tablespoon olive oil
2 tablespoons minced fresh herbs, such as parsley, chives, sage, rosemary, or a mix

1. Preheat the oven to 375°F. Lightly grease the baking dish with olive oil.

2. If using frozen ravioli, bring a large pot of water to a boil. Salt generously and cook the ravioli according to package directions. Drain and set aside.

3. In a large deep skillet, melt the butter over medium heat. Slowly sauté the garlic over medium-low to medium heat, without letting it color or burn. After about 10 minutes, whisk in the flour. Cook over medium heat, whisking constantly, until the butter and flour are a smooth, well-combined paste.

4. Slowly add the milk, whisking constantly. Whisk until the flour mixture and the milk are smooth and completely combined. Whisk for another 2 to 3 minutes over medium heat, until the mixture just begins to thicken, then remove from the heat. Stir in the nutmeg and salt.

5. Remove the sauce from the heat and season to taste with pepper. Stir in 1 cup of the Parmesan cheese.

6. In a food processor or chopper, combine the remaining ¼ cup of Parmesan cheese, the bread crumbs, olive oil, herbs, and a pinch of salt and pepper. Blend until well combined. Toss the ravioli with the white sauce and spread in the prepared dish. Spread the bread crumbs over the ravioli.

7. Cover the dish tightly with foil and bake for 25 minutes. Remove the foil and turn the heat up to 450°F. Bake for an additional 15 minutes, or until the sauce is bubbling and the top is golden brown. Let stand for 5 minutes before serving.

Whole Wheat Pasta with Chicken Sausage, Chickpeas, and Garlicky Greens

YOU CAN WHIP UP THIS DISH with fresh and wholesome ingredients that probably just happen to live in your pantry and freezer. Frozen spinach, canned tomatoes, and canned chickpeas are all great staples to have on hand, and combined with pasta they make a very quick and nutritious casserole.

o *Serves 6*

CASSEROLE DISH: 9 × 13-inch baking dish
BAKE TIME: 25 minutes

1 pound whole wheat rotini
1 tablespoon olive oil
4 cloves garlic, minced
¾ pound smoked or cured chicken sausage
One 16-ounce bag frozen chopped spinach, thawed and drained
2 tablespoons reduced-sodium soy sauce
One 10-ounce can whole chickpeas, rinsed and drained
One 14.5-ounce can diced tomatoes, drained
Freshly ground black pepper
1 cup grated Parmesan cheese

1. Preheat the oven to 375°F. Lightly grease the baking pan with olive oil. Fill a large pot halfway with water, salt it generously, and bring to a boil. Add the pasta and cook according to package directions until just al dente. Drain, return to the cooking pot, and set aside.

2. Place a large deep skillet over medium heat and add the olive oil. When the oil is hot but not smoking, add the garlic and turn the heat to low. Cook, stirring frequently, until the garlic is golden and fragrant. Add the sausage and cook for about 5 minutes, or until it is lightly golden brown. Add the spinach and cook, stirring frequently, on medium heat until the spinach is hot. Stir in the soy sauce and taste, adding more soy sauce if necessary.

3. Add the sausage mixture to the cooked pasta in the pot, along with the chickpeas, diced tomatoes, and black pepper to taste. Stir in the Parmesan cheese and spread the mixture in the prepared baking dish. (At this point the casserole may be covered and refrigerated for up to 24 hours.)

4. Bake, uncovered, for 25 minutes, or until the cheese is melted and the top is golden brown. Let stand for 5 minutes before serving.

Smoked Sausage and Sage Pasta Casserole

SMOKED SAUSAGE is such an easy shortcut to a flavorful meal. So are caramelized onions, and they're piled on together in this quick and delicious savory pasta bake. It's one-dish cooking at its finest. All you need to add is a simple green salad and you have a meal. ○ *Serves 4 to 6*

CASSEROLE DISH: 9 × 13-inch baking dish
BAKE TIME: 30 minutes

1 pound whole wheat rotini
2 tablespoons unsalted butter
3 small onions, thinly sliced
1 pound smoked sausage, such as andouille or chorizo

4 cups baby spinach

6 to 10 fresh sage leaves

4 cloves garlic, minced

2 cups shredded mozzarella cheese

1 teaspoon salt

1 teaspoon freshly ground black pepper

½ cup grated Parmesan cheese

1. Preheat the oven to 350°F and lightly grease the baking dish with olive oil. Fill a large pot halfway with water, salt generously, and bring to a boil. Add the pasta and cook according to package directions until just al dente. Drain, return to the cooking pot, and set aside.

2. Meanwhile, heat the butter in a heavy skillet over medium heat. Add the onions and cook slowly over medium-low heat until they are golden brown. This will take between 15 and 20 minutes.

3. While the pasta and onions are cooking, thinly slice each link of smoked sausage into coin-shaped rounds. Coarsely chop the spinach and fresh sage.

4. In the cooking pot, toss the cooked pasta, caramelized onions, sausage, spinach, sage, minced garlic, mozzarella, and salt and pepper. Spread in the prepared casserole dish. Sprinkle the Parmesan cheese on top. (At this point the casserole may be covered and refrigerated for up to 24 hours. Let come to room temperature before baking.)

5. Bake, uncovered, for 30 minutes, or until the top is lightly browned and the mozzarella is bubbly. Let rest for 5 minutes before serving.

Variation: If you are making this late in the fall or in winter, when fresh baby spinach isn't easily available, substitute a winter green like chard or kale. These are a little meatier but just as delicious as the spinach.

Handy Caramelized Onions

Slice and caramelize a few extra onions while you're cooking the ones for this recipe. Freeze them in individual plastic bags for quick and easy additions to future casseroles, soups, and sandwiches.

Mixed Greens Pasta Casserole with Cheesy Topping

THIS CASSEROLE IS AN ODE to dark, leafy greens. I love them dearly, and I think that people should eat more of them. This isn't just a matter of principle, though; it's also a matter of taste, since the slightly sweet chew of good pasta, baked slowly with earthy bitter greens and melted salty cheese, is a great pleasure. If you have a bunch or two of Swiss chard, kale, collard greens, turnip tops, mustard greens, or any other green leafy vegetable, throw them in here.

o *Serves 6*

CASSEROLE DISH: 9 × 13-inch baking dish
BAKE TIME: 30 minutes

1 pound rotini
½ pound kale
½ pound Swiss chard
2 tablespoons unsalted butter
1 large onion, finely chopped
6 cloves garlic, sliced
Juice and zest of 1 lemon
½ cup low-sodium chicken broth
1 teaspoon salt
Freshly ground black pepper
8 ounces whole-milk mozzarella cheese
½ cup grated Parmesan cheese

1. Preheat the oven to 350°F and lightly grease the baking pan with olive oil. Fill a large pot halfway with water, salt generously, and bring to a boil. Add the pasta and cook according to package directions until barely al dente. Drain, return to the cooking pot, and set aside.

2. Meanwhile, wash and dry the kale and chard. Prepare the greens by slicing out and discarding the thick center rib. Tightly roll the leaves and slice them in half lengthwise, then crosswise into ribbons.

3. Heat the butter in a large, deep skillet or Dutch oven over medium heat. Add the onion and cook, stirring frequently, until translucent and soft, about 10 minutes. Add the garlic and cook for another 5 minutes.

4. Turn the heat to high and add the greens, stirring to combine them with the olive oil and onions. Pour the lemon juice and chicken broth over them and cook, tossing, until they are wilted. Turn off the heat, and stir the wilted greens, along with any liquid in the pan, into the cooked pasta. Season with salt, pepper, and the lemon zest, and spread in the prepared baking dish.

5. Cut the mozzarella into small cubes, and scatter them over the pasta in the dish. (At this point the casserole may be covered and refrigerated for up to 24 hours. Let come to room temperature before baking.) Spread the Parmesan on top and bake, uncovered, for 30 minutes, or until the top is lightly browned and the cheese is bubbly. Let rest for 5 minutes before serving.

Micah's Mac and Cheese

THIS DISH IS NAMED AFTER a young friend of mine who likes macaroni and cheese very much. He has particular requirements, however: bowtie pasta (farfalle) is his favorite shape, and the cheese should be only Parmesan. I like Parmesan very much, too, so this simple, flavorful baked mac and cheese is among my favorite dishes. ○ *Serves 6 to 8*

CASSEROLE DISH: 9 × 13-inch baking dish
BAKE TIME: 35 minutes

1 pound farfalle
¼ cup (½ stick) unsalted butter
¼ cup all-purpose flour
2½ cups milk
1¾ teaspoons salt
2 cups grated Parmesan cheese
Freshly ground black pepper

1. Preheat the oven to 350°F. Lightly grease the baking pan with olive oil. Bring a large pot of water to a boil over high heat, and salt the water generously. Cook the pasta for about 2 minutes less than recommended by the package directions. Drain and return to the pot.

2. In a medium saucepan, melt the butter over medium-high heat. Add the flour, 1 tablespoon at a time, stirring constantly with a wooden spoon. Cook for another minute, still stirring, until the flour and butter paste pulls away from the bottom of the pan.

3. Slowly add the milk, whisking constantly. Whisk in ¾ teaspoon salt. Cook, stirring constantly, until the sauce thickens. This will take anywhere from 2 to 5 minutes. Remove from the heat, stir in 1 cup of the Parmesan cheese, and set aside.

4. Stir ½ cup of the Parmesan cheese into the cooked pasta. Then pour in the white sauce and mix thoroughly. Stir in the remaining 1 teaspoon of salt and black pepper to taste.

5. Spread in the prepared dish and sprinkle with the remaining ½ cup of Parmesan. (At this point the casserole may be covered and refrigerated for up to 24 hours. Let come to room temperature before baking.) Cover tightly with aluminum foil and bake for 30 minutes, or until hot and bubbling. Uncover and bake for an additional 5 minutes, or until golden on top. Let stand for 5 minutes before serving.

Ground Beef and Ziti with Spicy Red Sauce

HERE'S A HOT AND SPICY TAKE on a traditionally mild pasta casserole. A bit of smoky chipotle chile and a lot of crispy fried meat: This is a casserole that anyone who wants a little extra heat will love. ● *Serves 6*

CASSEROLE DISH: 9 × 13-inch baking dish
BAKE TIME: 30 minutes

1 pound ziti
Olive oil
1 pound ground beef or pork
1 large onion, finely chopped

2 cloves garlic, minced

1 tablespoon tomato paste

2 teaspoons chipotle chile powder

1 tablespoon Worcestershire sauce

One 28-ounce can tomato sauce

1 teaspoon sugar

1½ teaspoons salt

Freshly ground black pepper

2 large eggs, beaten

2 tablespoons unsalted butter

¾ cup dry bread crumbs

1. Preheat the oven to 350°F and lightly grease the baking pan with olive oil. Fill a large pot halfway with water, salt generously, and bring to a boil. Add the pasta and cook according to package directions until barely al dente. Drain, toss with a drizzle of olive oil, return to the cooking pot, and set aside.

2. Meanwhile, heat a drizzle of olive oil in a wide, deep skillet. Add the ground beef and cook over medium-high heat, stirring and breaking into crumbles, until crispy and well browned.

3. Add the onion and garlic to the meat and turn the heat to medium-low. Cook slowly for about 10 minutes, or until the onion and garlic are fragrant and soft. Add the tomato paste and chipotle and sauté them with the beef and onions for a minute or two.

4. Stir in the Worcestershire and tomato sauce and bring the sauce to a simmer. Simmer for about 10 minutes, or until slightly reduced. Set aside to cool for at least 5 minutes. Season with the sugar, salt, and pepper to taste. When the sauce has cooled slightly, stir in the beaten eggs. Spread the cooked pasta in the prepared baking dish, then pour the sauce over the top. Stir a little (no need to combine thoroughly).

5. In a small skillet, heat the butter over medium heat and add the bread crumbs. Cook until the bread crumbs have absorbed most of the butter. Spread over the pasta in the dish. (At this point the casserole may be covered and refrigerated for up to 24 hours, or frozen for up to a month. Let come to room temperature before baking.)

6. Bake, uncovered, for 30 minutes or until the bread crumbs are browned and the sauce is bubbling. Let stand for several minutes before serving.

Butternut Squash Pasta Casserole with Gruyère and Pecans

MOST SQUASH CASSEROLES call for the squash to be roasted beforehand, a rather time-consuming process. This recipe still calls for cooking the squash before baking it with the pasta, but here it is simmered quickly in milk, which also becomes the sauce for the pasta. ○ *Serves 6*

CASSEROLE DISH: 9 × 13-inch baking dish
BAKE TIME: 30 minutes

1 pound rotini, radiatore, or medium shells
4 slices bacon, cut into ½-inch pieces
1 small onion, minced
10 to 12 sage leaves, coarsely chopped
One 2-pound butternut squash, peeled and chopped into 1-inch chunks (page 113)
1½ cups milk or cream
1 teaspoon salt
Freshly ground black pepper
½ teaspoon ground nutmeg
1 cup grated Gruyère cheese
1 cup pecans, toasted and coarsely chopped

1. Preheat the oven to 375°F and lightly grease the baking dish with olive oil. Fill a large pot halfway with water, salt generously, and bring to a boil. Add the pasta and cook for about 5 minutes less than recommended by the package directions. Drain and set aside.

2. In a large pot (you can use the rinsed pasta pot) over medium heat, cook the bacon, stirring occasionally, until it is crisp and the fat has rendered. Add the onion and sage and cook with the bacon until the onion is tender and translucent, about 5 minutes.

3. Add the chopped squash and cook with the onions and bacon for 3 to 4 minutes. Pour in the milk and bring to a simmer. Turn the heat to low and cover the pot. Cook just until the squash is barely tender when pierced with a fork. The cooking time will depend both on the squash and size of the chunks, but it should be around 10 minutes.

4. Add the salt, black pepper to taste, and the nutmeg. Stir in the pasta and cheese. Spread in the prepared baking dish and top with the chopped pecans. (At this point the casserole may be covered and refrigerated for up to 24 hours. Let come to room temperature before baking.) Bake, uncovered, for 30 minutes, or until the cheese is bubbling. Let stand for 5 minutes before serving.

Ruffly Radiatore

Different pasta shapes are better for different sorts of sauces and casseroles. One favorite for baked casseroles is the curled, ruffled radiatore, which is just the right size for cheese-laden bites. Its ridges catch the sauce and the inner curve holds chunks of meat or vegetable. If you find radiatore at the grocery store or a specialty shop, give it a try in one of these casseroles.

Orecchiette, Red Bean, and Almond Bake

TOSS TOGETHER A FEW STAPLES in an unexpected way for an unexpectedly delicious result. This dish features pasta shaped like small ridged ovals (*orecchiette* means "little ears"), kidney beans, and crunchy almonds, all in a creamy sauce of yogurt, eggs, and cheese. It's quick and easy and full of delicious textures. In fact, this may be my favorite among the pasta casseroles in my repertoire. ○ *Serves 6*

CASSEROLE DISH: 9 × 13-inch baking dish
BAKE TIME: 30 to 35 minutes

1 pound orecchiette
1 cup whole-milk plain yogurt
2 large eggs, beaten
1 teaspoon salt
1 teaspoon smoked paprika
Freshly ground black pepper
One 12-ounce can kidney beans, rinsed and drained
¾ cup blanched sliced almonds
1 small onion, diced
2 cups shredded cheddar or aged Gouda cheese

1. Preheat the oven to 375°F and lightly grease the baking dish with olive oil.

2. Fill a large pot halfway with water, salt generously, and bring to a boil. Add the pasta and cook for about 2 minutes less than recommended by the package directions. Drain, return to the cooking pot, and set aside.

3. Mix the yogurt with the beaten eggs in a small bowl and season with the salt, smoked paprika, and black pepper to taste. Pour the mixture into the pasta and stir in the kidney beans, almonds, onion, and about 1½ cups of the cheese. Spread in the prepared baking dish and sprinkle the remaining ½ cup of cheese on top. (At this point the casserole may be covered and refrigerated for up to 24 hours. Let come to room temperature before baking.)

4. Bake, uncovered, for 30 to 35 minutes, or until the cheese is bubbling and the top is golden. Serve immediately.

Baked Shells with Zucchini, Gouda, and Herbs

THIS CASSEROLE is one I like to think of as a baked pasta salad. It has all the merits of a truly good pasta salad: lots of different textures and tastes, with a summery flavor. The crunchy, toasty pine nuts, gooey cheese, and tender pasta are delicious without being too rich or filling, and the summer zucchini and herbs are refreshingly bright. ○ *Serves 6*

CASSEROLE DISH: 9 × 13-inch baking dish
BAKE TIME: 30 to 35 minutes

1 large zucchini, grated
2 teaspoons salt
1 pound small or medium pasta shells
⅔ cup pine nuts
1 cup plain yogurt
1 large egg, beaten
Freshly ground black pepper
1⅓ cups grated Gouda cheese
Small handful (about ¼ cup) fresh flat-leaf parsley, minced
2 large sprigs fresh mint (leaves only), minced

1. Preheat the oven to 375°F and lightly grease the baking dish with olive oil.

2. Place the grated zucchini in a bowl and stir in the salt. Set aside.

3. Fill a large pot halfway with water, salt generously, and bring to a boil. Add the pasta and cook for about 2 minutes less than recommended by the package directions. Drain, return to the cooking pot, and set aside.

4. Heat a large skillet over medium heat and add the pine nuts. Cook carefully for 2 to 4 minutes, frequently shaking the pan or stirring, until the pine nuts start to turn golden brown and smell toasted. Remove from the heat.

5. Stir the yogurt and beaten egg together in a small bowl and season generously with black pepper. Drain off as much water as possible from the grated zucchini, then blot dry with a paper towel.

6. When the pasta has cooled slightly, stir in the grated zucchini, toasted pine nuts, yogurt mixture, and about 1 cup of the grated Gouda cheese. Stir in the parsley and mint, and spread in the prepared baking dish. Sprinkle the top with the remaining ⅓ cup of cheese. (At this point the casserole may be covered and refrigerated for up to 24 hours. Let come to room temperature before baking.)

7. Bake, uncovered, for 30 to 35 minutes, or until the cheese on top has melted and the pasta is lightly golden. Serve immediately.

Creamy Stuffed Shells with Ricotta and Broccoli

STUFFED SHELLS ONLY LOOK LIKE A LOT OF WORK. They're filled individually, by hand, but they truly don't take as long as you might think. This dish has a homemade white sauce with Parmesan and a creamy filling featuring earthy broccoli and bright lemon. It's rather light, unlike more traditional stuffed shells, and you can pull it together in less than an hour. ○ *Serves 6*

CASSEROLE DISH: 9 × 13-inch metal baking pan
BAKE TIME: 32 minutes

FOR THE PASTA AND STUFFING:

1 pound jumbo pasta shells

One 32-ounce bag frozen broccoli florets

15 ounces ricotta cheese

1 large egg, beaten

2 cloves garlic, minced

Juice and zest of 1 lemon

Salt and freshly ground black pepper

FOR THE SAUCE:

¼ cup (½ stick) unsalted butter

¼ cup all-purpose flour

2 cups milk

¼ teaspoon salt

2 cups grated Parmesan cheese

1. Preheat the oven to 350°F. Lightly grease the baking dish with olive oil. Bring a large pot of water to a boil over high heat, and salt the water generously. Cook the pasta shells according to package directions, drain, and spread out on a clean kitchen towel to cool.

2. While the pasta is boiling, cook the broccoli florets. Steam them in a steamer insert on the stovetop for about 5 minutes, or put them in a microwave-safe bowl with ¼ cup of water, cover, and microwave for 5 minutes. Drain the cooked broccoli and chop into small pieces.

3. In a large bowl, mix the ricotta, beaten egg, garlic, lemon juice and zest, about 1 teaspoon of salt, and pepper to taste. Stir in the chopped broccoli.

4. To make the sauce, in a medium saucepan, melt the butter over medium-high heat. Add the flour, 1 tablespoon at a time, stirring constantly with a wooden spoon. Cook for another 3 to 4 minutes, still stirring, until the flour and butter paste is bubbly and just beginning to turn brown.

5. Slowly add the milk, whisking constantly. Whisk in the salt. Cook, stirring constantly, until the sauce just begins to thicken. This will take anywhere from 2 to 5 minutes. Remove from the heat, stir in 1½ cups of the Parmesan cheese, and set aside.

6. Spoon ½ cup of the white sauce over the bottom of the prepared baking dish. Fill each cooked pasta shell with a spoonful of the ricotta and broccoli mixture, and place the shells in the dish with the filling facing sideways. Spread the remaining white sauce over the shells. Sprinkle with the remaining ½ cup of Parmesan. (At this point the casserole may be covered and refrigerated for up to 24 hours. Let come to room temperature before baking.)

7. Cover the dish tightly with foil and bake for 30 minutes, or until heated through and bubbling. Turn the oven to broil, remove the foil, and broil for 2 minutes, or until bubbling and golden on top. Let stand for 10 minutes before serving.

Saucy Shells Stuffed with Spiced Tofu

MANY BAKED PASTA DISHES are deliciously cheesy and fatty, and while it's wonderful to indulge once in a while, not every pasta casserole needs to be that heavy. This casserole is far lighter; in fact, there's no cheese in it at all! This vegan dish will still be welcomed by omnivores, however. It has some zing and a kick, and the tofu is perfectly creamy, just like ricotta. ○ *Serves 6*

CASSEROLE DISH: 9 × 13-inch baking dish
BAKE TIME: 45 minutes

FOR THE SAUCE:
2 tablespoons olive oil
1 small onion, diced
6 cloves garlic, minced
1 green bell pepper, cored and diced
1 red bell pepper, cored and diced
One 28-ounce can plum tomatoes, with their juices,
    crushed with the back of a spoon
1 teaspoon sugar
2 tablespoons balsamic vinegar
Salt and freshly ground black pepper

FOR THE PASTA AND STUFFING:

1 pound jumbo pasta shells

¼ cup short-grain white rice

1 pound silken tofu, very well drained (page 172)

One 16-ounce bag frozen spinach, thawed and drained

1 teaspoon chili powder

1 teaspoon ground ginger

1 teaspoon salt

Freshly ground black pepper

1. To make the sauce, heat the olive oil in a large, deep skillet over medium heat. Add the onion and cook for 5 minutes, or until the onion is translucent and fragrant. Add the garlic and bell peppers, stirring frequently and cooking until soft, about 5 more minutes.

2. Pour in the tomatoes and their juices and stir in the sugar, vinegar, salt, and pepper. Bring to a simmer and cook until slightly thickened, about 10 minutes.

3. Preheat the oven to 350°F. Lightly grease the baking pan with olive oil. Bring a large pot of water to a boil over high heat, and salt the water generously. Cook the pasta shells according to package directions, drain, and spread out on a clean kitchen towel to cool.

4. In the pasta pot, bring another few cups of water to a boil. Cook the rice for 10 minutes, then drain and set aside. The rice will not be fully cooked.

5. Crumble the tofu into a medium bowl and mix it with the rice, spinach, chili powder, ginger, salt, and pepper. Stir in about 1 cup of the tomato sauce.

6. Spoon 1 cup of the tomato sauce over the bottom of the prepared baking dish. Fill each cooked pasta shell with the tofu mixture, and place the shells, filling side up, in the dish. Pour the remaining tomato sauce over the shells. (At this point the casserole may be covered and refrigerated for up to 24 hours. Let come to room temperature before baking.)

7. Cover the dish tightly with foil and bake for 40 minutes, or until heated through and bubbling. Uncover and bake for an additional 5 minutes. Serve immediately.

Chicken and Tomato Pasta Rolls

T HIS RECIPE CALLS FOR STUFFING MANICOTTI with warmly spiced ricotta cheese and shredded chicken (a great way to use up a cup or two of leftover roast chicken) and topping it with a simple homemade tomato sauce. If you want to enjoy the delicious stuffing, but you also want to forego the process of stuffing those slippery manicotti tubes, try the shortcut variation that follows.

o *Serves 6*

CASSEROLE DISH: 9 × 13-inch baking dish
BAKE TIME: 50 minutes

1 pound manicotti

FOR THE TOMATO SAUCE:
2 tablespoons olive oil
6 cloves garlic, minced
Two 28-ounce cans diced tomatoes, with their juices
1 teaspoon sugar
1 tablespoon balsamic vinegar
Salt and freshly ground black pepper

FOR THE FILLING:
3 cups shredded or chopped cooked chicken
15 ounces ricotta cheese
1½ cups grated Parmesan cheese
1 cup shredded mozzarella cheese
2 large eggs, beaten
2 teaspoons smoked paprika
1 teaspoon salt
½ teaspoon freshly ground black pepper
Small handful (about ¼ cup) fresh flat-leaf parsley, chopped

1. Preheat the oven to 350°F and lightly grease the baking dish with olive oil. Bring a large pot of water to a boil over high heat, and salt the water generously. Cook the manicotti according to the package directions, drain, and spread out on a clean kitchen towel to cool.

2. To make the sauce, heat the olive oil in a large, deep skillet or wide saucepan over medium heat. When it is hot, add the garlic and turn the heat down to low. Cook the garlic until golden and fragrant, about 4 minutes.

3. Add the tomatoes and their juices, crushing the tomatoes with the spoon as you stir them into the hot oil. Bring to a boil, then lower the heat and simmer for at least 15 minutes, while you make the filling and stuff the pasta tubes. When you are ready to use the sauce, stir in the sugar, vinegar, and salt and pepper to taste. Turn off the heat and set aside.

4. For the filling, combine the chicken, ricotta, 1 cup of the Parmesan, the mozzarella, eggs, paprika, salt, pepper, and parsley. Mix well and set aside.

5. Spread the bottom of the baking dish evenly with about 1 cup of sauce. Use a small teaspoon to stuff each manicotti tube with filling, and place the tubes in the baking dish. Top evenly with the remaining sauce, making certain that the pasta is completely covered. Sprinkle the remaining ½ cup of Parmesan cheese on top. (At this point the casserole may be covered and refrigerated for up to 24 hours, or well-wrapped and frozen for up to a month. Let come to room temperature before baking.)

6. Cover the dish with aluminum foil and bake for about 40 minutes. Remove the foil and bake for an additional 10 minutes, or until the cheese is melted and golden. Let stand for 10 minutes before serving.

Variation: If you don't want to stuff those little manicotti tubes, substitute an equal quantity of lasagna noodles. Spread a spoonful of filling on each cooked lasagna noodle, then roll it up from the short end, like a tube, and assemble and bake as directed above.

Orzo and Pesto Bake

DO YOU HAVE FRESH PESTO AROUND? Do you want to show it off in a fresh, easy pasta dish? This is the one! It really showcases the fresh tastes of summer, with yellow pepper, onion, and all the garlicky goodness of fresh pesto. If you don't have homemade pesto, substitute the best store-bought version you can find. This dish is also rather healthier than many pasta casseroles, with just enough cheese to make it taste rich, but not so much that it overwhelms the clear taste of the pesto. ○ *Serves 6*

CASSEROLE DISH: 9 × 13-inch baking dish
BAKE TIME: 25 minutes

1 pound orzo
2 tablespoons olive oil
2 cloves garlic, minced
1 yellow bell pepper, cored and diced
1 small onion, minced
⅔ cup fresh basil pesto
1 cup shredded mozzarella cheese
Salt and freshly ground black pepper
½ cup grated Parmesan cheese

1. Preheat the oven to 400°F and lightly grease the baking pan with olive oil.

2. Heat 4 cups of water to boiling in a medium saucepan and salt the water generously. Add the orzo and cook for precisely 7 minutes. Drain and return to the pot.

3. Heat the olive oil in a wide, heavy skillet over medium heat. Add the garlic, bell pepper, and onion and cook over medium heat for about 5 minutes, or until the vegetables are just beginning to soften and become fragrant. Combine the vegetables with the orzo in the pot.

4. Stir in the pesto, mozzarella, and salt and pepper to taste. Spread in the prepared baking dish and sprinkle with the Parmesan. (At this point the casserole may be covered and refrigerated for up to 24 hours.) Bake for 25 minutes, or until the cheese is gooey and the orzo is tender but still al dente. Let stand for 5 minutes before serving.

Baked Spaghetti with Tomatoes and Pine Nuts

SPAGHETTI MAKES A WONDERFUL PASTA CASSEROLE, since it bakes into a dense concoction that can be cut and sliced like a frittata. This is a saucy vegetarian version of baked spaghetti with the bright flavors of tomato, lemon, and red pepper flakes. ○ *Serves 6*

CASSEROLE DISH: 9 × 13-inch baking dish
BAKE TIME: 30 minutes

1 pound thin spaghetti
Olive oil
Large pinch of red pepper flakes
4 large cloves garlic, minced
One 28-ounce can diced tomatoes, drained
Zest of 1 lemon, grated
1 teaspoon salt
Freshly ground black pepper
2 cups ricotta cheese
8 large eggs, beaten
½ cup grated Parmesan cheese
¾ cup pine nuts, toasted

1. Preheat the oven to 400°F and lightly grease the baking dish with olive oil. Bring a large pot of water to a boil over high heat, and salt the water generously. Cook the spaghetti for about 2 minutes less than recommended by the package directions. Drain and return to the cooking pot, then toss with a generous amount of olive oil.

2. Heat 2 tablespoons olive oil in a large deep skillet over medium-low heat. When the oil is hot, add the red pepper flakes and garlic. Cook, stirring frequently, for about 3 minutes, or until the garlic is golden and fragrant. Don't let it burn or turn crisp.

3. Add the drained diced tomatoes and cook, stirring frequently, until hot. Add the lemon zest, ½ teaspoon of salt, and black pepper to taste. Take the skillet off the heat and set aside.

4. In a large bowl, whisk together the ricotta and eggs and season with more black pepper and the remaining ½ teaspoon of salt. Stir in the Parmesan cheese and pine nuts.

5. Add the cooked pasta to the bowl, then stir in the tomato mixture. Spread in the prepared baking dish and drizzle with olive oil. (At this point the casserole may be covered and refrigerated for up to 24 hours.) Bake, uncovered, for 30 minutes, or until the center is set but still moist. Let stand for 5 minutes before cutting into squares.

Baked Spaghetti Carbonara

SPAGHETTI CARBONARA IS PERHAPS THE ULTIMATE Italian comfort food and is an easy dish to prepare. It generally calls for bacon, a little white wine, and gently cooked eggs all tossed together with hot spaghetti. Heaven in a dish! This baked version takes its inspiration from the original, but adds a little extra milk for moistness. ○ *Serves 6*

CASSEROLE DISH: 9 × 13-inch baking dish
BAKE TIME: 30 minutes

1 pound spaghetti
Olive oil
8 slices bacon, cut into 2-inch lengths
4 cloves garlic, minced
½ cup white wine
6 large eggs
1½ cups milk
2 cups grated Parmesan cheese
1 teaspoon salt
¼ teaspoon ground nutmeg
Freshly ground black pepper

1. Preheat the oven to 400°F and lightly grease the baking dish with olive oil. Bring a large pot of water to a boil over high heat, and salt the water generously. Cook the spaghetti for about 2 minutes less than recommended by the package directions. Drain and return to the cooking pot, then toss with a generous amount of olive oil.

2. Place the bacon pieces in a large, deep skillet and turn the heat to medium. Cook the bacon slowly until it is crispy, about 10 minutes. Add the garlic and cook over medium heat for an additional 4 minutes, or until the garlic is fragrant and golden.

3. Turn the heat to medium-high and add the white wine. Bring to a boil and simmer for 5 minutes, or until the wine is slightly reduced. Turn off the heat and set the skillet aside.

4. In a large bowl, beat the eggs thoroughly and whisk in the milk and Parmesan cheese. Stir in the salt, nutmeg, and a generous quantity of black pepper. Add the spaghetti and toss thoroughly. Pour in the bacon mixture and toss again.

5. Spread the pasta mixture in the prepared baking dish. (At this point the casserole may be covered and refrigerated for up to 24 hours.) Bake, uncovered, for 30 minutes, or until set. Let cool for 5 minutes before cutting into squares and serving.

Bread and Onion Panade with Spicy Greens

MOST OF THE baked bread casserole recipes are back in the breakfast section, but here's one classic bread dish that deserves a place on the dinner table. This is my adaptation of a classic dish, repopularized by Alice Waters's and Judy Rodgers's wonderful cookbooks. It's a hot dish of onions, broth, cheese, and leftover bread—peasant eating at its best. This is inexpensive and delicious, and a comforting food to eat in the dead of winter. For a milder taste, use Swiss chard or kale; for a slightly spicy edge, use mustard greens. o *Serves 6*

CASSEROLE DISH: 2-quart baking dish or Dutch oven
BAKE TIME: 65 to 75 minutes

¾ pound good-quality sourdough bread, cut into 2-inch cubes

2 tablespoons unsalted butter

1½ pounds onions, sliced into thin half-moons

Salt

4 cloves garlic, minced

½ pound mustard greens, broccoli rabe, or Swiss chard, cut into fine ribbons

Freshly ground black pepper

1 cup grated Parmesan or Gruyère cheese

4 cups low-sodium chicken or vegetable broth

Olive oil

1. Preheat the oven to 350°F and lightly grease the baking dish or Dutch oven with olive oil or butter. Spread the bread cubes on a large baking sheet and toast for 45 minutes in the oven while preparing the rest of the ingredients.

2. Heat the butter in a deep, heavy skillet over medium heat. When the butter foams up, add the onions and sprinkle them lightly with salt. Cook over low heat for about 25 minutes, stirring occasionally. When they are soft, turn up the heat a notch or two and cook them for another 5 to 10 minutes or until they are golden brown. Stir frequently to keep them from burning.

3. Turn down the heat and add the garlic. Cook for 5 minutes or until golden and fragrant. Add the greens and cook, stirring frequently. Sprinkle the greens with salt and pepper as they cook. When they are wilted and soft, take them off the heat.

4. Layer half of the toasted bread cubes in the bottom of the prepared dish. Spread half of the greens mixture over the bread cubes and pack it down into the gaps between the bread. Sprinkle with about half of the cheese. Make another layer of the remaining bread cubes and remaining greens. Cover with the remaining cheese.

5. Heat the broth to a simmer in a small saucepan and carefully pour it into the baking dish. The bread and greens will look rather drowned and soupy; this is correct. Drizzle the top with olive oil. (At this point the panade may be covered and refrigerated for up to 24 hours.)

6. Cover and bake for 45 minutes, then uncover the dish and bake for another 20 to 30 minutes, or until the top is golden brown and crisp. Let stand for at least 10 minutes before serving hot.

Chewy Udon Baked with Mushrooms, Egg, and Beef

MOST PASTA CASSEROLES use Italian noodles: spaghetti, macaroni, rotini. But Asian noodles also offer some wonderful possibilities for baked casseroles. Udon noodles are chubby and have a silky texture, especially when served in soup. Their sturdy bite makes this savory, eggy casserole especially satisfying. ○ *Serves 6*

CASSEROLE DISH: 9 × 13-inch baking dish
BAKE TIME: 25 minutes

1 pound dried udon noodles
1 pound ground beef
4 cloves garlic, minced
½ pound white mushrooms, sliced
½ cup low-sodium beef or chicken broth
¼ cup reduced-sodium soy sauce
4 large eggs, beaten
One 1-inch piece fresh ginger, peeled and grated
1 small bunch scallions, sliced into ½-inch pieces
Freshly ground black pepper

1. Preheat the oven to 350°F and lightly grease the baking dish with nonstick cooking spray. Cook the udon in boiling salted water until barely al dente, then drain and rinse with cold water. Set aside.

2. In a large skillet, cook the ground beef over medium-high heat for 10 minutes or until crispy and browned. Stir frequently to help it brown evenly. Turn the heat to low and add the garlic. Cook slowly until the garlic is golden and fragrant. Push the beef and garlic to the side of the pan, add the mushrooms, and cook without stirring for 5 minutes. Flip the mushrooms over and stir in the beef. Cook for another few minutes.

3. Turn the heat to high and add the broth and soy sauce. Cook, stirring to scrape up any beef on the bottom of the pan. Simmer for a few minutes, then turn off the heat.

4. In a large bowl, whisk the eggs with the ginger and scallions, then add the noodles and toss. Add the beef and mushroom mixture and season with black pepper.

5. Spread the mixture in the prepared baking dish. (At this point the casserole may be covered and refrigerated for up to 24 hours.) Bake, uncovered, for 25 minutes, or until set. Let stand for 5 minutes before cutting and serving.

Baked Quinoa with Sweet Potatoes and Almonds

QUINOA IS A SUPERGRAIN, one that has way more protein than rice or wheat and a complete set of nutrients. Well, it doesn't hurt that it's so nutritious, but I just like its nutty, slightly bitter flavor and its light and fluffy texture. This recipe is a fast, foolproof recipe for baked quinoa, with sweet potatoes to mellow out the quinoa's edge and almonds for crunchy interest.

o Serves 6

CASSEROLE DISH: 3-quart baking dish or Dutch oven
BAKE TIME: 65 minutes

2 cups quinoa
1 medium onion, diced
1 pound (about 2 large) sweet potatoes, peeled and diced into ½-inch chunks
1 cup fresh flat-leaf parsley, finely chopped
1 cup grated Parmesan cheese
1 cup toasted sliced almonds
½ teaspoon ground cinnamon
Pinch of ground nutmeg
2 teaspoons salt
Freshly ground black pepper
5 cups low-sodium vegetable or chicken broth

1. Preheat the oven to 350°F and grease the baking dish or Dutch oven with olive oil. Rinse the quinoa in a mesh strainer, shaking it and rubbing it to rinse it well. Drain.

2. In a large bowl, toss the quinoa with the onion, sweet potatoes, parsley, Parmesan, and ½ cup of the almonds. Stir in the cinnamon, nutmeg, salt, and pepper to taste. Meanwhile, bring the broth to a simmer in a saucepan or in the microwave.

3. Spread the quinoa mixture in the prepared baking dish and pour in the simmering broth. Cover with a double layer of aluminum foil or with a lid. Bake for 50 minutes, then remove the lid and sprinkle the remaining almonds on top. The dish may look soupy or full of liquid; this is normal, and it will thicken considerably as it finishes baking and as it stands. Return the quinoa to the oven uncovered. Bake for an additional 15 minutes. Let stand for 10 minutes before serving.

Harvest Mixed-Grain Pilaf with Mushrooms

THIS DISH IS BASED ON A FAVORITE (and classic) Martha Stewart recipe. I love the combination of grains and the foolproof method of cooking them all at once, mixed together. I adjusted the recipe, adding an extra vegetable or two for color and some lentils for a little softness. ● *Serves 6*

CASSEROLE DISH: 4-quart Dutch oven or other stovetop-to-oven pot with lid
BAKE TIME: 45 minutes to 1 hour

3½ cups low-sodium chicken or vegetable broth
1 tablespoon unsalted butter
1 large portobello mushroom cap, diced
1 red onion, diced
1 red or yellow bell pepper, cored and diced
2 cloves garlic, minced
1 cup pearl barley
½ cup soft winter wheat berries

¼ cup millet
¼ cup red lentils
¼ cup wild rice, rinsed and drained
¼ cup white wine
¼ cup chopped fresh herbs, such as flat-leaf parsley, thyme, and oregano
1 cup grated Parmesan cheese
2 teaspoons salt
Freshly ground black pepper

1. Preheat the oven to 350°F. Put the broth in a medium saucepan and bring to a simmer over medium heat, then turn the heat down to low and keep the broth hot without letting it boil again.

2. In the Dutch oven, melt the butter over medium-high heat. When the butter foams, add the mushrooms and let them cook without stirring at all for about 5 minutes. Stir them once, flipping them over, then let them cook for an additional 5 minutes. When they are quite well browned, add the onion, bell pepper, and garlic and cook, stirring frequently, until soft and fragrant, about 10 minutes.

3. Add the barley, wheat berries, millet, lentils, and wild rice, stirring to coat them with the butter and onion mixture. Add the wine and cook, stirring frequently, for about 10 minutes.

4. Stir in the broth, herbs, cheese, salt, and pepper to taste. Cover and bake for 45 minutes. Check after 45 minutes; if the grains are still al dente but soft, remove and let stand, covered, for 10 minutes before serving. Or, if necessary, bake for an additional 15 minutes. Serve hot.

Pearl Couscous Gratin with Goat Cheese and Spinach

THIS IS A QUICK AND EASY CASSEROLE with deliciously chewy pearl couscous, also known as Israeli couscous. These rolled pearly nubs are pasta-like and perfectly round. Here they're cooked up quickly with chicken broth, a scoop of low-fat cottage cheese, and fresh spinach, with some almonds for crunch.

o *Serves 4 to 6*

CASSEROLE DISH: 8-inch square baking dish
BAKE TIME: 30 minutes

2 tablespoons olive oil
1½ cups pearl couscous
2 cups low-sodium chicken or vegetable broth
Juice and zest of 1 lemon
1 shallot, minced
2 cups loosely packed fresh spinach, cut into ribbons
½ cup toasted sliced almonds
2 large eggs
1½ cups cottage cheese
4 ounces goat cheese, crumbled
1 teaspoon salt
Freshly ground black pepper

1. Preheat the oven to 350°F. Lightly grease the baking dish with olive oil.

2. Heat the 2 tablespoons olive oil in a medium saucepan over medium heat. When the oil is hot, add the couscous and cook, stirring frequently, until the couscous smells toasted and is slightly golden brown. Add the broth and lemon juice and bring to a boil. Cover, turn the heat to low, and cook for 14 minutes, or until most of the liquid has been absorbed. Uncover, fluff with a fork, and take off the heat.

3. In a large bowl, mix the couscous with the lemon zest, shallot, spinach, and almonds. In a separate bowl, whisk the eggs, then stir in the cottage cheese and about three-quarters of the crumbled goat cheese. Add this cheese and egg mixture to the couscous and stir well. Add the 1 teaspoon salt and pepper to taste.

4. Spread the couscous mixture in the prepared baking dish, top with the remaining goat cheese crumbles, and drizzle with olive oil. Bake for about 30 minutes, or until the cheese is melted. Let stand for 5 minutes before serving.

Hearty Barley Casserole with Lamb and Mushrooms

CHEWY BARLEY GRAINS are a great complement to the dark, rich flavors of browned mushrooms and lamb. This dish tastes complex and rich, but it comes together fast, with a minimum of fuss and fancy ingredients. The result is more than the sum of its parts, and the leftovers are just as delicious (or more so) on the second day. ○ *Serves 6*

CASSEROLE DISH: 3-quart Dutch oven or other stovetop-to-oven pot with lid
BAKE TIME: 1 hour

Vegetable oil
½ pound lamb stew meat, trimmed of fat and cut into ½-inch pieces
3 tablespoons unsalted butter
½ pound white mushrooms, thinly sliced
1 large onion, sliced into half moons
4 cloves garlic, minced
2 sprigs fresh rosemary
1 cup pearl barley
½ cup toasted pine nuts
1½ teaspoons salt
Freshly ground black pepper
2½ cups low-sodium beef broth

1. Preheat the oven to 350°F. Heat the Dutch oven over medium-high heat and add a drizzle of vegetable oil. When it is very hot, so that water sizzles instantly when flicked onto the surface, add the lamb. Sauté the lamb for about 5 minutes, flipping it constantly. When the lamb is well browned on all sides, remove it from the pan and place it in a large bowl, along with any juices it may have released.

2. Wipe out the Dutch oven, then heat the butter in it over medium heat. When the butter foams up, add the mushrooms. Let them cook without turning or stirring for 4 minutes. Scrape them up and turn them, then let them cook for another 3 or 4 minutes without stirring.

3. Add the onions and garlic to the skillet and cook for about 10 minutes, or until the onions are translucent and the garlic is fragrant. Don't let the garlic burn; stir if necessary to keep it from browning or sticking. Add the rosemary sprigs and barley and sauté for an additional minute or two. Stir in the pine nuts, salt, and pepper.

4. Return the lamb to the Dutch oven, and add the broth. Bring to a simmer, cover, and bake for 1 hour. Remove and let sit, covered, for 10 minutes before serving.

Poultry, Meat, and Seafood Bakes

Most of the chapters in this book include at least a few recipes with meat. But if you want a meat-centric main dish, this is the place to find it. In this chapter, meat isn't just used for flavor: It's the star.

I have included some updated classics, like Baked Chicken and Rice (page 217)—a family favorite. There are easy, hearty dishes for a crowd, like Tangy Corned Beef Hash Casserole (page 244) and Spiced Oven Carnitas (page 238), as well as some fresh twists and new flavors. One of my own favorite dinners is Asian Cabbage Rolls with Spicy Pork (page 232).

Baking is one of the easiest and most dependable ways to cook fish and other seafood, so I have included some of my favorite go-to recipes for fish, like Baked Fish Packets with Fennel and Tomatoes (page 256) and a saucy baked tilapia with ginger and cilantro (page 257).

There are great recipes for dinner parties, like Oven Paella with Chicken, Shrimp, and Chorizo (page 250), and there are simple, homey dishes for weeknight meals, like Turkey Enchiladas with Spinach and Cheese (page 226). Regardless of the occasion, the season, the budget, or the time limit, I think you'll find something to enjoy in this chapter.

Baked Chicken and Rice

BAKED CHICKEN AND RICE CASSEROLE is one of those classic recipes found on the label of a can of cream of mushroom soup, right? Well, here's a different version that's still easy and quick but doesn't call for any canned soup. Instead, it substitutes fresh mushrooms, browned for savory flavor, and creamy, tangy yogurt. Serve this with a good green salad and a glass of white wine, and you have a very satisfying evening meal. ○ *Serves 6*

CASSEROLE DISH: 9 × 13-inch baking dish or 3-quart casserole
BAKE TIME: 1 hour

1 cup white rice
1 small sprig fresh rosemary
2½ pounds boneless, skinless chicken thighs or breasts
Salt and freshly ground black pepper
Olive oil
½ pound white mushrooms, sliced
1 small white onion, diced
2 cloves garlic, minced
1⅔ cups low-sodium chicken broth
1 teaspoon smoked paprika
¾ cup whole-milk yogurt

1. Preheat the oven to 350°F and lightly grease the baking dish or casserole with olive oil. Spread the rice in an even layer in the casserole dish. Place the sprig of rosemary in the center.

2. Cut the chicken into bite-size pieces and season them lightly with salt and pepper. Heat a drizzle of olive oil in a large skillet over medium-high heat. When the pan is hot, add the chicken. Sauté, in batches, just until browned, flipping and stirring the chicken as it cooks. When the chicken is golden brown on both sides, remove it from the pan and place it on top of the rice in the baking dish.

3. Add the mushrooms to the skillet and let them cook, without stirring, for about 5 minutes. Then flip them over and let them cook for an additional 3 minutes on the other side, or until they are well browned. Add an extra drizzle of olive oil, then add the onion and garlic. Turn the heat to medium-low and slowly cook the onion and garlic with the mushrooms until the onion is translucent and tender, about 10 minutes.

4. Raise the heat to high and add the broth. Bring to a simmer, scraping the pan constantly to release any browned bits from the bottom of the pan. Remove from the heat and stir in the smoked paprika, 1½ teaspoons of salt, and the yogurt.

5. Pour the broth mixture over the rice and chicken. Cover the dish tightly with foil or a lid and bake for 55 minutes. Remove the foil or lid and bake for an additional 5 minutes. Let stand for 10 minutes before serving.

Lemony Chicken Pot Pie with Parsley Biscuit Crust

CHICKEN POT PIE is one of those things that I always really want to like, but almost never do. It's usually too thick and goopy, with stringy chicken and pallid vegetables. So I set to work making up a chicken pot pie that I would like, one more tuned to my own tastes. This one has very little thickener, and it uses fresh vegetables that stand up to long cooking much better than those frozen peas or minced carrots. So it's more like a hearty oven chicken stew with fluffy, tender biscuits on top and fresh, lemony flavors throughout. ● *Serves 6*

CASSEROLE DISH: 9 × 13-inch baking dish
BAKE TIME: 40 minutes

FOR THE BISCUIT TOPPING:
1¼ cups all-purpose flour
2 teaspoons baking powder
½ teaspoon salt
¼ cup fresh flat-leaf parsley, very finely chopped
¼ cup (½ stick) unsalted butter, cold, cut into pieces
½ cup milk

FOR THE CHICKEN:

2 pounds boneless, skinless chicken breasts

¼ cup all-purpose flour

Salt and freshly ground black pepper

Olive oil

1 large onion, diced

1 fennel bulb, cored and chopped into small pieces

4 cloves garlic, minced

1½ pounds Yukon Gold potatoes, cut into ½-inch chunks

Juice and zest of 1 lemon

1 cup dry white wine

2 cups low-sodium chicken broth

⅔ cup grated Parmesan cheese

1. Preheat the oven to 400°F and lightly grease the baking dish with olive oil.

2. Prepare the biscuit dough. Mix the flour in a medium bowl with the baking powder, salt, and parsley. Cut in the cold butter and work it in with your fingers or a pastry blender until the flour mixture resembles soft bread crumbs. Add the milk, stirring just until the dough comes together. Set aside.

3. Cut the chicken breasts into large bite-size pieces. Toss the pieces in a bowl with the flour and 1 teaspoon each of salt and pepper. Set aside.

4. Heat a generous drizzle of olive oil in a large Dutch oven or sauté pan over medium-high heat. When the oil is hot enough to sizzle when a drop of water is flicked in, add the chicken and brown for about 6 minutes, turning halfway through. Remove the chicken with a slotted spoon and set aside.

5. Reduce the heat to medium. Add the onion, fennel, and garlic, and cook for about 5 minutes, or until they are start to turn tender and fragrant. Add the potatoes and turn the heat up a little. Sauté the potatoes for a few minutes with the onion, then add the lemon zest, lemon juice, and wine and bring to a simmer, scraping up any browned bits from the bottom of the pan. Add the broth and chicken, and season the stew with about 1 teaspoon of salt and plenty of black pepper.

6. Spread the stew in the prepared baking dish. Drop the biscuit dough on top in 6 to 8 evenly spaced mounds and sprinkle the Parmesan cheese over the top. Bake, uncovered, for about 40 minutes, or until the chicken is fully cooked and the biscuit topping is golden. Serve hot.

Tomato and Ginger Oven Chicken Curry

THIS IS A QUICK VERSION of a spicy tomato chicken curry, a tangy and piquant dish for a cold night that's terrific over white rice or couscous, with a cucumber salad on the side. This nods to traditional Indian curries, but it doesn't go through the more labor-intensive steps of creating a real curry. It still gives you that fresh, spicy taste, though, with tender chicken and warm flavors.

o *Serves 8*

CASSEROLE DISH: 5- or 6-quart Dutch oven or other stovetop-to-oven pot with lid
BAKE TIME: 55 minutes

2 pounds boneless, skinless chicken thighs
Salt and freshly ground black pepper
¼ cup vegetable oil
2 medium onions, diced
6 cloves garlic, minced
One 3-inch piece fresh ginger, peeled and grated
2 tablespoons curry powder
1 tablespoon garam masala
1 cinnamon stick
1 bay leaf
1 whole dried red chile (optional)
One 6-ounce can tomato paste
Two 14.5-ounce cans diced tomatoes, with their juices
2 teaspoons salt

1. Preheat the oven to 325°F. Cut the chicken into 1-inch pieces and pat it dry. Toss with salt and pepper.

2. Put the Dutch oven on the stove over medium-high heat and add a drizzle of the vegetable oil. When the oil is hot, add the chicken and lightly sear it on all sides, in batches if necessary. Remove the chicken from the pot with a slotted spoon and set aside.

3. Add the remaining vegetable oil to the pot, and when it's hot, add the onions. Turn the heat to medium and cook the onions, stirring frequently, until they are tender and translucent, about 8 minutes.

4. Add the garlic, ginger, curry powder, garam masala, cinnamon stick, bay leaf, and chile pepper, if using. Sauté the spices with the onions for about 5 minutes, then add the tomato paste. Sauté for another minute or two, then return the chicken to the pot. Pour the tomatoes over the top, and bring to a simmer. Stir in the salt.

5. Cover the pot and bake for 45 minutes, or until the chicken is cooked through and tender. Remove the lid and cook for an additional 10 minutes to let the sauce thicken slightly. Serve hot.

Chicken Thighs with Balsamic Vinegar and Ginger Rice

THIS IS A QUICK, EASY, DELICIOUS baked chicken dish that becomes intensely flavorful in the oven. There are only a few ingredients, but they meld into a vibrant whole. The chicken is baked until it is tangy and melting off the bone, with a pile of tender ginger rice below it and plenty of sauce to pour over it all. ◦ *Serves 4*

CASSEROLE DISH: 9 × 13-inch baking dish
BAKE TIME: 50 minutes

4 pounds bone-in chicken thighs
Salt and freshly ground black pepper
¾ cup white rice
One 2-inch piece fresh ginger, peeled and grated
2 cloves garlic, minced, or 2 teaspoons garlic paste
1 cup dry white wine
1 cup low-sodium chicken broth
¼ cup balsamic vinegar
2 teaspoons ground ginger
½ cup grated Parmesan cheese

1. Preheat the oven to 400°F. If the thighs are not skinless, cut away the skin from the meat and discard. Pat the thighs dry and sprinkle them with salt and pepper.

2. Put the rice in the baking dish and mix with the grated ginger and garlic, rubbing them together with your fingers. Place the chicken thighs on top of the rice.

3. In a separate bowl, whisk together the white wine, chicken broth, balsamic vinegar, ground ginger, and a generous amount of black pepper. Pour this over the chicken thighs and rice. Cover the dish tightly with aluminum foil and bake for 45 minutes, or until the juices of the chicken run clear when pierced with a knife.

4. Remove the foil and sprinkle the chicken with the Parmesan cheese. Return to the oven and bake for an additional 5 minutes, or until the Parmesan is melted. Serve immediately.

Herbed Chicken Meatballs with Coconut Sauce

YOU CAN'T BEAT A MEATBALL for sheer comfort food, at least in my household. These tender herbed meatballs, made with chicken and a touch of lemon, are a little lighter than your typical meatball. The sauce is rich and creamy, and simmering the meatballs in it after they've browned gives them both flavor and tenderness. ❍ *Serves 4*

CASSEROLE DISH: 9 × 13-inch baking dish
BAKE TIME: 35 minutes

¼ cup milk
¾ cup dry bread crumbs
1 small onion, peeled
2 cloves garlic, peeled
1 pound ground chicken
1 tablespoon olive oil
1 large egg, beaten
¼ cup minced fresh cilantro, plus extra for garnish
Zest of 1 lemon
1 teaspoon salt
Freshly ground black pepper

FOR THE SAUCE:

One 14-ounce can coconut milk

2 teaspoons cornstarch

1 tablespoon vegetable oil

One 2-inch piece fresh ginger, peeled and grated

¼ cup minced fresh chives

½ cup low-sodium chicken broth

½ teaspoon salt

¼ teaspoon chili powder

Juice of 1 lemon

1. Preheat the oven to 400°F and lightly grease the baking dish with nonstick cooking spray. Combine the milk and bread crumbs in a large bowl.

2. Use a box grater or food chopper to finely grate the onion and garlic. Put the grated onion and garlic in the large bowl with the milk and bread crumbs and mix in the ground chicken, olive oil, beaten egg, cilantro, and lemon zest. Add the 1 teaspoon salt and a generous quantity of black pepper. Mix thoroughly with your hands.

3. Form the mixture into about 16 meatballs and place in the prepared baking dish. Roast for about 15 minutes, or until the meatballs are well browned and have reached an internal temperature of 165°F.

4. While the meatballs are baking, prepare the sauce. Pour a little coconut milk into a small bowl and whisk in the cornstarch. Heat the vegetable oil in a small saucepan and add the ginger and chives. Cook for a minute or two, then add the remaining coconut milk, chicken broth, salt, and chili powder. Bring to a simmer, then add the cornstarch mixture. Whisk and cook over low heat until the sauce has thickened slightly. Stir in the lemon juice.

5. Pour the sauce over the meatballs in their dish and turn the heat down to 325°F. Bake for an additional 20 minutes, or until the sauce is bubbling and the meatballs are tender. Serve immediately, garnished with extra cilantro.

Tender Chicken Meatballs

For best flavor and tenderness when making meatballs (or any other dish) with ground chicken, use ground chicken thighs instead of chicken breasts. The meat is more tender and slightly higher in fat, so it will stay moister.

Pot Chicken and Potatoes
Baked in Cinnamon-Saffron Milk

F YOU TRY JUST ONE RECIPE from this chapter, make it this one. This is adapted from a dish by Jamie Oliver: chicken in milk. Sounds odd, right? But it's based on classic Italian recipes; this cooking method gives the meat a tender sweetness and a thick golden sauce, full of chicken drippings. This version, with a touch of saffron, is easy and mind-blowingly delicious. ❍ *Serves 4 to 6*

CASSEROLE DISH: 5- or 6-quart Dutch oven or other stovetop-to-oven pot just large enough for the chicken

BAKE TIME: 1½ hours

2 cups milk
Pinch of saffron threads
One 3- to 4-pound chicken, giblets removed
Salt and freshly ground black pepper
¼ cup (½ stick) unsalted butter
2 tablespoons olive oil
1½ pounds small red potatoes, cut into quarters
Zest of 2 lemons, finely chopped
10 cloves garlic, unpeeled
1 cinnamon stick

1. Preheat the oven to 375°F. Warm the milk in a small saucepan or in the microwave and crumble in the saffron. Set aside to steep. Pat the chicken dry and rub it all over with salt and pepper.

2. Place the Dutch oven or pot over medium-high heat and add the butter and olive oil. When it foams up and begins to sizzle, put the chicken in the pot, breast down. Brown it for about 6 minutes, then flip, using tongs and a spatula. Brown the chicken on all sides, until it is golden and beginning to look crispy. This will take about 20 minutes total.

3. Take the pot off the heat and transfer the chicken to a plate. Discard about half of the fat in the pot. Spread the potatoes in the bottom of the pan, then add the warmed saffron milk, lemon zest, garlic cloves, and cinnamon stick. Place the chicken back in the pot, breast side down, on top of the potatoes and milk. Put the lid on the pot and put it in the oven for 1½ hours, basting occasionally. Remove the lid for the final 10 minutes so that the chicken skin can become crispy. The dish is finished when the chicken is very tender and about to slide off the bone and the potatoes are cooked through. The internal temperature of the chicken (taken in the thickest part of the thigh) will be 165°F or higher. Serve immediately.

Tortilla Chicken Casserole

THIS IS A TAKEOFF on an old favorite from childhood, but without the canned soup and with the addition of some shredded cooked chicken. Serve with vinaigrette coleslaw for a fast and easy dinner! ○ *Serves 4 to 6*

CASSEROLE DISH: 9-inch pie pan
BAKE TIME: 30 minutes

3 tablespoons unsalted butter
3 tablespoons all-purpose flour
½ cup low-sodium chicken broth
½ cup milk
One 4-ounce can mild green chiles, chopped
Eight 8-inch flour tortillas
2 cups finely shredded cooked chicken
2½ cups shredded cheddar cheese

1. Preheat the oven to 350°F and lightly grease the pie pan with nonstick cooking spray.

2. Melt the butter in a small saucepan over medium heat, then add the flour. Cook, stirring, until the mixture forms a paste. Whisk in the broth and milk and stir until the mixture thickens, about 3 minutes. Stir in the chiles.

3. Place a tortilla in the pie pan and top with a couple tablespoons of the sauce, a small handful of shredded chicken, and a small handful of cheese. Repeat with remaining tortillas, and top the whole stack with a sprinkle of cheddar cheese. Cover the pie pan loosely with foil, and bake for 30 minutes. Let stand for 5 minutes before cutting into wedges to serve.

Turkey Enchiladas with Spinach and Cheese

T URKEY ENCHILADAS ARE A HIGHLIGHT of the post-Thanksgiving meal repertoire. After the turkey sandwiches, and the turkey soup, these are a really delicious way to use up the rest of the leftover turkey meat. Well, you don't need to wait for Thanksgiving to serve this. If you don't have turkey, substitute roast chicken or even browned ground chicken or beef. ○ *Serves 6*

CASSEROLE DISH: 9 × 13-inch baking dish
BAKE TIME: 25 minutes

FOR THE SAUCE:
Olive oil
8 cloves garlic, halved
1¼ pounds fresh baby spinach
1 cup chicken or turkey broth
1 bunch scallions, sliced
2 cups fresh cilantro leaves, chopped
1 fresh jalapeño pepper, sliced (optional)
Juice of 1 lime
Salt and freshly ground black pepper

FOR THE ENCHILADAS:
Twelve 6-inch corn tortillas
4 cups chopped roasted turkey
2 cups shredded mozzarella cheese

1. Preheat the oven to 450°F. Lightly grease the baking dish with olive oil.

2. To make the sauce, heat a drizzle of olive oil in a large skillet over medium heat. Add the garlic and cook for about 5 minutes. Add the spinach and cook just until wilted, then add the chicken broth and bring to a simmer. Remove from the heat, then add the scallions, cilantro, and jalapeño, if using. Let cool slightly, then blend in a food processor or blender until smooth. Whiz in the lime juice, and season to taste with salt and pepper.

3. Overlap half of the tortillas in the prepared baking dish. Sprinkle half of the turkey over the tortillas, and pour half of the spinach sauce over the top. Sprinkle with half of the cheese. Repeat with the remaining tortillas, turkey, sauce, and cheese. Sprinkle with salt and pepper.

4. Bake for 25 minutes, or until the sauce is bubbly and the cheese is golden and melted. Cool the enchiladas for at least 15 minutes before serving warm.

Tender Turkey with Sausage and Mushrooms

THIS RECIPE IS BASED ON Mark Bittman's fabulous braised turkey, published a few years ago in the *New York Times*. It was the first turkey recipe I actually enjoyed, and its rich, dark flavors are so different from dry Thanksgiving turkey that you may decide to serve this version for your next holiday.

o *Serves 6*

CASSEROLE DISH: 9 × 13-inch roasting pan
BAKE TIME: 2 hours

1 cup boiling water
1 ounce dried morels, porcini, or mixed wild mushrooms, roughly chopped
8 slices bacon, chopped into 1-inch pieces
1 pound spicy fresh Italian sausage, cut into 2-inch chunks
2 turkey thighs
2 turkey drumsticks
Salt and freshly ground black pepper
1 pound cremini or white mushrooms, sliced
3 large carrots, peeled and diced
3 large stalks celery, diced
1 large onion, diced
2 cloves garlic, minced
1 cup dry white wine
1 long sprig fresh rosemary

1. Preheat the oven to 325°F. Rub the bottom of the roasting pan with olive oil and set aside. Pour the boiling water over the dried mushrooms in a small bowl. Set aside to steep.

2. Place a large, deep skillet over low heat and add the bacon. Cook slowly until the bacon fat begins to render out, about 8 minutes. Add the sausage chunks and turn the heat to high. Cook for about 5 minutes, or just until the sausage has browned. Remove the sausage and bacon from the pan with a slotted spoon and set them aside on a plate lined with paper towels.

3. Pat the turkey pieces dry and sprinkle them with salt and pepper. Turn the heat under the skillet to medium-high and add the turkey. Brown the turkey well on both sides. This will take about 10 minutes. Take the turkey out of the pan and set aside with the browned sausage and bacon.

4. Turn the heat to medium and add the fresh mushrooms. Cook without moving or stirring for 5 minutes, then flip them over and cook for another 3 minutes, or until they are well browned. Add the carrots, celery, onion, and garlic and cook slowly over medium heat for about 10 minutes, or until all the vegetables are tender.

5. Drain the reconstituted dried mushrooms into a bowl, reserving their steeping liquid. Add these mushrooms to the vegetable mixture in the skillet and turn off the heat. Combine the vegetables with the bacon and sausage in the roasting pan and nestle the browned turkey pieces into the vegetables. Add the reserved steeping liquid from the mushrooms and the white wine, along with the rosemary sprig.

6. Cover the pan tightly with aluminum foil. Roast for 1½ hours, then remove the foil and roast for an additional 30 minutes, or until the turkey is so tender it can be pulled from the bone with a fork. Serve hot.

Shredded Duck with Sausage and White Beans

DUCK IS OFTEN CONSIDERED a luxury meat these days, which is a pity. Duck meat is dark and tender, with a warmth of flavor that is so homey and comforting. This casserole, based on the classic French cassoulet of white beans, sausage, and duck, is delicious enough to serve to company, but you may want to hoard it for a couple of nights of leftovers instead. ○ *Serves 6*

CASEROLE DISH: 5- or 6-quart Dutch oven or other stovetop-to-oven pot with lid
BAKE TIME: About 2 hours

2 duck breast fillets (about 1 pound total)
Salt and freshly ground black pepper
1 tablespoon olive oil
¾ pound pork chops or pork stew meat, cut into 1-inch pieces
1 pound fresh spicy sausage, cut into 1-inch pieces
4 slices bacon, chopped into 1-inch pieces
½ pound carrots, peeled and diced
½ pound celery, diced
1 large onion, diced
4 cloves garlic, minced
1 pound dried small navy beans
2 sprigs fresh thyme
2 sprigs fresh rosemary
1 bay leaf
5 cups low-sodium chicken broth

FOR THE BREAD CRUMB TOPPING:
⅓ cup fresh bread crumbs
¼ cup grated Parmesan cheese
2 tablespoons chopped fresh flat-leaf parsley
1 clove garlic
½ teaspoon salt
½ teaspoon freshly ground black pepper
Olive oil

1. Preheat the oven to 325°F. Using a small, very sharp knife, trim the skin and layer of fat off the duck breasts, and set it aside. Pat the breasts dry and sprinkle them lightly with salt and pepper.

2. Heat the olive oil in the Dutch oven over medium-high heat and sear the duck breasts for about 3 minutes on each side. Remove the duck breasts and set them aside.

3. Place the reserved fat from 1 duck breast in the Dutch oven and turn the heat to low. Very slowly let the duck fat render until it is mostly liquid. Add the pork chop pieces and sausage and let them brown well in the duck fat, stirring frequently. Remove the pork and sausage and set aside.

4. Add the bacon to the pan and cook for 5 minutes, or until the bacon is beginning to curl up. Add the carrots, celery, onion, and garlic and cook for about 10 minutes, or until the onions are fragrant and translucent. Add the dried beans and cook for about 5 more minutes, then return the pork and sausage pieces to the pan. Add the herb sprigs, bay leaf, and chicken broth. Bring to a simmer, then place the duck breasts on top of the beans, cover the pan, and bake for 1½ hours.

5. While the casserole is baking, prepare the bread crumb topping. Whiz the bread crumbs, cheese, parsley, garlic, salt, and pepper in a food processor. Drizzle in a bit of olive oil and whiz again until the mixture is the texture of wet sand and green and gold in color.

6. After 1½ hours, check the beans. They should be quite tender. If they are not, return the dish to the oven for 15 minutes. Take the dish out of the oven and remove the duck breasts. Shred all the meat (it should be meltingly tender) and stir it back into the beans. Sprinkle the top with the bread crumbs and return to the oven, uncovered, for about 20 minutes, or until the top is golden and crusty. Serve immediately.

Sweet and Smoky Cabbage Rolls with Lamb and Tomato

STUFFED CABBAGE is such a warm and homey dish. I didn't appreciate it until I was an adult; when I was a kid, ground meat rolled up in cabbage seemed rather unappealing, to say the least. Now, however, it's just the sort of comfort food I love. This recipe pares down the work of the traditional version and substitutes leaner, yet more flavorful, lamb for the beef. ○ *Serves 4 to 6*

CASSEROLE DISH: 9 × 13-inch baking dish
BAKE TIME: 45 minutes

1 large head napa cabbage
1 tablespoon unsalted butter
1 pound ground lamb

Salt

1 medium onion, diced

4 cloves garlic, minced

One 28-ounce can diced tomatoes, with their juices

1 tablespoon brown sugar

2 tablespoons red wine vinegar

1 cup cooked white rice, from ⅓ cup rice steamed in ⅔ cup water

¼ cup Worcestershire sauce

½ teaspoon freshly ground black pepper

1 teaspoon smoked paprika

1. Preheat the oven to 375°F. Lightly grease the baking dish with olive oil or nonstick cooking spray.

2. Remove 8 of the largest outer cabbage leaves and roll them gently with a rolling pin until they are flattened and pliable. Core the remaining cabbage and chop half of it very finely. Refrigerate the unused half for another use.

3. Heat a large, deep skillet or wide saucepan over medium heat. Add the butter. When it foams up, add the ground lamb and cook, stirring frequently, for about 10 minutes, or until the lamb is well browned. Add the chopped cabbage and sprinkle with salt. Cook for an additional 5 minutes, or until the cabbage is wilted and tender. Remove the lamb and cabbage from the pan and set aside in a large bowl, leaving any drippings behind in the pan.

4. Add the onion and garlic to the skillet and turn the heat to low. Cook, stirring frequently, for 10 minutes, or until the onion is translucent and fragrant.

5. Add the tomatoes and their juices, brown sugar, vinegar, and 1½ teaspoons of salt. Bring to a boil, and then turn the heat to low and simmer for 10 minutes, stirring occasionally. While the tomatoes are simmering, mix the cooked rice, Worcestershire sauce, pepper, and smoked paprika with the browned lamb and cabbage. Add 1 cup of the cooked tomato mixture.

6. Lay a prepared cabbage leaf on a work surface with the stem end facing you. Place about ½ cup meat mixture onto the stem end. Fold in the sides and roll up the leaf, then place the bundle, seam side down, in the prepared baking dish. Repeat with the rest of the cabbage leaves and meat mixture. Top each cabbage roll with a spoonful of sauce. Ladle any remaining sauce around the cabbage rolls. (At this point the rolls can be covered and refrigerated for up to 24 hours.)

7. Cover with foil and bake for 45 minutes. Let rest for 5 minutes before serving.

Asian Cabbage Rolls with Spicy Pork

T HESE CABBAGE ROLLS take more than a cue from the spicy gingered pork inside Chinese dumplings. They're stuffed with the fresh flavors of cilantro, soy sauce, sesame, and scallion. This recipe makes a double pan, since you will definitely want leftovers of this light and delicious dinner! ○ *Serves 8*

CASSEROLE DISH: Two 9 × 13-inch baking dishes
BAKE TIME: 35 minutes

2 large heads napa cabbage
2 teaspoons salt
1 pound ground pork
1 cup cooked white rice, from ⅓ cup rice steamed in ⅔ cup water
½ pound shiitake mushrooms, finely chopped
2 large eggs, beaten
1 tablespoon toasted sesame oil
¼ cup reduced-sodium soy sauce
One 3-inch piece fresh ginger, peeled and grated
4 cloves garlic, minced or 1 tablespoon garlic paste
Freshly ground black pepper
1 bunch scallions, chopped
2 cups fresh cilantro, chopped

FOR THE SAUCE:
¼ cup reduced-sodium soy sauce
¼ cup rice vinegar
1 cup low-sodium chicken broth
1 tablespoon toasted sesame oil
1 teaspoon sugar
1 teaspoon sriracha or other hot chili sauce (optional)

1. Preheat the oven to 400°F. Remove 24 large outer leaves from the heads of cabbage (take 12 from each). Roll each leaf with a rolling pin gently to flatten and smooth it. Core the remaining cabbage and chop it very fine. Sprinkle it with the salt and set aside in a colander.

2. In a large bowl, mix the pork, rice, mushrooms, beaten eggs, sesame oil, soy sauce, ginger, garlic, and a generous amount of black pepper. Stir in the scallions and cilantro. Press and drain any remaining water off the salted cabbage and stir the cabbage in as well.

3. Lay a prepared cabbage leaf down with the stem end facing you. Place about ⅔ cup meat mixture onto the stem end of the cabbage leaf. Fold in the sides and roll up the leaf, then place the bundle, seam side down, in one of the baking dishes. Repeat with the rest of the cabbage leaves and meat mixture, placing 2 rows of 6 rolls in each dish. (If you have any leftover mixture it can be rolled into meatballs and tucked between the cabbage rolls to bake with them.)

4. To make the sauce, whisk together all the ingredients in a small bowl and pour it over the cabbage rolls, dividing it between the 2 baking dishes. (At this point the rolls can be covered and refrigerated for up to 24 hours. You can also freeze one dish for later use. Before adding the sauce, place the dish in the freezer and let the rolls freeze completely, then remove the rolls from the dish and stack them in a freezer bag or container. To bake, thaw the rolls in the refrigerator overnight, place in a baking dish, pour the sauce over them, and bake as directed below.)

5. Bake, uncovered, for 35 minutes, or until an instant-read thermometer inserted into a roll at the center of the dish registers 160°F. Serve drizzled with the pan juices.

Oven Pot Roast with Yorkshire Pudding

O H, POT ROAST, stewing gently in its juices: It's the traditional smell of Sunday afternoons and weekend evenings. A pot roast may be a dish served to company (especially with the golden eggy puff of Yorkshire pudding), but it's also the dead-easiest way to cook up something reliably delicious. My favorite way to cook this inexpensive cut of meat is in the oven. I feel that the oven does the best job at getting the meat really tender, what with the way the heat surrounds the dish and envelops it in a slow, humid warmth. This recipe is very simple, without too many steps or too much fussiness. All you need is a pot roast and a lazy afternoon. ● *Serves 6*

CASSEROLE DISH: 5-quart covered Dutch oven, 9 × 13-inch baking dish
BAKE TIME: 3½ to 4 hours for the pot roast, 50 minutes for the Yorkshire pudding

4 pounds beef shoulder, boneless chuck roast, or brisket, at room temperature
Salt and freshly ground black pepper
2 tablespoons olive oil
1 large yellow onion, thickly sliced
6 cloves garlic, halved
1 long sprig fresh rosemary
1 cup low-sodium beef broth

FOR THE YORKSHIRE PUDDING:
2 cups all-purpose flour
1 teaspoon salt
Pinch of freshly ground black pepper
3 large eggs, beaten
2 cups milk
2 tablespoons unsalted butter, melted
⅓ cup drippings from the roast beef

1. Preheat the oven to 250°F. Pat the meat very dry and season it liberally with salt and pepper.

2. Heat the Dutch oven over medium-high heat. Add the olive oil and, when it is quite hot, add the meat. Sear the meat for at least 6 minutes on each side. If the meat is a larger piece, you may need to cut it in half and do this in batches. There should be room around the meat in the pan so that it sizzles, rather than steams. Get the meat quite brown, even a little burnt around the edges. This is where all the flavor comes from, so brown as deeply as you dare.

3. When the meat is well browned, lift it out of the Dutch oven. Spread the onion slices in the bottom of the pan and add the garlic and rosemary sprig. Put the meat back on top and pour in the beef broth. Bring to a simmer, then put the lid on, place in the oven, and bake for 3½ to 4 hours, checking after 3½ hours to see if the meat is tender. If it shreds easily with a fork, it is done.

4. An hour or so before the pot roast is finished, make the batter for the Yorkshire pudding. Whisk together the flour, salt, and pepper in a large bowl. Whisk in the eggs, milk, and butter. Blend with a whisk or in a blender until the mixture is completely smooth, with no lumps. Cover and set aside until the roast is done.

5. Remove the meat from the oven; drain off and reserve ⅓ cup of the drippings. Partially cover the Dutch oven with its lid and let the meat rest in its juices.

6. Raise the oven temperature to 450°F. Pour the ⅓ cup pan drippings into the 9 × 13-inch baking dish and put it in the oven for 15 minutes. When the dish is quite hot, pour in the Yorkshire pudding batter and bake for 20 minutes. Lower the heat to 350°F and bake for an additional 15 minutes.

7. Slice the Yorkshire pudding and serve immediately with shredded pot roast and its juices.

Pork Cutlets Rolled with Olives, Sun-Dried Tomatoes, and Prosciutto

PORK LOIN IS A VERY LEAN CUT OF MEAT, and it's often sold in thin slices or cutlets. This recipe puts those pre-cut slices of pork to good use in a fast recipe that is nevertheless quite fancy enough for company. This was my husband's go-to dish when he was a bachelor, and it definitely impressed quite a few of his single friends! ○ *Serves 4*

CASSEROLE DISH: 9 × 13-inch metal baking pan
BAKE TIME: 22 minutes

2 pounds pork loin cutlets (10 to 12 cutlets)
Salt and freshly ground black pepper
Olive oil
1 small onion, diced
4 cloves garlic, minced
¾ cup finely chopped sun-dried tomatoes (dry or oil-packed)
1 cup chopped green olives
1 cup toasted dry bread crumbs
8 leaves fresh sage, chopped
2 long sprigs fresh rosemary (leaves only), chopped
1½ cups grated Parmesan cheese
10 to 12 thin slices prosciutto

1. Preheat the oven to 375°F. Lightly grease the baking dish with olive oil or non-stick cooking spray. Pat the pork cutlets dry and lightly season them with salt and pepper.

2. Heat a generous drizzle of olive oil in a heavy skillet set over medium heat. Add the onion and cook until fragrant and translucent, about 10 minutes. Add the garlic and cook for an additional 5 minutes. Remove from the heat.

3. In a large bowl, stir together the onion, garlic, sun-dried tomatoes, olives, bread crumbs, sage, rosemary, and 1 cup of the Parmesan cheese. Add a little olive oil until it clumps together, and season with salt and pepper.

4. On a work surface, place each loin cutlet on top of a slice of prosciutto. Spread about ⅓ cup of the stuffing in the center of each loin cutlet, and roll it (and the prosciutto) up so that the prosciutto wraps around the pork and holds it together. Place seam side down in the prepared baking dish. Spread any leftover stuffing around the meat. (At this point the rolled-up cutlets can be covered and refrigerated for up to 24 hours.)

5. Bake the pork loin rolls, uncovered, for 20 minutes, or until the internal temperature of the stuffing reaches 155°F. Take the pan out of the oven, and turn the heat up to broil. Sprinkle the rolls with the remaining ½ cup of Parmesan, and broil for 2 minutes, or until the cheese is melted. Serve immediately.

Gouda-Stuffed Pork Chops

THESE HEFTY PORK CHOPS OOZE with aged Gouda cheese and the taste of browned bread crumbs and garlic. Baked on top of apples, they get just a touch of sweetness, which enhances the dish without overwhelming it.

○ *Serves 4*

CASSEROLE DISH: 10-inch cast-iron skillet
BAKE TIME: 30 minutes

FOR THE BRINE:
4 cups water
2 tablespoons cider vinegar

¼ cup salt

3 tablespoons brown sugar

1 tablespoon whole peppercorns

FOR THE PORK CHOPS:

4 thick-cut bone-in pork chops (1½ inches thick)

¼ cup olive oil

2 cloves garlic, minced

½ cup dry bread crumbs

1 small handful (about ¼ cup) fresh flat-leaf parsley, minced

8 fresh sage leaves, minced

1 cup grated aged Gouda cheese

Salt and freshly ground black pepper

1 large apple, peeled and sliced

1 large onion, peeled and thinly sliced

½ cup dry white wine

1. For the brine, bring the water and vinegar to a boil in a small saucepan, and add the salt, brown sugar, and peppercorns. Stir until the salt and sugar are dissolved. Put the pork chops in a large baking dish and pour the brining liquid over them. Cover and refrigerate for 24 hours.

2. Preheat the oven to 350°F. Remove the pork chops from the brine and rinse thoroughly, then pat very dry with paper towels. Set them aside to air-dry a little longer, while you make the stuffing.

3. Film a large cast-iron skillet with olive oil and set it over medium-high heat. Heat the olive oil, then add the garlic. Turn the heat to low, and cook the garlic for 5 minutes. Add the bread crumbs and cook, stirring constantly, for another 3 to 4 minutes, or until the bread crumbs brown.

4. Put the garlic and bread crumbs in a medium bowl and mix with the parsley, sage, Gouda cheese, and a sprinkling of salt and pepper.

5. Take each pork chop and slice it almost in half lengthwise, so that it has an open pocket in the center. Stuff the Gouda mixture into each pocket. (At this point the pork chops can be covered and refrigerated for up to 24 hours.)

6. Heat the skillet again over medium-high heat and film it with olive oil. Carefully add the stuffed pork chops. Brown on each side for 2 minutes, or until the pork chops are golden brown. Remove the chops and spread the apple and onion slices in the skillet. Place the pork chops on top and pour in the white wine. Cover the skillet with aluminum foil.

7. Bake for 30 minutes, or until the internal temperature of the stuffing registers 160°F on an instant-read thermometer and the Gouda is melted. Serve immediately.

Spiced Oven Carnitas

PULLED AND SHREDDED PORK, also known as carnitas, is a wonderfully easy and delicious oven dish for a crowd. It's my go-to dish when I have to serve a lot of people; this recipe will easily serve 8 and could probably be stretched to 12. Serve with tortillas, salsa, chopped zucchini or cucumber, and plenty of guacamole. **o** *Serves 8*

CASSEROLE DISH: 5- or 6-quart Dutch oven or other stovetop-to-oven pot with lid
BAKE TIME: 2½ hours

5- to 6-pound pork butt roast (also called shoulder roast)
Salt and freshly ground black pepper
¼ cup olive oil
½ teaspoon red pepper flakes
2 tablespoons ground cumin
2 teaspoons ground allspice
1 teaspoon ground cinnamon
4 sprigs fresh oregano
6 cloves garlic, halved
Juice and zest of 1 orange
Juice and zest of 1 lemon
½ cup white wine

1. Preheat the oven to 350°F. Cut the pork roast into 4 evenly sized pieces. Pat them quite dry and season them lightly with salt and pepper. Heat the olive oil in the Dutch oven over medium-high heat. Sear the pork pieces, one at a time, for several minutes on each side, until they are well browned. Remove from the heat.

2. Nestle the pork pieces back in the Dutch oven. Sprinkle with the red pepper flakes, cumin, allspice, and cinnamon. Tuck the oregano sprig and garlic cloves between the pieces, and sprinkle in the lemon and orange zests. Pour in the orange and lemon juices and the white wine.

3. Cover and bake for 2½ hours. When the pork is extremely tender, take it out of the oven and let it rest, still covered, for about 20 minutes. Remove the lid and shred with 2 forks. Serve hot.

Easy Payoff Oven Short Ribs

SHORT RIBS ARE ONE OF MY FAVORITE THINGS to bake in the oven. They undergo such a transformation: from cheap, tough little hunks of meat with a bone sticking out of the middle to silky, sumptuous bits of meat just sliding off the bone. They are crowd-pleasers, and inexpensive, too. Like pot roast, I think that short ribs are best made in the oven, where the enveloping heat makes them really tender. This recipe is a fairly simple preparation, but you can get fancier if you want by adding more spices to the rub and lots of vegetables during the braise.

○ *Serves 6*

CASSEROLE DISH: 5- or 6-quart Dutch oven or other stovetop-to-oven pot with lid
BAKE TIME: 3 hours

2 teaspoons salt
2 teaspoons freshly ground black pepper
2 teaspoons ground mustard
4 pounds bone-in short ribs
¼ cup olive oil
2 tablespoons tomato paste
1 large onion, diced
2 cups low-sodium chicken or beef broth
2 cups dry red wine
2 sprigs fresh thyme
1 long sprig fresh rosemary
1 bay leaf
10 cloves garlic, unpeeled

1. Preheat the oven to 300°F. Mix the salt, pepper, and mustard in a small bowl. Pat the short ribs very dry, then pat them all over with the seasoning mix.

2. Heat the olive oil in the Dutch oven over medium-high heat. Working in batches, sear the short ribs in the olive oil until they are very well browned, about 4 minutes on each side. Remove the browned short ribs to a plate.

3. Add the tomato paste and onion to the pot and cook for about 5 minutes. Add the broth and wine and bring to a simmer. Add the herbs and garlic cloves, then return the short ribs to the pot. Cover and put in the oven.

4. Cook for about 3 hours, or until the ribs are very tender and falling off the bone. At this point, they can be served immediately or refrigerated for up to 3 days. (In fact, short ribs, like other braised meats, are even better on the second or third day after their initial cooking.) To serve refrigerated short ribs, skim any solid fat off the surface of the sauce, then reheat, covered, in a 350°F oven for about 30 minutes.

Green Peppers Stuffed with Pork and Rice

STUFFED PEPPERS ARE SIMPLE, easy, and wholesome. This recipe varies from traditional versions by picking up gently on Asian flavors, with crispy pan-fried pork, soy, and a hint of ginger. ○ *Serves 6*

CASSEROLE DISH: 9 × 13-inch baking dish
BAKE TIME: 30 minutes

1½ cups cold water
1½ teaspoons salt
1 cup white rice
6 large green peppers, tops cut off and reserved, insides cleaned out
1 pound ground pork
2 cloves garlic, minced
1 small onion, minced

Freshly ground black pepper

1 teaspoon ground ginger

1 tablespoon reduced-sodium soy sauce

1 tablespoon rice vinegar

2 tablespoons olive oil

½ cup hot water

1. Preheat the oven to 375°F. Bring the cold water to a boil in a small saucepan. Stir in ½ teaspoon of the salt and the rice. Cover, turn the heat to low, and cook for 18 minutes. Remove from the heat and keep covered.

2. Discard the stems of the peppers, but finely dice the tops themselves. Place a large, deep skillet over medium-high heat and add the ground pork. Cook, stirring frequently, for about 10 minutes, or until the meat begins to get browned and crispy. Add the diced pepper tops, garlic, and onion and turn the heat down to medium. Cook for another 5 minutes.

3. Add the cooked rice to the skillet, along with the remaining 1 teaspoon of salt, black pepper to taste, and the ginger. Mix well. Fill each of the green peppers with the rice and pork mixture, and place them, cut side up, in the baking dish. (At this point the stuffed peppers can be covered and refrigerated for up to 24 hours.)

4. Whisk together the soy sauce, rice vinegar, and olive oil and drizzle it over the stuffed peppers. Pour the hot water into the baking dish, around the peppers. Bake for 30 minutes. Serve immediately.

Lamb Pastitsio

LAMB PASTITSIO IS A WONDERFUL GREEK DISH that deserves to be better known. Maybe if you are Greek your mother made this, but those of us who aren't were not so lucky. There is something about the layers of meat, pasta, and fluffy egg topping that is just so delicious! This recipe is a little lengthy, but it's worth it. ○ *Serves 8*

CASSEROLE DISH: 9 × 13-inch baking dish
BAKE TIME: 30 minutes

FOR THE MEAT SAUCE:
Olive oil
1 pound ground lamb
1 small onion, diced
4 cloves garlic, minced
One 14.5-ounce can diced tomatoes, with their juices
1 sprig fresh rosemary
1 teaspoon salt
½ teaspoon sugar
1 tablespoon red wine vinegar
Freshly ground black pepper

FOR THE PASTA:
1 pound small elbow macaroni
3 large eggs, separated
¼ cup grated Parmesan cheese

FOR THE EGG TOPPING:
½ cup (1 stick) unsalted butter
1 cup all-purpose flour
4 cups milk
¾ cup grated Parmesan cheese
½ teaspoon ground nutmeg
½ teaspoon salt
½ teaspoon freshly ground black pepper

1. Preheat the oven to 350°F and lightly grease the baking dish with olive oil.

2. To make the sauce, place a large, deep skillet over medium-high heat and add a drizzle of olive oil. When it shimmers, add the lamb. Cook for about 10 minutes, or until the lamb is well browned. Add the onion and garlic and turn the heat to medium-low. Cook for about 10 minutes, stirring frequently, until the onion is translucent and fragrant.

3. Add the tomatoes and their juices, as well as the rosemary sprig, salt, sugar, vinegar, and pepper to taste. Bring to a simmer, then turn the heat to low and simmer the sauce for about 30 minutes.

4. While the sauce is cooking, bring a large pot of salted water to a boil over high heat. Add the pasta and cook for about 4 minutes less than recommended by the package directions. Drain the pasta and return it to the cooking pot. Toss the cooked pasta with the egg whites (reserve the yolks for the egg sauce) and Parmesan cheese.

5. While the sauce and pasta are still cooking, make the béchamel, or egg sauce, that will top the dish. In a wide saucepan, melt the butter over medium heat. When the butter foams up, stir in the flour. Cook the flour with the butter for about 5 minutes, or until it starts to smell fragrant. Gradually whisk in the milk, whisking constantly to remove any lumps. Cook for about 3 minutes, or just until the mixture begins to thicken, then remove from the heat. Whisk in the cheese, reserved egg yolks, nutmeg, salt, and pepper.

6. Spread two-thirds of the cooked pasta mixture in the bottom of the prepared baking dish. Remove the rosemary sprig from the meat sauce, then spread the sauce evenly on top of the pasta, and spread the remaining pasta on top of the meat sauce. Pour the egg sauce over the pasta. Bake for 30 minutes, or until the egg topping is golden brown. Let stand for at least 30 minutes before cutting and serving warm.

Tangy Corned Beef Hash Casserole

RICH AND SALTY CORNED BEEF is a great addition to casseroles. Here's a delicious way to use up leftover corned beef from St. Patrick's Day; toss it with potatoes and a little onion for a hearty, filling hash. This recipe brings a fresh, interesting twist to the heavy, old-fashioned version, with yogurt's light tanginess, Gruyère cheese, and fresh herbs. ○ *Serves 8*

CASSEROLE DISH: 9 × 13-inch baking dish
BAKE TIME: 25 to 30 minutes

3 pounds (about 4 medium) potatoes, diced into ½-inch cubes
3 cups chopped corned beef
1½ teaspoons salt
½ teaspoon freshly ground black pepper
2 cups chopped red or green cabbage
1 large red onion, diced
4 cloves garlic, minced
3 tablespoons fresh flat-leaf parsley, chopped
4 sprigs fresh thyme (leaves only)
2 cups plain yogurt
2 large eggs, beaten
1 cup grated Gruyère cheese

1. Preheat the oven to 350°F and lightly grease the baking dish with olive oil or nonstick cooking spray. Bring a large pot of salted water to a boil over high heat. Add the potatoes and cook for 10 to 12 minutes, or until the potatoes are tender. Drain and rinse with cold water.

2. Toss the potatoes in a large bowl with the corned beef, salt, pepper, cabbage, red onion, and garlic. In a small bowl, stir together the parsley, thyme, yogurt, and eggs, and toss with the potato mixture. Stir in ½ cup of the cheese.

3. Spread the mixture in the prepared baking dish and sprinkle the top with the remaining ½ cup of cheese. (At this point the casserole can be covered and refrigerated for up to 24 hours.) Bake, uncovered, for 25 to 30 minutes, or until heated through and golden on top. Serve hot.

Cinnamon Lamb Orzo Bake

LAMB AND CINNAMON ARE WONDERFUL TOGETHER; their warmth complements each other beautifully. This dish has plenty of both, baked together with an underlayer of orzo pasta. This recipe is adapted from a Greek recipe by the wonderful chef Vefa Alexiadou. o *Serves 6*

CASSEROLE DISH: 5- or 6-quart Dutch oven or other stovetop-to-oven pot with lid
BAKE TIME: 2 hours

2 tablespoons olive oil
One 3-pound boneless lamb leg, trimmed of fat and cut into 1-inch pieces
6 cloves garlic, minced
1 large onion, diced
One 28-ounce can diced tomatoes, with their juices
1 tablespoon red wine vinegar
1 teaspoon sugar
2 cinnamon sticks
1 fresh rosemary sprig
2 teaspoons salt
Freshly ground black pepper
3 cups low-sodium chicken broth
1 pound orzo
¾ cup shredded Parmesan cheese

1. Preheat the oven to 325°F. Heat the olive oil in the Dutch oven over medium-high heat. Brown the lamb in 3 batches, making sure the pieces brown deeply on all sides. This will take about 8 minutes per batch. Set the lamb aside.

2. Add the garlic and onion to the fat in the pan and cook for about 5 minutes, or until the onion is just turning translucent. Return the lamb to the pan, along with the tomatoes and their juices, vinegar, sugar, cinnamon sticks, rosemary sprig, salt, and pepper to taste. Remove from the heat.

3. Meanwhile, in a medium saucepan, bring the chicken broth to a boil. Stir the orzo into the Dutch oven and pour the boiling broth over the top. Cover and bake for 1½ hours, then uncover, sprinkle with the Parmesan cheese, and return to the oven, uncovered. Bake for 30 minutes more, or until the orzo is al dente. Serve immediately.

Mediterranean Tuna Casserole
with Olives and Capers

WHEN IT COMES TO CASSEROLES, is there anything more ubiquitous than tuna casserole? Let's face it, that cheesy tuna dish was actually pretty good; we have fond memories of it from childhood. But our tastes grew up along with the rest of us, so this dish gives you some of that guilty pleasure but with much more sophisticated flavors. Salty capers, artichoke hearts, fresh herbs, and high-quality tuna bring this into the grown-up world. ● *Serves 6*

CASSEROLE DISH: 9 × 13-inch baking dish
BAKE TIME: 25 minutes

10 ounces wide egg noodles
Olive oil
1 pound small red potatoes, sliced ¼ inch thick
¼ cup (½ stick) unsalted butter
¼ cup all-purpose flour
2 cups milk
2 teaspoons salt
Freshly ground black pepper
Four 6-ounce cans tuna in olive oil, drained
One 9-ounce box frozen artichoke hearts, thawed and halved
¾ cup capers, rinsed and drained
½ cup sliced black olives
4 scallions, thinly sliced
½ cup minced fresh flat-leaf parsley
¾ cup finely grated Parmesan cheese

1. Preheat the oven to 400°F and lightly grease the baking dish with olive oil. Bring a large pot of salted water to a boil, and cook the noodles for 2 minutes less than recommended by the package directions. Drain the noodles, and dump them into a large bowl. Toss them immediately with a drizzle of olive oil so they don't clump together.

2. Fill the pot with water again and bring to a boil. Blanch the potato slices for 4 minutes, then drain and return them to the pot.

3. While the noodles and potatoes are cooking, heat the butter in a small saucepan. When it foams up, add the flour and stir. Cook for about 5 minutes, then whisk in the milk. Cook, stirring constantly, for about 5 minutes, or until the sauce thickens slightly. Stir in 1 teaspoon of salt and pepper to taste.

4. Mix the egg noodles in with the potatoes in the pot, then pour the sauce over them. Stir in the tuna, artichoke hearts, capers, olives, scallions, parsley, and ½ cup of the Parmesan. Stir in the remaining 1 teaspoon of salt. Spread in the prepared baking dish, and sprinkle with the remaining ¼ cup of Parmesan. (At this point the casserole can be covered and refrigerated for up to 24 hours.) Bake, uncovered, until bubbly, about 25 minutes. Serve warm.

Quick Lemony Scallops with Bread Crumbs and Wine

USED TO THINK OF SCALLOPS AS A LUXURY, but then I realized that portions for just a few people really don't cost that much. They're perfect for a quick weeknight meal, too, since they cook so quickly. This recipe, for instance, is foolproof and uses the oven; it will be ready in less than 20 minutes. Serve with crusty bread and the vegetable of your choice. ○ *Serves 4*

CASEROLE DISH: 9 × 13-inch baking dish or 3-quart gratin dish
BAKE TIME: 15 minutes

1 pound large sea scallops
⅔ cup Japanese panko crumbs
¼ cup grated Parmesan cheese
¼ cup fresh flat-leaf parsley, minced
Juice and zest of 1 lemon
½ teaspoon salt
½ teaspoon freshly ground black pepper
¼ cup (½ stick) unsalted butter, melted
2 tablespoons white wine

1. Preheat the oven to 400°F and lightly grease the baking dish with olive oil or nonstick cooking spray. Pat the scallops dry.

2. Use the tips of your fingers to work the bread crumbs, Parmesan, parsley, lemon zest, and salt and pepper together in a small bowl. Roll each of the scallops in this bread crumb mixture and arrange them in a single layer in the prepared dish.

3. Whisk the lemon juice, melted butter, and white wine together until thick and emulsified. Pour over the crumb-coated scallops. Sprinkle the remaining bread crumb mixture over the top. Bake for 15 minutes, or until the topping is golden and the scallops are opaque. Do not overcook! Serve immediately.

Squid Gratinée with Bread Crumbs and Herbs

F YOU THINK YOU DON'T LIKE SQUID, try this recipe and see if you reconsider your opinion. This makes tender little morsels of fresh squid, coated in golden herbed bread crumbs. They're crispy, chewy, and savory. Serve with garlic butter or spicy mayo for dipping. ○ *Serves 4*

CASSEROLE DISH: 9 × 13-inch baking dish or 3-quart gratin dish
BAKE TIME: 8 minutes

2 pounds cleaned squid
Salt and freshly ground black pepper
⅓ cup olive oil
2 cloves garlic, minced
1 cup fine dry bread crumbs
1 small sprig fresh rosemary (leaves only), minced
4 sprigs fresh thyme (leaves only)

1. Preheat the oven to 500°F. Slice the squid bodies into thin rings, and trim the tentacles into evenly sized pieces. Pat them as dry as you can. It's helpful to leave them in the fridge for a few hours after cutting them up to dry out more thoroughly. Toss them with a very light sprinkle of salt and pepper and a drizzle of olive oil.

2. Heat a large skillet over medium heat with the ⅓ cup olive oil. When the oil is hot, add the garlic and turn the heat to low. Cook slowly, letting the garlic infuse the oil with its flavor. When the garlic is golden and fragrant, remove it from the oil with a slotted spoon and discard.

3. Turn the heat to high and add the bread crumbs. Cook, stirring frequently, for about 8 minutes, or until the bread crumbs are golden and fragrant. Remove from the heat and stir in the rosemary and thyme leaves.

4. Toss the squid with the bread crumbs, coating the squid well. Spread in the baking dish and roast for about 8 minutes, stirring twice. Serve immediately.

Jambalaya with Bacon, Artichokes, and Shrimp

T**HIS IS A DELICIOUS COLD-WEATHER DISH** that relies heavily on cupboard staples, so it's easy to whip up without doing too much shopping first. It's suffused with the delicious taste of bacon, tangy artichokes, and olives, and it's wonderful with a glass of white wine and a piece of crusty bread. **o** *Serves 6*

CASSEROLE DISH: 3-quart Dutch oven
BAKE TIME: 25 minutes

1 pound small shrimp, peeled and deveined
Salt and freshly ground black pepper
4 slices bacon, chopped into 1-inch pieces
½ teaspoon red pepper flakes (optional)
One 12-ounce bag frozen artichoke hearts, thawed, drained, and quartered
1½ cups short-grain white rice
1 tablespoon balsamic vinegar
One 28-ounce can diced Italian tomatoes, well drained
1½ cups pitted whole black olives, drained
3 cups low-sodium chicken broth

1. Preheat the oven to 350°F. Pat the shrimp dry and sprinkle them lightly with salt and pepper. Set aside.

2. Put the bacon in the Dutch oven and turn the heat to medium. Cook slowly for about 10 minutes, or until it is just starting to crisp up and has released all its fat.

3. Add the pepper flakes (if using), artichokes, and rice, and stir to coat with the bacon fat. Cook for about 5 minutes, or until fragrant, then add the vinegar, tomatoes, and olives. Sauté for a few moments, then add the chicken broth, and bring to a boil. Stir in the shrimp.

4. Cover the Dutch oven tightly and put it in the oven to bake for 25 minutes, or until the rice is cooked through and the shrimp are pink. Serve immediately.

Oven Paella with Chicken, Shrimp, and Chorizo

PAELLA IS A GLORIOUS SPANISH DISH of rice and seafood, full of meaty shrimp and tender mussels still in their black shells. It makes a wonderful presentation at the table. This baked recipe shows that it doesn't have to be too difficult or time-consuming to prepare. ● *Serves 6 to 8*

CASSEROLE DISH: 5- or 6-quart Dutch oven or other large stovetop-to-oven pot with lid
BAKE TIME: 40 minutes

½ teaspoon saffron threads
1 tablespoon hot water
Olive oil
½ pound smoked chorizo, sliced into ½-inch-thick coins
2 pounds boneless, skinless chicken thighs, cut into bite-size pieces
1 large onion, diced
1 green bell pepper, cored and diced
1 red bell pepper, cored and diced
6 cloves garlic, minced
2¼ cups Arborio or other short-grain white rice
One 28-ounce can diced tomatoes, drained
1 cup white wine

4 cups low-sodium chicken broth

2 teaspoons salt

Freshly ground black pepper

1 pound small shrimp, peeled and deveined

½ pound mussels, cleaned

2 tablespoons unsalted butter, melted

Smoked paprika, for garnish

1. Preheat the oven to 375°F. Crumble the saffron threads into a small bowl and pour the hot water over them. Let them soak while preparing the meat.

2. Put the Dutch oven over medium-high heat and add a drizzle of olive oil. When the oil is hot, add the sausage and cook until browned on both sides, about 6 minutes. Remove and set aside. Add the chicken pieces and cook for another 10 minutes, or until the chicken is light golden brown, turning and stirring as they brown. (Do this in batches if necessary.) Remove the chicken and set aside with the sausage.

3. Add the onion, bell peppers, and garlic to the drippings and fat left behind in the pan, and turn the heat down to medium. Cook, stirring frequently, for 5 to 10 minutes, or until the onion is tender and translucent and the garlic is golden. Add the rice and stir and cook for another few minutes.

4. Add the tomatoes and turn the heat to high. Cook, stirring, for about 2 minutes, then add the white wine, chicken broth, and saffron mixture. Stir in the salt and a generous amount of black pepper. Bring to a simmer, then stir in the browned chicken and sausage.

5. Bake, covered, for 30 minutes, or until the chicken is cooked through. Rinse the shrimp and pat them dry. Season lightly with salt and pepper. Uncover the paella dish and add the shrimp and mussels, arranging them evenly in the rice and pushing them down a bit. Bake, uncovered, for an additional 10 minutes, or until the shrimp are pink and the mussels have opened. Discard any unopened mussels.

6. Drizzle the finished paella with melted butter and dust lightly with smoked paprika. Serve immediately.

Slow-Baked Cioppino

CIOPPINO IS A "CHOPPED" STEW of mixed seafood in a broth of tomatoes and white wine. It's totally delicious, especially in the wintertime or in the cool and windy weather that's typical of the city most identified with cioppino: San Francisco. This oven-baked version is simple and nourishing. ○ *Serves 6*

CASSEROLE DISH: 9 × 13-inch baking dish
BAKE TIME: 45 minutes

Olive oil
4 stalks celery, cut into ½-inch slices
1 large onion, diced
5 cloves garlic, minced
1 teaspoon red pepper flakes
Salt and freshly ground black pepper
1 cup white wine
1 cup low-sodium chicken broth
One 28-ounce can whole plum tomatoes, drained and crushed
½ cup fresh flat-leaf parsley, minced
Zest of 1 lemon
12 large sea scallops
2½ pounds halibut or cod, cut into bite-size pieces
12 jumbo shrimp, peeled and deveined

1. Preheat the oven to 400°F. Heat a generous drizzle of olive oil in a large, deep skillet or wide saucepan. Add the celery, onion, garlic, and red pepper flakes and cook for about 5 minutes, or until the vegetables are just beginning to get tender. Season generously with salt and pepper. Transfer the vegetables to the baking dish.

2. Add the white wine, chicken broth, and tomatoes to the skillet and bring to a boil. Turn off the heat and stir the parsley and lemon zest into the sauce.

3. Pat the scallops, fish, and shrimp dry, then season them with salt and pepper. Lay the seafood in a single layer on top of the vegetables in the baking dish, and pour the tomatoes and liquid on top of everything.

4. Bake for about 45 minutes, or until the fish is tender. Serve immediately.

Crab-Stuffed Tomatoes

JUICY, TANGY TOMATOES and sweet, mellow crab were meant to go together! This dish is based on a recipe for Creole stuffed prawns from Emeril Lagasse, but it's adapted to be a little less work and a little more suited to a full dinner. This makes a good starter, too (one tomato per person should suffice). Serve with a little crusty garlic bread and a crisp green salad. ● *Serves 3*

CASSEROLE DISH: 9 × 13-inch baking dish
BAKE TIME: 20 minutes

6 large ripe tomatoes
Salt and freshly ground black pepper
Olive oil
1 small onion, minced
2 stalks celery, minced
1 green bell pepper, cored and minced
4 cloves garlic, minced
1 pound lump crabmeat, picked over to remove any bits of shell and cartilage
1 large egg, beaten
¼ cup grated Parmesan cheese
1 cup dry bread crumbs
1 tablespoon unsalted butter
½ teaspoon cayenne pepper or smoked paprika

1. Preheat the oven to 375°F. Cut off the top of each tomato, discard the hard core on top, and scoop out the insides, reserving the tomato pulp in a separate bowl. (If the tomatoes don't want to stand up, cut off their bottoms instead and stand them on their heads.) Place the tomatoes in the baking dish, and sprinkle their insides lightly with a pinch of salt and black pepper. Drain off any really juicy liquid from the bowl of tomato pulp, leaving the flesh and seeds behind.

2. Heat a generous drizzle of olive oil in a large skillet over medium-high heat. When the pan is hot, add the onion, celery, bell pepper, and garlic. Cook for about 5 minutes, or until the vegetables are beginning to turn tender and translucent.

3. Remove the skillet from the heat and let its contents cool slightly. Stir in the crabmeat. Stir in the beaten egg, cheese, and ⅓ cup of the bread crumbs. Spoon this filling into the hollowed-out tomatoes.

4. Heat the skillet over medium-high heat again and add the butter. When it foams up, add ½ cup of the reserved tomato flesh and mash it as it cooks. Add the cayenne, as well as a pinch of salt and pepper. Cook for about 5 minutes, or until the tomato and butter have reduced slightly. Spoon this evenly over the tops of the tomatoes. Top each tomato with the remaining ⅔ cup of bread crumbs and drizzle them with olive oil. (At this point the tomatoes can be covered and refrigerated for up to 24 hours.)

5. Roast the tomatoes, uncovered, for 20 minutes, or until they are golden on top and hot all through. Let stand for 5 minutes, then serve.

Halibut Wrapped in Chard with Thyme Butter

WRAPPING FISH IN LARGE CHARD LEAVES helps keep both tender and moist in the oven, and the chard gives the fish a lovely, delicate flavor. Here that flavor is built upon with a compound butter of thyme and shallots. This is an easy yet special company dish. ○ *Serves 4*

CASSEROLE DISH: 9 × 13-inch baking dish
BAKE TIME: 12 to 14 minutes

½ cup (1 stick) unsalted butter, at room temperature
Juice and zest of 1 lemon, plus 4 lemon slices
2 sprigs fresh thyme (leaves only)
1 shallot, minced
Salt and freshly ground black pepper
Four 1-inch-thick halibut fillets (½ pound each)
Olive oil
4 very large Swiss chard leaves, halved lengthwise, center stems removed

1. Preheat the oven to 450°F. Lightly grease the baking dish with olive oil. Blend the butter, lemon juice and zest, thyme leaves, and shallot in a small bowl. Season lightly with salt and pepper.

2. Pat the fish fillets dry and lightly season them with salt and pepper. Heat a heavy large skillet (preferably cast-iron) over high heat until very hot. Add a drizzle of olive oil and swirl the pan to coat. Place the fillets, seasoned side down, in the skillet. Cook until very brown on the bottom, about 1 minute. Turn off the heat and remove the seared fillets from the pan.

3. Place 4 squares of baking parchment on a clean countertop. On each square, overlap a pair of Swiss chard leaf halves so that they form an X. Place one fillet in the center of each X, then spread with some of the lemon-thyme butter. Top each with a lemon slice.

4. Fold the leaves over the fillets, forming a sort of rough packet. Roll up the parchment around the packet and lay it, seam side down, in the prepared baking dish. Bake until the fish is just opaque in the center, 12 to 14 minutes. Transfer the packets to plates, open the parchment, and serve.

Baked Fish Packets with Fennel and Tomatoes

THINK THAT OVEN-BAKING is the most reliable and easiest way to prepare fish. This recipe is totally foolproof: The fish is basically steamed inside foil packets with vegetables and garlic, so it's infused with flavor during its very quick baking time. Experiment, too, by substituting whatever seasonal vegetables you enjoy.

○ Serves 4

CASSEROLE DISH: 9 × 13-inch baking dish
BAKE TIME: 20 minutes

4 thick Pacific halibut or cod fillets (about 1½ pounds total)
Salt and freshly ground black pepper
Zest of 1 orange
¼ teaspoon red pepper flakes
2 cloves garlic, minced
¼ cup olive oil
1 small onion, very thinly sliced
1 bulb fresh fennel, very thinly sliced
1 large tomato, thinly sliced
1 cup green olives, pitted and halved lengthwise

1. Preheat the oven to 400°F. Lay out 4 squares of aluminum foil, each large enough to wrap completely around a fish fillet. Pat the fish dry with a paper towel, then season it lightly with salt and pepper.

2. Combine the orange zest, red pepper flakes, garlic, and olive oil in a small bowl. Set aside.

3. Layer onion, fennel, and tomato slices in each of the foil squares. Season with salt and pepper, and place one fish fillet on top of each vegetable stack. Scatter ¼ cup sliced olives on top of each fish fillet, and drizzle with the olive oil mixture. Fold the foil over the ingredients and crimp the edges to seal the packets.

4. Place the packets in the baking dish and bake for about 20 minutes, or until the fish is opaque inside and flakes easily with a fork. Serve immediately.

Fast Tilapia with Asian Flavors

THIS IS ONE OF THE FASTEST, EASIEST, most crowd-pleasing baked dishes you can make. It's a spicy, salty, sweet baked fish with soy sauce and ginger. Add a little brown rice and some steamed spinach, and it's a quick and healthy meal that will have your guests licking their plates. ○ *Serves 4*

CASSEROLE DISH: 9 × 13-inch baking dish
BAKE TIME: 8 minutes

4 large tilapia (or similar thin white fish) fillets (about 1½ pounds total)
Salt and freshly ground black pepper
1 fresh jalapeño pepper (optional), chopped
3 cloves garlic, minced
One 2-inch piece fresh ginger, peeled and grated
¼ cup reduced-sodium soy sauce
⅓ cup white wine
2 teaspoons toasted sesame oil
⅓ cup chopped fresh cilantro, plus extra for garnish
Scallions, chopped, for garnish

1. Preheat the oven to 475°F. Pat the fish fillets dry with a paper towel and sprinkle them with salt and pepper. Lay them in a single layer in the baking dish.

2. Put the jalapeno pepper (if using), the garlic, ginger, soy sauce, wine, sesame oil, and cilantro in a small food processor and whiz until blended. Pour the sauce over the fish, rubbing it in a little. Bake for about 8 minutes, or until the fish flakes easily and is cooked through. It will be opaque instead of transparent in the center, but it should still be quite moist and flaky.

3. Serve immediately, garnished with chopped scallions and cilantro.

Sweet Goodness from the Oven

What are your favorite desserts?

Do you like simple, homey fruit crumbles and crisps, or do you prefer elaborate pastries from the bakery? Do you love crunchy cookies and crisp wafers, or do you go for smooth puddings and rich pies? Chocolate or vanilla? Fruit or nuts? There are so many choices when it comes to dessert!

This chapter holds many sweet options to accompany your home-cooked casseroles, and many of these desserts can be considered casseroles themselves. They all bake at temperatures similar to the ones used for your casseroles, so it's easy to whip these up and slip them into the oven as your casserole supper bakes, too.

These recipes lean toward the homey side; I confess to preferring simple, rustic desserts, like Deep-Dish Frosted Sugar Cookie Bars (page 271), Chocolate and Banana Bread Pudding (page 274), and Layered Pumpkin Crumb Cake (page 278), which are easy to make on a weeknight. I love seasonal fruit desserts like Rhubarb-Lavender Oat Crisp (page 264), made with fresh rhubarb in the springtime, or Apple and Quince Crumble (page 266) in the autumn. I make Strawberry-Blueberry Buckle (page 268) in the summertime with fresh fruit, and I make it in the winter with bags of berries from the freezer.

And just in case your oven is full, I've included a few desserts that don't need to bake at all, like the creamy refrigerated pudding Panna Cotta (page 288) and my family's favorite no-bake casserole: No-Bake Boston Cream Pie Strata (page 286), with vanilla pudding and chocolate frosting layered between graham crackers.

Basic Oat Crisp with Fruit

ALTHOUGH THERE ARE RECIPES HERE for fruit cobblers and crisps, I do think the best fruit crisps are made on the spur of the moment, with seasonal fruit thrown together with just a hint of sugar and spice. Here's a crispy oat topping for any sort of fruit mixture. ○ *Serves 8*

CASSEROLE DISH: 9 × 13-inch baking dish
BAKE TIME: 45 minutes

 8 to 10 cups sliced fruit or whole berries
1½ cups old-fashioned rolled oats
½ cup all-purpose flour
1 cup packed light brown sugar
1 teaspoon mixed ground spices, such as cinnamon, nutmeg, ginger, or coriander
¼ teaspoon salt
1 cup (2 sticks) cold unsalted butter
½ cup chopped nuts of your choice (optional)

1. Preheat the oven to 375°F and fill the baking dish with the fresh fruit, cut into small, evenly sized pieces. If you are using small berries such as raspberries or blackberries, you can leave these whole.

2. Mix the dry ingredients together in a bowl, then cut the butter into pieces and gently work it into the dry ingredients with your fingers until the mixture resembles coarse crumbs. Mix in the nuts, if using. Sprinkle the fruit with the crumbs evenly. (At this point the crisp may be covered and refrigerated for up to 24 hours.)

3. Bake, uncovered, for about 45 minutes, until the topping is golden and crisp and the fruit is tender when pierced with a knife.

Basic Buttery Cobbler with Fruit

HAVE AN INDISCRIMINATE LOVE OF FRUIT DESSERTS, pans of seasonal fruit baked until bubbly with crispy toppings of oats or tender cobbler dough. But when it comes to those cobblers, I do prefer a soft, biscuit-like dough. This recipe is cobbled together—as it were—from two old favorites, and to me it represents the perfect melding of a quick and easy recipe with a truly tender, toothsome biscuit topping. ○ *Serves 8*

CASSEROLE DISH: 9 × 13-inch baking dish
BAKE TIME: 30 minutes

8 to 10 cups sliced fruit or whole berries
2 cups all-purpose flour
⅓ cup plus 3 tablespoons sugar
1 tablespoon baking power
¼ teaspoon ground nutmeg (optional, depending on
    what kind of fruit you are using)
½ teaspoon salt
½ cup (1 stick) unsalted butter, cut into small pieces
1 large egg, beaten
¾ cup milk

1. Preheat the oven to 400°F and fill the baking dish with the fruit. If you're using firm fruit, like pears or apples, bake it in the oven for about 15 minutes, while preparing the dough, to let it begin to cook.

2. Mix the flour, ⅓ cup sugar, baking powder, nutmeg, and salt in a large bowl, then add the butter and work it in with your fingers or a pastry cutter until the dough is crumbly. Stir in the egg and milk just until the dough comes together; don't overmix.

3. Spoon the filling over the fruit in 8 to 12 even mounds. Sprinkle the mounds with the remaining 3 tablespoons of sugar. Bake for about 30 minutes, or until the topping is golden. Serve warm.

Quick and Easy Fruit Galette

O NE OF THE EASIEST DESSERTS I know how to make is a galette, or free-form tart. You make up a simple pie dough (or biscuit dough; a biscuit galette is quite tasty), roll it into a rough circle, put fruit on top, then draw up the sides to form a rustic-style tart. Pop it in the oven and you're done! Here's a quick dough suitable for a 10-inch galette, or for a 9-inch single-crust fruit pie or tart. ○ *Serves 8*

CASSEROLE DISH: Large baking sheet
BAKE TIME: 50 minutes

2 cups all-purpose flour
¾ teaspoon salt
1 tablespoon sugar, plus extra for sprinkling
14 tablespoons (1¾ sticks) unsalted butter, plus
   2 tablespoons to assemble galette
⅓ to ½ cup ice water
About 6 cups sliced fruit

1. Pulse the flour, salt, sugar, and butter in a food processor until crumbly. (Or mix the flour in a medium bowl with the salt and sugar, and work in the butter with your fingers or a pastry blender until crumbly.)

2. Slowly add the ice water just until the mixture comes together in a dough. Wrap it in plastic wrap and refrigerate for about an hour.

3. Preheat the oven to 425°F. Take the dough out of the fridge and roll it out on a well-floured surface. Form the dough into a large, rough circle on a baking sheet. Cover the dough with a pinwheel of thinly sliced fruit, leaving an uncovered border of a couple of inches all the way around the edge. Dot with butter and sprinkle with a little extra sugar. Fold the uncovered dough up around the fruit. It should look rustic and a little rough.

4. Bake for about 50 minutes, or until browned and crispy on the bottom.

Rhubarb-Lavender Oat Crisp

RHUBARB IS A WONDERFUL TREAT in the spring. I love the tangy tartness of fresh rhubarb and its beautiful green and red color. This crisp plays up rhubarb's gentle herbal flavors with a tiny pinch of dried lavender, which gives a subtle herbed taste to the sweet, golden crisp without overwhelming it. Dried lavender can be found with the spices and dried herbs at many large grocery stores or in the bulk sections of natural-foods markets. Serve this with whipped cream or strawberry ice cream. ○ *Serves 6*

CASSEROLE DISH: 9 × 13-inch baking dish
BAKE TIME: 40 to 45 minutes

2 pounds fresh rhubarb, leaves removed and discarded
½ cup granulated sugar
¼ cup honey
½ teaspoon dried lavender buds
1½ cups old-fashioned rolled oats
½ cup all-purpose flour
¾ cup light brown sugar
¼ teaspoon salt
½ cup (1 stick) unsalted butter
¾ cup toasted sliced almonds

1. Preheat the oven to 375°F. Lightly grease the baking dish with butter or non-stick cooking spray.

2. Cut the rhubarb stalks into small, even pieces about the size of your knuckle. Toss in a bowl with the granulated sugar and honey. Rub the lavender between your hands, and add the crushed lavender to the rhubarb. Stir everything together and spread evenly in the baking dish.

3. In a small bowl, mix the oats, flour, ½ cup brown sugar, and salt. Melt 6 tablespoons of the butter and mix it with the dry ingredients, then spread this crumble topping over the rhubarb.

4. Melt the remaining ¼ cup of brown sugar and 2 tablespoons butter, along with the toasted almonds, together in the microwave or in a small saucepan, and dot the mixture over the crumble topping. (At this point the crisp may be covered and refrigerated for up to 24 hours.)

5. Bake, uncovered, for 40 to 45 minutes, or until the topping is lightly browned. Let stand for at least 15 minutes, then serve warm.

Baked Apples with Toasted Oats and Cream Cheese

F YOU'VE NEVER HAD A BAKED APPLE, then these will be a delightful treat. Warm, cinnamon-spiced cream cheese is a surprise inside these old-fashioned baked apples, along with nutty toasted oats. **○** *Serves 4*

CASSEROLE DISH: 8-inch square baking dish
BAKE TIME: 30 minutes

4 large, firm baking apples, such as Fuji, Rome, or Golden Delicious
¼ cup old-fashioned rolled oats
¼ cup golden raisins
¼ cup walnuts, chopped
¼ cup dark or light brown sugar
1 teaspoon ground cinnamon
¼ teaspoon ground nutmeg
Pinch of salt
4 ounces cream cheese
1 tablespoon unsalted butter, cut into 4 squares
½ cup boiling water

1. Preheat the oven to 375°F. Core the apples with an apple corer, or use a paring knife to cut a 1-inch cylinder in the center of each apple. Leave about ½ inch of apple on the bottom. Use a paring knife or peeler to remove any remaining core or seeds.

2. Heat a small skillet over medium-high heat. Add the oats and toast them, stirring frequently. When they smell toasty and are beginning to brown, take them off the heat and transfer them to a small bowl.

3. Stir the raisins, walnuts, brown sugar, cinnamon, nutmeg, and salt into the toasted oats. Cut the cream cheese into small pieces and stir into the oat mixture as well.

4. Place the apples in the baking dish. Use a teaspoon to stuff each apple with the oat and cream cheese mixture. Top each apple with one of the butter squares. (At this point the apples may be covered and refrigerated for up to 24 hours.)

5. Pour the boiling water into the pan, surrounding the apples. Bake, uncovered, for about 30 minutes, until the apples are tender. Pour any pan juices over the apples when you remove them from the oven. Let stand for 10 minutes before serving.

Apple and Quince Crumble

THE TOPPING FOR THIS FAVORITE autumn dessert is adapted from Marian Burros's sublime plum and ginger crumble. It's halfway between a cookie and a crumble topping—crispy and moist at the same time, and supremely satisfying on top of the sweet spiced fruit. A note on the quinces: Don't avoid this recipe if you can't find them; just substitute firm pears or extra apples. But if you do happen to find (and poach) a few quinces, you will be richly rewarded. ○ *Serves 6*

CASSEROLE DISH: 9 × 13-inch baking dish
BAKE TIME: 45 minutes

3 cups water
½ cup granulated sugar (if using quinces)
2 medium quinces, peeled and cored (or 2 firm pears, peeled and cored)
6 medium apples, peeled and cored
¾ cup dried cherries
¼ cup crystallized ginger, finely chopped
1¼ cups dark brown sugar
2¼ cups all-purpose flour
3 teaspoons ground cinnamon
½ teaspoon ground nutmeg
2 teaspoons baking powder
½ teaspoon salt

2 large eggs, beaten

⅓ cup raw or turbinado sugar

¾ cup (1½ sticks) unsalted butter, melted

1. To poach the quinces: Bring the water to a boil in a medium saucepan and stir in the granulated sugar until it dissolves. Cut the peeled and cored quinces into slices. Add the slices to the pan and turn the heat to low. Simmer for 30 to 60 minutes, or until they turn an orangey pink and can be easily pierced with a knife. Remove from the heat and strain away the liquid. (Keep the liquid; it's delicious when further reduced into a syrup. Serve it over fruit, stirred into soda water, or drizzled on ice cream.)

2. Preheat the oven to 375°F and lightly grease the baking dish with butter or nonstick cooking spray.

3. Cut the peeled and cored apples into slices. Toss the cooked quince slices with the apples and dried cherries. Stir in the crystallized ginger, ¼ cup brown sugar, ¼ cup flour, and 1 teaspoon cinnamon. Spread the fruit mixture in the prepared baking dish.

4. In a separate bowl, combine the remaining 1 cup of brown sugar, 2 cups of flour, 2 teaspoons of cinnamon, the nutmeg, baking powder, and salt. Add the eggs and mix lightly with the tips of your fingers until it forms a dry crumble.

5. Evenly sprinkle or spread this dry mixture over the fruit in the baking dish. Sprinkle the top with the raw sugar, then pour all the melted butter over the top of that. Bake for 45 minutes, or until the top is golden brown and craggy and the apples are tender. Let stand for 10 minutes before serving

About Quinces

Quinces are an old-fashioned fruit that have fallen out of favor in modern times. They're ugly and knobbly, with patches of gray fuzz on their greenish-yellow skin. They look rather like apples, but, unlike apples, their mouth-puckering astringency makes them inedible when raw. Quinces must be cooked before eating.

This cooking process, though, is a kitchen miracle. Slip slices of peeled quince into a bath of poaching liquid and cook for an hour, and they turn a deep rosy pink. They become intensely sweet and fragrant, and the aroma as they cook will steal through your house like perfume. Quinces are such a sweet surprise that I think everyone should try cooking them at least once.

Strawberry-Blueberry Buckle

MAYBE FRESH STRAWBERRIES are in season—or maybe you're craving them in the middle of February. The good news is that frozen strawberries and blueberries, flash-frozen at the peak of ripeness, are a very good substitute for fresh summer berries. In fact, they are preferable to the huge, tasteless strawberries and small, insipid blueberries, shipped from removed regions, that you find at the supermarket in the middle of winter. Go with frozen berries; they're a better deal, and tastier, too. This recipe works equally well with frozen or fresh. And if you're wondering about the name, a "buckle" is a dead-easy cake-like topping for fruit. This will take you maybe six minutes to stir up and put in the oven, and about two minutes to clean up. ○ *Serves 6*

CASSEROLE DISH: 9 × 13-inch baking dish
BAKE TIME: 40 minutes

10 ounces fresh or frozen blueberries
2 cups (16 ounces) fresh or frozen strawberries
½ cup chopped almonds
Juice and zest of 1 lemon
½ cup granulated sugar
1 cup light or dark brown sugar
4 large eggs
1 cup (2 sticks) unsalted butter, melted
1 teaspoon vanilla extract
2 cups all-purpose flour
¼ teaspoon salt
¼ teaspoon ground nutmeg

1. Preheat the oven to 350°F. Lightly grease the baking dish with butter.

2. Spread the fruit in the bottom of the pan and lightly mix it with the almonds, lemon juice, and ¼ cup of the granulated sugar.

3. In a medium bowl, whisk together the lemon zest, brown sugar, eggs, melted butter, and vanilla. Stir in the flour, salt, and nutmeg, and pour the batter over the fruit.

4. Sprinkle the top of the batter with the remaining ¼ cup of granulated sugar and bake for 40 minutes, or until the top is golden and set. Let cool before serving.

Brownie Bake with Cherries and Cream Cheese Swirl

WHO DOESN'T LOVE BROWNIES? These are a real crowd-pleaser, and here they're dressed up a little with juicy ripe cherries and a sweet, indulgently creamy swirl. ○ *Serves 8 to 10*

CASSEROLE DISH: 9 × 13-inch baking dish
BAKE TIME: 35 to 40 minutes

FOR THE BROWNIES:
6 ounces unsweetened chocolate
4 ounces semisweet chocolate
½ cup (1 stick) unsalted butter, at room temperature
1 cup sugar
4 large eggs
1 cup all-purpose flour
1 teaspoon baking powder
½ teaspoon salt
1 teaspoon vanilla extract
1½ cups halved, pitted cherries (fresh or thawed frozen)

FOR THE CREAM CHEESE SWIRL:
8 ounces cream cheese, at room temperature
¼ cup (½ stick) unsalted butter, at room temperature
¼ cup sugar
1 teaspoon almond extract

1. Preheat the oven to 375°F and lightly grease the baking dish with butter or non-stick cooking spray.

2. To make the brownies, combine the chocolates, butter, and sugar in a double boiler or a saucepan over very low heat. Heat carefully until melted and smooth, stirring frequently at the end as the chocolate melts. Set aside to cool slightly.

3. Beat the eggs until pale and lightened—at least 6 minutes in an electric mixer—then slowly mix in the melted chocolate mixture. Add the flour, baking powder, and salt to the bowl, along with the vanilla. Mix just until combined, then stir in half of the cherries. Spread the brownie batter in the prepared pan.

4. To make the cream cheese swirl, whip the cream cheese with the butter, sugar, and almond extract until light and fluffy. Stir in the remaining cherries. Drop the cream cheese mixture on top of the brownie batter in 6 evenly spaced spoonfuls, then take a thin knife and swirl the cream cheese through the batter. Bake for 35 to 40 minutes, or until just set. Let cool for at least 15 minutes before cutting and serving.

Raspberry Meringue Layer Bars

THIS IS AN EASY AND FOOLPROOF layered dessert, but its components are rather fancy, with buttery cake-like cookie on the bottom, tangy jam in the middle, and a crispy, airy layer of meringue on top. It feels delicate and special enough for a party, and my guests always love it. ● *Serves 24*

CASSEROLE DISH: 10½ × 15½-inch jelly-roll pan
BAKE TIME: 30 minutes

3 large eggs, separated
¾ cup (1½ sticks) unsalted butter, at room temperature
¾ cup sugar
1 teaspoon vanilla extract
2¼ cups all-purpose flour
¼ teaspoon baking soda
¾ teaspoon baking powder
½ teaspoon salt
1 cup seedless raspberry jam
1 cup finely chopped walnuts

1. Preheat the oven to 300°F. Lightly grease the jelly-roll pan with nonstick cooking spray.

2. In the bowl of an electric mixer, whip the egg whites on high speed until they form stiff peaks. Use a spatula to scrape them out into a separate small bowl, and set aside. Be careful to just gently tip the egg whites into the bowl and not to deflate them.

3. In the bowl of the mixer, cream the butter and sugar for several minutes, or until they are creamy and fluffy. Add the egg yolks and vanilla extract, and beat for a full 5 minutes, or until the volume has increased by half and the mixture is smooth.

4. In a separate bowl, whisk the flour with the baking soda, baking powder, and salt. Stir into the butter mixture with a wooden spoon or your hands just until it comes together.

5. Scrape the dough into the prepared jelly-roll pan and pat it out into an even layer. Spread the dough with the jam, and sprinkle ½ cup walnuts over the jam. Spread the beaten egg whites evenly over the nuts, and sprinkle the remaining ½ cup nuts over the egg whites.

6. Bake for 30 minutes. Watch carefully to avoid overbaking the egg white topping; it should be crisp but not brown. Let cool completely, and cut into small squares. These bars will keep, tightly covered, for up to 5 days, but the egg white topping will lose some of its crispness and become slightly chewy after the first day or so.

Deep-Dish Frosted Sugar Cookie Bars

LOVE PLAIN SUGAR COOKIES, topped with a smear of buttery frosting. But it's a lot of extra work to roll out and cut all those cookies. This recipe gives you all that sweet sugar rush, but with much less work. Here the sugar cookie dough is baked casserole-style in a baking pan, then frosted and cut into squares. Easy!

o *Serves 6*

CASSEROLE DISH: 10½ × 15½-inch jelly-roll pan
BAKE TIME: 35 minutes

FOR THE COOKIES:

1 cup (2 sticks) unsalted butter, at room temperature

4 ounces cream cheese, at room temperature

1 cup granulated sugar

1 cup light brown sugar

4 large eggs

2 teaspoons vanilla extract

3½ cups all-purpose flour

Zest of 1 lemon

1 teaspoon salt

1¼ teaspoons baking powder

FOR THE FROSTING:

1 cup (2 sticks) unsalted butter, at room temperature

Zest of 1 lemon

1 teaspoon vanilla extract

Pinch of salt

3½ cups confectioners' sugar

¼ cup milk

Colored sprinkles (optional)

1. Position an oven rack in the center of the oven. Preheat the oven to 375°F, and lightly grease the jelly-roll pan with butter or nonstick cooking spray. If you want to be able to lift these (or any other bar cookie) out of the pan before cutting them, then line your pan with parchment paper. Use an extra-long piece, laid crosswise so that the long sides of the pan have a bit of parchment hanging over them.

2. To make the cookies, in the bowl of an electric mixer, cream the butter, cream cheese, and sugars until lightened and fluffy, about 5 minutes at high speed. Add the eggs and vanilla and mix thoroughly.

3. Add the flour, lemon zest, salt, and baking powder. Mix just until thoroughly blended, then pat the dough into the prepared pan. Bake on the center rack for 35 minutes, or until a toothpick inserted in the center comes out clean. If you've lined the pan with parchment, after the cookie bars have cooled for a few minutes, run a sharp knife around the sides of the pan to loosen them, then lift out the parchment. Place the pan on a wire rack and cool completely before frosting.

4. To make the frosting, in the bowl of an electric mixer, whip the butter until it is lightened and creamy. Add the lemon zest, vanilla, salt, confectioners' sugar, and milk, and whip until combined and fluffy. Add a little more milk if it is too thick, or a little more sugar if it is too loose. Spread the frosting over the cooled cookie bars, and top with sprinkles, if desired.

Salted Caramel and Walnut Slice

THIS "SLICE," OR BAR COOKIE, is practically the national dessert of Australia and New Zealand. It's also called millionaire's shortbread, and it definitely tastes like a million bucks! It consists of a firm layer of cookie shortbread, followed by a layer of gooey caramel, and topped by a thin and crispy layer of chocolate. I like the richness of walnuts worked into the shortbread base and a sprinkle of flaky sea salt on top; both of these additions to the classic recipe help balance out the sweetness of the other layers. ○ *Serves 12*

CASSEROLE DISH: 8-inch square baking dish
BAKE TIME: 15 minutes

FOR THE SHORTBREAD BASE:
1 cup all-purpose flour
½ cup light brown sugar
½ cup walnuts, finely ground
¼ cup unsweetened dried coconut (see Note on page 149)
Pinch of salt
½ cup (1 stick) unsalted butter, melted
½ teaspoon vanilla extract

FOR THE CARAMEL FILLING:
¼ cup honey
2 tablespoons unsalted butter
One 14-ounce can sweetened condensed milk
¼ teaspoon salt

FOR THE CHOCOLATE TOPPING:
6 ounces bittersweet chocolate, broken into pieces
1 tablespoon unsalted butter
1 tablespoon vegetable oil
Flaky sea salt

1. Preheat the oven to 400°F and line the baking dish with parchment paper so that the ends hang over 2 of the sides. Lightly grease the parchment with nonstick cooking spray.

2. To make the shortbread, stir the flour, brown sugar, walnuts, and coconut together in a medium bowl. Stir in the salt, melted butter, and vanilla. Press into the prepared baking dish in a thin, even layer. Bake for 15 minutes, or until golden.

3. To make the filling, while the base is baking pour the filling ingredients into a small pan or double boiler and set it over low heat. Cook, whisking constantly, until the mixture boils. Let it boil for about 5 minutes, or until it thickens and pulls away from the sides of the pan.

4. Remove the shortbread base from the oven and pour the caramel filling on top. Spread it evenly and put the pan in the fridge to chill.

5. To make the chocolate layer, in a small saucepan combine the chocolate with the butter and oil. Cook over low heat until melted and smooth. Whisk thoroughly to remove any lumps, then spread evenly over the chilled caramel layer. Sprinkle lightly with flaky sea salt and refrigerate to harden chocolate. Serve in very small squares; this stuff is extremely rich!

Chocolate and Banana Bread Pudding

CHOCOLATE AND BANANAS were meant for each other. This rich yet not too sweet bread pudding is moist and fluffy, mellow and homey, with a hint of cinnamon and bites of creamy banana scattered throughout. Serve this with caramel sauce or whipped cream. ○ *Serves 6*

CASSEROLE DISH: 3-quart soufflé dish or Dutch oven
BAKE TIME: 45 minutes

18 ounces day-old brioche, challah, or other egg-enriched bread
2 ripe yet firm bananas
2 cups milk
1 cup cream

½ cup light brown sugar

½ teaspoon ground cinnamon

¼ teaspoon salt

8 ounces bittersweet chocolate, finely chopped

6 large eggs

1 teaspoon vanilla extract

2 tablespoons unsalted butter, cut into bits

1. Preheat the oven to 325°F and generously grease the soufflé dish or Dutch oven with butter.

2. Cut the bread into 1-inch cubes. Peel the bananas and cut into small chunks. Toss with the bread and spread evenly in the prepared dish.

3. Warm the milk, cream, brown sugar, cinnamon, and salt in a medium saucepan over low heat. When bubbles form around the edges of the milk, but before it comes to a boil, remove from the heat and add the chocolate. Let it stand for a few minutes so the chocolate can melt, then whisk until smooth.

4. Beat the eggs and vanilla in a separate bowl, then gradually add to the chocolate and milk. Whisk to combine, then pour over the bread and bananas. Dot the top of the bread pudding with the butter. (At this point the bread pudding may be covered and refrigerated for up to 24 hours.) Bake, uncovered, for about 45 minutes, or until set. The pudding will continue to firm up as it cools. Serve slightly warm.

Cranberry Cake with Walnut Praline Topping

THIS IS A FRUITCAKE for people who hate fruitcake. It's fresh, festive, and full of bright flavors. But it's also rich and moist and a great treat for holiday gatherings. *And* it's really, really easy and quick to make—the ultimate one-bowl cake. ○ *Serves 10*

CASSEROLE DISH: 10-inch springform pan or 9 × 13-inch baking dish
BAKE TIME: 45 to 65 minutes

FOR THE CAKE:

3 large eggs

2 cups granulated sugar

¾ cup (1½ sticks) unsalted butter, slightly softened and cut into chunks

1 teaspoon vanilla extract

Zest of 1 orange

2 cups all-purpose flour

½ teaspoon salt

¼ teaspoon ground nutmeg

One 12-ounce bag (2½ cups) fresh cranberries

FOR THE TOPPING:

¼ cup (½ stick) unsalted butter

¼ cup light or dark brown sugar

1 cup coarsely chopped walnuts

1. Preheat the oven to 350°F. Lightly grease the springform pan or baking dish with butter.

2. To make the cake, put the eggs and sugar in the bowl of a stand mixer. Beat for 6 to 8 minutes on high speed, until the eggs thicken considerably and turn pale yellow. They will double in volume and stream into ribbons when you lift the beaters.

3. Add the butter, vanilla, and orange zest and beat for an additional 2 minutes. Stir in the flour, salt, and nutmeg. Fold in the cranberries. Pour the batter into the prepared pan and set aside.

4. To make the walnut praline, heat the butter in a skillet over medium-high heat. When the butter foams up, add the brown sugar and stir. Add the walnuts and cook for several minutes, stirring, until the mixture is shiny and smooth and the nuts smell toasted. Spread over the cake batter.

5. Bake for about 45 minutes if using a 9 × 13-inch pan, or about 65 minutes if using a springform pan. Check internally with a skewer or toothpick to make sure the center of the cake is not still gooey; when the tester comes out with crumbs clinging to it instead of liquid batter, the cake is done. If the cake is browning too quickly, tent the top with foil to keep it from burning. Cool completely before serving. This cake keeps very well, if you wrap it securely in plastic wrap after it has cooled completely. It also freezes well.

Note: You may have noticed that this cake does not contain any baking powder or baking soda. All the leavening is provided by the beaten eggs, so it's important to beat them until they are quite thick and creamy. This produces a cake that is not dry or airy, but moist and a little dense.

Baked Rice Pudding with Lemon

THIS IS AN ADAPTATION OF AN ADAPTATION: Laurie Colwin's marvelous take on Jane Grigson's classic oven-baked rice pudding. This is an extremely easy (although long-cooked) rice pudding. There aren't any eggs included, and there's very little hands-on time. You simply cook this pudding low and slow, for nearly three hours, until the rice has almost dissolved and the milk has reduced into a thick, creamy pudding. Feel free to try other varieties of citrus zest. I hardly need to mention that this lightly sweetened pudding is great for breakfast.

◦ *Serves 8*

CASSEROLE DISH: 9 × 13-inch baking dish
BAKE TIME: 2½ to 3 hours

¾ **cup white rice**
6 **cups whole milk**
Zest of 2 lemons
½ **cup sugar**
½ **teaspoon salt**
2 **tablespoons rum (optional)**

1. Preheat the oven to 250°F. Mix the rice, milk, lemon zest, sugar, salt, and rum, if using, in the baking dish. Bake, uncovered, until the rice pudding is quite soft and the milk has been somewhat reduced; it will take at least 2½ hours and up to 3 hours. Stir it every 45 minutes.

2. Let the pudding stand and cool for at least 20 minutes before serving. It will thicken considerably as it cools.

Layered Pumpkin Crumb Cake

T HIS IS ONE OF MY FAVORITE FALL DESSERTS. The ingredient list looks lengthy, but the cake is actually very straightforward, and, unlike similar recipes, this one does not rely on a cake mix. It's a tender, moist, from-scratch cake with a warm pumpkin filling and a crumbly, cinnamon-spiced topping.

o *Serves 8 to 10*

CASSEROLE DISH: 9 × 13-inch baking dish
BAKE TIME: 45 minutes

FOR THE DRY MIX:
1 cup granulated sugar
3 cups all-purpose flour
1 teaspoon salt
3 teaspoons baking powder

FOR THE CAKE:
½ cup (1 stick) unsalted butter, at room temperature
2 large eggs
1 teaspoon vanilla extract

FOR THE PUMPKIN FILLING:
3 large eggs, beaten
1½ cups homemade or store-bought pumpkin puree
1 cup dark brown sugar
⅔ cup milk
2 teaspoons ground cinnamon
1 teaspoon ground ginger
½ teaspoon ground cloves
½ teaspoon ground nutmeg

FOR THE CRUMB TOPPING:
½ teaspoon ground cinnamon
½ teaspoon ground cloves
½ teaspoon ground ginger
½ cup (1 stick) unsalted butter, at room temperature
1 tablespoon water, as needed

1. Preheat the oven to 350°F. Grease the baking dish with butter. To make the dry mix, combine the sugar, flour, salt, and baking powder in a medium bowl.

2. To make the cake, in the bowl of an electric mixer, beat the butter until whipped and creamy. Then beat in the eggs and vanilla. Beat in about 2 cups, or half, of the dry mix. Pat this cake dough into the prepared pan.

3. To make the filling, in a clean bowl, whisk together the eggs, pumpkin puree, brown sugar, milk, and spices. Spread the mixture over the cake in the pan.

4. To make the crumb topping, mix the cinnamon, cloves, and ginger into the remaining dry mix. Work in the butter, mixing with your fingers until crumbly. Add 1 tablespoon of water if needed and continue mixing with your fingers until loose and crumbly. Spread this topping over the pumpkin filling.

5. Bake for about 45 minutes, or until the filling is set inside. Let cool for at least 20 minutes before slicing. This is great warm, but also very good when chilled.

Oven-Poached Pears in Red Wine with Cinnamon

PEARS POACHED IN RED WINE are a delicious, elegant, and rather healthful way to end a meal. Traditionally, fruit is poached on top of the stove, but I have found that oven-poaching makes the pears more uniformly tender. It also saves you from having to clean a wine-splattered stovetop. ○ *Serves 6*

CASSEROLE DISH: 5- or 6-quart Dutch oven or other stovetop-to-oven pot with lid
BAKE TIME: 30 minutes

1 cup sugar
3 cups dry red wine
Zest of 1 lemon
2 cinnamon sticks
2 bay leaves
2 cups water
6 firm yet ripe pears, preferably with stems attached, peeled

1. Preheat the oven to 325°F. Mix the sugar, wine, lemon zest, cinnamon sticks, and bay leaves in the Dutch oven, along with the water. Place over medium-low heat and cook until the sugar is dissolved.

2. Lay the pears down in the wine mixture. Cover and bake for 30 minutes. Halfway through, turn the pears over so that the wine covers the other side. Cook until the pears are tender when pierced with a knife.

3. Remove the pears from the oven and let cool completely in the liquid. After the pears are completely cool, remove them from the Dutch oven and cook the liquid down on the stovetop for about 15 minutes, or until reduced to a thick syrup. Serve the pears drizzled with the poaching liquid.

Baked Custard with Port Wine Sauce

BAKED CUSTARD is an old-fashioned and very simple oven dessert. This one is smooth and creamy, a little wobbly, and very soothing. It's delicious with the port wine sauce that accompanies it; the wine is a rich and robust contrast to the custard's understated creaminess. You can also make this custard in individual cups for a more elegant presentation. Bake in 6-ounce ramekins for about 20 minutes, or until just barely set. ○ *Serves 6*

CASSEROLE DISH: 9 × 13-inch baking dish
BAKE TIME: 1 hour

FOR THE CUSTARD:
4 large eggs
4 large egg yolks
3 cups milk
1 cup heavy cream
1 teaspoon vanilla extract
1 cup sugar
¼ teaspoon salt
Ground nutmeg

FOR THE SAUCE:

1 cup ruby port

3 tablespoons sugar

1 cinnamon stick

1 strip lemon peel

1 teaspoon balsamic vinegar

1. Preheat the oven to 325°F. Lightly grease the baking dish with nonstick cooking spray.

2. To make the custard, put the eggs and egg yolks in a blender and whiz until thoroughly beaten. Blend in the milk, cream, vanilla, sugar, and salt and whiz until frothy. Pour into the prepared baking dish and sprinkle with nutmeg.

3. Bake for 20 minutes, then stir once. Bake for 40 minutes longer, or until the custard is just barely set. The center will still seem very jiggly and wobbly, but a knife inserted at the very edge of the custard will come out clean. Remove from the oven and immediately place in the refrigerator. This stops the custard from cooking any further. You can serve the custard warm (in fact, I prefer it that way); just take it out of the fridge when it's no longer hot and serve while still warm. But you can also chill it completely and serve it cold with the sauce.

4. To make the port wine sauce, combine the ruby port, sugar, cinnamon stick, lemon peel, and vinegar in a small saucepan. Bring to a boil and cook, stirring, until the sugar dissolves. Turn down the heat and let the sauce simmer for 15 minutes, or until reduced by about half. Remove from the heat and let cool.

5. Serve the warm or chilled custard in small bowls with the wine sauce drizzled on top.

Smooth Egg Custards

Baked egg custards like this one are generally cooked in a water bath, which helps them bake evenly and can prevent cracks from forming on top. But I find water baths too much trouble for such a simple treat, so I tend not to use them. I also find that blending the ingredients in the blender and stirring once while baking tend to mitigate any ill effects from the absence of a water bath. But if you want a very reliably smooth texture, then try baking this in a water bath: Just set your dish of custard inside a larger pan and pour about 1 inch of boiling water into the larger pan, then bake as directed in the recipe.

Hot Applesauce with a Meringue Cap

WAS INTRODUCED TO THIS REFRESHINGLY SIMPLE and not-too-sweet dessert by Molly Wizenberg at the wonderful blog Orangette. Molly learned this dish from a friend in France, and I love the simplicity of it. It's also a good opportunity to slip in a recipe for oven-baked applesauce, which is one of the very easiest ways to make a delicious homemade treat. ○ *Serves 8*

CASSEROLE DISH: 9 × 13-inch baking dish or 3-quart Dutch oven
BAKE TIME: 45 minutes for the apples; 2 hours for the meringue cap

FOR THE APPLESAUCE:
4 pounds very tart apples, such as Granny Smith, peeled, cored,
    and cut into small chunks
½ cup apple juice, cider, or water
¼ cup pure maple syrup
Pinch of salt
2 cinnamon sticks or 1½ teaspoons ground cinnamon
Juice of 1 lemon

FOR THE MERINGUE:
5 large egg whites
½ teaspoon cream of tartar
Pinch of salt
1¼ cups sugar
¼ teaspoon ground nutmeg

1. Preheat the oven to 350°F. To make the applesauce, in the baking dish, combine the apples with the apple juice, maple syrup, salt, cinnamon, and lemon juice. Cover the pan tightly with foil or a lid. Bake for about 45 minutes, or until the apples are completely mushy.

2. Remove the apples from the oven and turn the temperature down to 225°F. Mash the apples with a potato masher until they form a soft, chunky sauce, or blend or puree them for a smooth sauce, then return them to the baking dish.

3. To make the meringue, put the egg whites into the bowl of a stand mixer, or use a large mixing bowl and a hand mixer. Beat the egg whites on medium speed with the whisk attachment until they are frothy, then sprinkle in the cream of tartar and salt. Continue to beat the egg whites until they are very foamy and starting to increase in volume. Turn the mixer speed to high and, while beating, add the sugar slowly, not more than ¼ cup at a time. Continue beating the egg whites until they are very glossy and hold stiff peaks. If you swoop your finger or the beaters into the egg white, the resulting peak should stand straight up, with just the tip flopping over a little. Beat in the nutmeg as the egg whites reach this stiff stage.

4. Use a large spatula to smooth the meringue over the applesauce in the baking dish. Bake for about 2 hours, or until the meringue is firm, crisp, and dry. Let cool for 20 minutes, then serve.

Orange and Cardamom Yogurt Pudding with Stewed Fruits

THIS VERY SIMPLE YET DELICIOUS PUDDING was inspired by a home cook's submission to *Australian Women's Weekly*. I loved the unusual combination of yogurt and sweetened condensed milk and the unexpected flavor of cardamom. This pudding can be served with fresh fruit, such as strawberries in their own juices when in season, or with stewed dried fruit and wine syrup, below, in winter. ○ *Serves 6*

CASSEROLE DISH: 8-inch square baking dish or 2-quart shallow baking dish
BAKE TIME: 30 minutes

FOR THE PUDDING:
4 cups plain yogurt
One 14-ounce can sweetened condensed milk
Pinch of salt
2 tablespoons honey, warmed
Zest of 1 orange
¼ teaspoon ground cardamom

FOR THE STEWED FRUIT:

1 cup dried apricots, halved

½ cup dried cherries

½ cup pitted prunes, halved

¼ cup sugar

1 cup red wine

1 cup water

¼ teaspoon freshly ground black pepper

Pistachios, chopped, for serving

1. Preheat the oven to 350°F. To make the pudding, in a large bowl, whisk together the yogurt, sweetened condensed milk, salt, warmed honey, orange zest, and cardamom. Spread in the baking dish.

2. Bake for 30 minutes, or until the pudding appears barely set around the edges. Remove from the oven and let cool for at least 15 minutes before serving.

3. To make the stewed fruits, combine the dried fruits with the sugar, red wine, water, and black pepper in a saucepan over medium heat. Bring to a simmer, then turn heat to low. Let cook for about 45 minutes, or until the liquid has reduced to a syrup and the fruit is plump. Set aside to cool.

4. This pudding is great served warm, and it's also very good cold. Serve with the warm fruit, sprinkled with pistachios.

Variation: An alternative, but equally wonderful, accompaniment for this pudding would be the Breakfast Fruit with Granola Streusel (page 35).

Sweet Potato Pudding with Winter Spices

THIS IS AN OLD-FASHIONED PUDDING—let's call it your grandmother's or your great-grandmother's. I love the way that sweet potatoes' natural sweetness is used to full effect here, played up with warm, spicy cinnamon and cloves. This recipe is based on food scientist Shirley Corriher's grandmother's recipe, so it has quite a pedigree. ○ *Serves 6*

CASSEROLE DISH: 9 × 13-inch baking dish or 3-quart baking dish
BAKE TIME: 1 hour

2 large eggs
4 large egg yolks
One 14-ounce can evaporated milk
½ cup heavy cream
1½ cups packed dark brown sugar
1 teaspoon salt
One 2-inch piece fresh ginger, peeled and grated
1½ teaspoons ground cinnamon
½ teaspoon ground cloves
⅓ cup coarsely ground yellow cornmeal
Zest of 1 orange
1 tablespoon vanilla extract
2 pounds sweet potatoes (about 3 large), peeled and grated
4 graham crackers
1 tablespoon granulated sugar
1 teaspoon ground ginger

1. Preheat the oven to 325°F and lightly grease the baking dish with nonstick cooking spray or butter.

2. Whisk the eggs and egg yolks in a large bowl until well beaten, then whisk in the evaporated milk and the heavy cream. Whisk in the brown sugar, salt, fresh ginger, cinnamon, cloves, cornmeal, orange zest, and vanilla. Stir in the grated sweet potatoes. Spread the mixture in the prepared baking dish.

3. In a food processor or in a plastic bag, crush the graham crackers into fine crumbs, and mix in the sugar and ground ginger. Sprinkle this evenly over the top of the sweet potato pudding.

4. Bake for 1 hour. Remove from the oven when the top is browned and the custard is firm. Let cool for 20 minutes before serving.

No-Bake Boston Cream Pie Strata

HERE IS AN UNUSUAL DESSERT: It looks and tastes like a dessert casserole, but it spends no time whatsoever in the oven. This is an absolutely delicious and irresistible pudding; I especially like to make it in summer. It's composed of layers and layers of graham crackers and fresh vanilla pudding, topped with fudge frosting. When it sits together in the fridge overnight, it melds into a cake-like texture. So yummy, and easy, too! ○ *Serves 6*

CASSEROLE DISH: 9 × 13-inch baking dish

About 20 ounces (4 sleeves) graham crackers

FOR THE VANILLA CUSTARD:
3 tablespoons cornstarch
2 large eggs
3 large egg yolks
5 tablespoons unsalted butter
¾ cup sugar
½ teaspoon salt
4 cups half-and-half
2 teaspoons vanilla

FOR THE CHOCOLATE FROSTING:
¼ cup (½ stick) unsalted butter
¼ cup unsweetened cocoa powder
¼ cup milk
2 cups confectioners' sugar
1 teaspoon vanilla extract

1. Line the bottom of the baking dish with graham crackers, using about a quarter of them and breaking some in half if necessary. Set aside.

2. To make the custard, place the cornstarch in a small bowl. In a second small bowl, whisk together the eggs and egg yolks. Set both aside.

3. In a deep, heavy saucepan, melt the butter over medium heat and stir in the sugar. Add the salt and half-and-half, and stir. Warm over medium heat until bubbles form around the edges of the liquid. Do not let it boil. When the half-and-half mixture is hot, turn off the heat.

4. Pour a ladleful of the hot half-and-half mixture into the cornstarch. Whisk vigorously to combine. The mixture should come together smoothly, with no lumps; if there *are* any lumps, add a little more liquid and whisk them out. Pour this cornstarch mixture into the beaten eggs. Whisk vigorously to combine.

5. Pour the egg mixture into the saucepan with the remaining half-and-half mixture, and turn the heat to medium. Whisk continuously and vigorously, working all the angles of the pot and scraping the bottom. Continue whisking for about 5 minutes, or until the custard becomes very thick and starts to boil, with large bubbles that slowly rise to the surface. Turn off the heat and stir in the vanilla.

6. Spread one-third of the pudding evenly over the graham crackers. Top with a layer of one-third of the remaining graham crackers, and spread half of the remaining pudding over that layer. Add a third layer of graham crackers and top with the remaining pudding. Cover the top of the pudding with a final layer of graham crackers. Set aside.

7. To make the frosting, melt the butter with the cocoa powder in a small saucepan. Bring to a light simmer over medium-low heat and let it bubble for 1 minute. Whisk in the milk and cook for 3 more minutes, letting the mixture bubble up around the edges. Remove from the heat and beat in the confectioners' sugar with a whisk or hand beater. When the mixture is smooth, beat in the vanilla. While the frosting is still quite hot and liquid, pour it over the top layer of graham crackers and smooth with a hot knife or spatula dipped in hot water.

8. Cover the layered dessert with a lid or aluminum foil and refrigerate. (If using foil, be careful not to let it touch the top of the dessert, as it will stick to the frosting and spoil the look.) Refrigerate for a minimum of 4 hours and up to 2 days before slicing and serving. Serve chilled.

Easy Creamy Panna Cotta

PANNA COTTA IS A COOL, CREAMY, no-bake dessert that is also nearly effortless. Like the cream pie strata (page 286), it's a no-bake casserole, and it looks impossibly elegant when served up in a shallow bowl or in individual ramekins. I like to unmold it directly on serving plates and spoon a little fruit sauce on top, with berries and mint for garnish. It looks like a picture-perfect dessert from a restaurant, but it will actually only take you five minutes to prepare.

o *Serves 6 to 8*

CASSEROLE DISH: 1-quart serving bowl, or 6 to 8 individual bowls or ramekins

One 0.25-ounce package powdered gelatin (about 3 teaspoons)
¼ cup cold water
2 cups cream
⅓ cup sugar
2 cups milk
1 teaspoon vanilla extract
Pinch of salt
Sliced strawberries or other berries, for serving

1. If you want to serve the panna cotta unmolded, lightly grease the serving bowl or individual ramekins with nonstick cooking spray or a flavorless vegetable oil. If you are going to serve the panna cotta in the bowls, you can skip this step.

2. Sprinkle the powdered gelatin over the cold water in a medium bowl. Set it aside to soften for about 5 minutes.

3. In a small saucepan, heat the cream and sugar to a light simmer, then turn off the heat. Whisk to help the sugar dissolve completely in the liquid, then whisk in the gelatin mixture. Whisk for at least 1 minute to make sure it is evenly distributed and no lumps remain. Whisk in the milk, vanilla, and salt.

4. Pour the mixture into the serving bowl, or divide it among the ramekins, and cover the bowl or each ramekin with plastic wrap. (If you want to avoid any "skin" forming on top of the pudding, make sure the plastic wrap completely touches the surface of the panna cotta.) Put in the fridge to set. The panna cotta will need at least 2 hours to set—depending on the depth and size of the bowl or ramekins—

but it is safer to wait at least 4 hours, especially if the puddings will be unmolded. (At this point the panna cotta can be refrigerated for up to 3 days.)

5. To unmold, if desired, lightly run a knife around the edge of the chilled pudding and invert onto a plate. If the panna cotta won't release easily from the ramekin or bowl, run hot water over the base of the dish briefly, then try again. Serve with sliced berries.

Variations: You can play with the flavor and presentation to suit the season or your meal. Some changes or additions to try:

- Stir sliced strawberries or whole blueberries into the warm, still-liquid panna cotta before putting it in the fridge to chill.

- Halfway through the chilling time, when the panna cotta has thickened but not completely set, swirl in a few spoonfuls of unsweetened fruit puree.

- Add 1 to 2 teaspoons of lemon, orange, or lime zest (or a combination) to the warm panna cotta for a citrus version.

- Steep tea leaves, spices, or dried herbs like lavender in the warmed cream to give the panna cotta a delicate flavor. Strain them out before proceeding with the recipe.

- Serve with chocolate or caramel sauce.

While It Bakes

Salads, Breads, and Soups

Simple casseroles like Baked Chicken and Rice (page 217) or Tortilla Chicken Casserole (page 225) can be made quickly on a weeknight and satisfy you and your household. But even the most complete casserole needs at least one complementary dish to round it out into a meal, and what I usually want is a salad.

This chapter has just a few simple recipes for salads and vinaigrettes to accompany your favorite casseroles. There are warm-weather salads like the Summer Salad with Spinach and Tomato (page 297) and sweet ones like Quick Fruit Salad with Honey (page 300).

There are other casserole complements here, too, like fluffy Oat Muffins with Raisins (page 305) and 5-Minute Miso Soup (page 308). These are just a few of my favorite recipes to help you turn your casserole cookery into complete meals.

Simple Balsamic Vinaigrette

A SIMPLE BALSAMIC VINAIGRETTE is one of the easiest ways to turn a bowl of your favorite greens into a salad. All you need are some mixed lettuces or even just a head of romaine, torn into bite-sized pieces. Dress the salad carefully, starting with as little as ¼ cup of dressing and tossing the salad thoroughly before adding any more. Taste and see if you need more or if the salad needs salt and pepper. (I prefer to add salt and pepper to my salad directly, instead of to the vinaigrette itself.) ○ *Makes 1 cup*

¼ cup balsamic vinegar
¾ cup olive oil
1 teaspoon sugar (optional)

1. Whisk the vinegar with the oil in a small bowl or tall cup, whisking vigorously until the dressing emulsifies. (This means that the oil and vinegar have been fully combined; the liquid will turn opaque and rather frothy.) Whisk in the sugar, if using.

2. Store leftover vinaigrette in the refrigerator. Shake or whisk before using, since the oil and vinegar will separate during refrigeration.

Variations: Try making this simple salad dressing with other oils and vinegars. Pale rice vinegar has a very light, crisp taste, and it makes a good dressing for delicate spring vegetables. Look for fruit- or herb-infused vinegars, too. A bottle of citrus or strawberry vinegar will last for a long time and give you many delicious and unusual salads. I also enjoy using other oils in salad dressing; try adding a few tablespoons of walnut or hazelnut oil in place of some of the olive oil.

About Balsamic Vinegar

Balsamic vinegar comes in many shapes and sizes. Inexpensive balsamic vinegar runs a few dollars at the grocery store, and it usually has a rather harsh taste. Pricey vinegars, at the other end of the spectrum, may cost up to $100 per bottle at specialty shops and taste as complex as fine wine. Pick something in between, but know that with balsamic vinegar you generally get what you pay for. I use a fairly inexpensive version that has complexity and smoothness but doesn't break my wallet.

Creamy Salad Dressing

MOST GARDEN SALADS need nothing more than a light touch of vinegar and oil, as in the Simple Balsamic Vinaigrette (page 293). But sometimes a richer, creamier salad dressing is nice to have on hand, and after you make this simple version, you'll never buy another bottle of commercial ranch dressing. ○ *Makes 1 cup*

½ cup mayonnaise
1 clove garlic, minced
2 tablespoons grated Parmesan cheese
3 tablespoons finely chopped fresh flat-leaf parsley
⅛ teaspoon salt
⅛ teaspoon freshly ground black pepper
¼ cup buttermilk

1. Mix the mayonnaise, garlic, cheese, parsley, salt, and pepper in a medium-size bowl. Add the buttermilk in a slow stream, whisking constantly. Whisk until the buttermilk has been completely incorporated into the dressing. Taste and adjust the seasonings if necessary.

2. Store any leftover dressing in the refrigerator, whisking it thoroughly before using.

Sweet Citrus Vinaigrette

THIS IS MY FAVORITE WAY to dress a green salad. Lemons have a brighter, fresher taste than balsamic vinegar or other vinegars, and I love the way citrus juices brighten up fresh greens. This dressing is very adaptable, too; use orange juice and leave out the sugar for a mellower dressing, or use lime juice and a touch of cayenne pepper for a spicy, zesty salad. Here's another instance where I prefer to add salt to the salad after I've dressed it rather than to the vinaigrette itself. ○ *Makes 1 cup*

¾ cup olive oil

Juice and zest of 1 lemon

2 teaspoons sugar (optional)

⅛ teaspoon freshly ground black pepper

1. Whisk the olive oil with the lemon juice in a small bowl or tall cup until completely emulsified. (This means that the olive oil and lemon juice have been fully combined; the liquid will turn opaque and rather frothy.) Beat in the lemon zest, the sugar (if using), and the black pepper. Taste and adjust the seasonings if desired.

2. Store any leftover dressing in the refrigerator, whisking it thoroughly before using, since the lemon juice and oil will have separated during refrigeration.

Arugula and Golden Raisin Salad with Carrot Noodles

ARUGULA IS A MILDLY SPICY, pungent green that is in season in the early spring and again in late summer and fall as the weather cools. It's a great cool-weather green; in some gardens with cold frames and greenhouses it will grow right up through Christmas, and again after Valentine's Day. This hardiness and a pleasantly spicy bite explain its increased popularity; you can find big bags of it at nearly any grocery store these days. Get the freshest baby arugula you can find for this salad. ○ *Serves 4 to 6*

1 cup golden raisins

1 pound baby arugula

3 large carrots, peeled

¾ cup shredded Parmesan cheese

1 teaspoon kosher salt

½ teaspoon freshly ground black pepper

¼ cup Sweet Citrus Vinaigrette (page 294), or more to taste

1. Put the golden raisins in a small heatproof bowl and pour boiling water over them to cover. Let them steep for 10 minutes or however long it takes for you to put the rest of the salad together. This will plump up the raisins and make them softer, juicier, and more easily speared with a fork!

2. If the arugula leaves are very large, tear them into pieces. Put the arugula in a large bowl. Using the largest holes on a box grater, shred the carrots into a separate bowl and pat dry of any excess moisture. Toss with the arugula. Add the Parmesan cheese, salt, and pepper and toss again.

3. Drain the raisins thoroughly and pat dry. Toss with the salad. (At this point the salad can be covered and refrigerated for up to 12 hours.) Add the salad dressing and toss to combine. Taste and adjust the dressing or seasonings as necessary and serve.

Spring Garden Salad with Shaved Radish and Celery

TENDER SPRING GARDEN GREENS, peppery radishes, and crunchy celery make up a simple, colorful salad that's wonderful with a slightly more indulgent dressing. If you think you don't like radishes (I thought so for a long time), try the smallest, sweetest radishes you can find, and look for different varieties. The standard huge supermarket red radishes are often very sharp. Look for the long, white-tipped French breakfast radishes or the beautiful Easter egg radishes. ● *Serves 4 to 6*

1 pound mixed salad greens, such as romaine, butterhead, and red leaf lettuce
1 pound small radishes
4 large stalks celery
¼ cup chopped fresh chives
1 teaspoon kosher salt
½ teaspoon freshly ground black pepper
½ cup Creamy Salad Dressing (page 294), or more to taste
1 cup toasted walnuts or pecans, chopped

1. Tear the greens into bite-sized pieces and put them in a very large bowl.

2. Trim off the radish tops and root ends. Using a mandoline or single-blade grater, slice the radishes very thin. Try to make them nearly translucent. Do the same for the celery, slicing each stalk into very thin half-moons. Add both to the bowl with the greens.

3. Toss all the vegetables with the chives, salt, and pepper. (At this point the salad can be covered and refrigerated for up to 12 hours.) Toss with the salad dressing. Taste and adjust the dressing or seasonings if necessary. Top with the chopped nuts and serve.

Summer Salad with Spinach and Tomato

DARK GREEN SPINACH and ripe red tomatoes provide some of summer's best eating. If you prefer heartier greens, try this with very fresh, young Swiss chard or kale. If you are making this ahead (see step 2), wait to slice and drain the tomatoes until shortly before serving. ○ *Serves 4 to 6*

½ pound tomatoes
Sugar
Fine salt
1 pound spinach or other dark leafy greens
½ cup fresh basil leaves
6 ounces mozzarella cheese, chopped into small chunks
¼ cup olive oil
2 tablespoons red wine vinegar
1 teaspoon kosher salt
½ teaspoon freshly ground black pepper

1. Line 2 large plates with paper towels. Cut each tomato in half from top to bottom and remove the core. Cut each half into thin slices and lay them on the plates. Sprinkle with a fine layer of sugar and salt. Let sit while you prepare the rest of the vegetables.

2. Tear the spinach leaves into bite-sized pieces, or cut them into thick ribbons, and place in a large bowl. Cut the basil leaves into coarse shreds and toss with the spinach. Add the mozzarella and toss again. (At this point the salad can be covered and refrigerated for up to 12 hours.)

3. Drain any remaining liquid from the tomatoes and toss them with the greens and cheese. Toss with the olive oil, and then sprinkle the vinegar, salt, and pepper over the salad and toss gently. Taste and adjust the seasonings as needed. Serve immediately.

Autumn Salad with Kale, Pecorino, and Olive Oil Croutons

KALE IS VERY DARK GREEN, with beautiful ruffled leaves, so it is often used as a garnish on plates and in deli cases. It's a pity to relegate it to the role of garnish, though, since it has a wonderful depth of flavor and is also extremely hardy. It grows straight up through the snow in winter, and after the first cold snap of fall it gets a little sweeter and mellower. So this salad is best in autumn, when its robust flavor can stand up to the rich, sweet dishes of cold weather.

o *Serves 4 to 6*

FOR THE CROUTONS:
One 10-ounce loaf day-old French bread or baguette, cut into 1-inch cubes
3 tablespoons olive oil
Kosher salt
Freshly ground black pepper

FOR THE SALAD:
1 pound kale, stems trimmed off and discarded
1 cup grated Pecorino Romano cheese
⅓ cup olive oil
2 teaspoons kosher salt
1 teaspoon freshly ground black pepper
Juice of 1 lemon

1. Preheat the oven to 325°F. Toss the bread cubes with the olive oil, a healthy sprinkle of kosher salt, and a sprinkle of black pepper. Spread in a single layer across a large, heavy baking sheet. Bake for 15 to 20 minutes, stirring frequently and flipping on all sides to let the cubes brown evenly. Remove when they are golden on all sides; let cool completely. Store in an airtight container. (The croutons can be stored at room temperature for up to 2 weeks or frozen in an airtight container or bag for up to 3 months.)

2. Roll several kale leaves into a tight cigar shape and slice into thin ribbons. Repeat for all the kale leaves and place in a large bowl.

3. Toss the kale with the cheese and croutons. Add the olive oil, salt, and pepper and toss. Add the lemon juice and toss. Taste and adjust the seasonings, if necessary. Serve immediately.

Winter Salad with Fennel, Cabbage, and Citrus

THE BEST WINTER SALADS aren't made with hothouse greens or spinach flown in from thousands of miles away. They're made with what's truly in season: bulb vegetables, cabbage, and citrus. Winter is the time to eat fresh, bright, and crunchy salads with lots of delicious snap and zest. ○ *Serves 6 to 8*

1 large bulb fennel, trimmed of feathery top
1 small head green or Savoy cabbage, loose outer leaves discarded
1 small head radicchio
⅓ cup canola oil
Juice and zest of 1 orange
Juice and zest of 1 lemon
1 teaspoon sugar
1 teaspoon kosher salt
½ teaspoon freshly ground black pepper

1. Cut the fennel bulb in half from top to bottom, then thinly slice each half crosswise with a mandoline or the slicer blade on a box grater. Cut the cabbage in quar-

ters and core it; cut each quarter into fine shreds. Do the same with the radicchio. Toss all the vegetables in a large bowl.

2. Add the canola oil, orange and lemon zests, sugar, salt, and pepper and toss. Add half the juices of the orange and lemon and toss, then taste and add additional juice if you like. Adjust the salt and pepper as needed. Refrigerate for 1 hour before serving; this salad is best served cold and snappy.

Quick Fruit Salad with Honey

A SWEET, REFRESHING FRUIT SALAD is a great accompaniment to a summer casserole. A good fruit salad can also stand in for dessert, especially when it's dressed with this light and easy mixture of honey and lemon. If you want to dress it up just a bit more for dessert, serve with dollops of whipped cream. ○ *Serves 6*

1 cantaloupe, halved and seeded
1 quart strawberries, hulled and cut into quarters
1 pint blueberries
Juice and zest of 1 lemon
½ teaspoon ground nutmeg
¼ cup loosely packed mint leaves, finely chopped
2 tablespoons honey
2 firm bananas, peeled and cut into ½-inch-thick coins

1. Cut each seeded cantaloupe half into fourths and cut the rind off with a small paring knife, then chop the fruit into 1-inch cubes. Toss in a large bowl with the strawberry quarters, blueberries, lemon zest, nutmeg, and mint.

2. Whisk the lemon juice with the honey in a small saucepan and warm over low heat until completely combined, or microwave in a cup for about 30 seconds. Whisk until the honey is completely dissolved, then pour over the fruit and toss to combine. Chill until ready to serve. Immediately before serving, toss with the bananas.

Simple Pot Bread

MANY HOT CASSEROLES just beg for a good loaf of bread to accompany them: Bread can wipe up the juices and soak up the sauce, and once the meal is over, leftover bread is transformed into bread crumbs to garnish the next baked hot dish. If you have a good bakery nearby, a plain baguette or loaf of whole-grain bread can serve you well, but making your own bread is also a simple proposition, and extremely rewarding.

This recipe takes the attention span of a child and demands zero bread-baking experience or instincts. It's based on the now-famous recipe for no-knead bread published in *The New York Times* a few years ago. Mark Bittman and Jim Lahey did us all a great service by showing just how simple slow-rise, no-attention bread can be. Start this bread in the morning and by supper you'll have an artisan-quality loaf. You really can't mess this up.

○ *Makes 1 large loaf, suitable for serving 4 to 6 people*

BAKING DISH: 5- or 6-quart Dutch oven or other stovetop-to-oven pot with lid
BAKE TIME: 45 minutes

3 cups all-purpose flour
¾ teaspoon regular yeast or ½ teaspoon instant yeast
1¼ teaspoons salt
1½ cups water

1. Make the dough in the morning, before you eat breakfast or go to work. Mix all the ingredients in a large bowl. The dough will be wet and slightly goopy. Spray the dough lightly with nonstick cooking spray or lightly rub the top with olive oil. Cover the bowl lightly with plastic wrap and leave it in the warmest spot in your kitchen. Let it rise for at least 6 hours, although up to 12 hours will be fine.

2. About 3 hours before dinner, lightly spray a work surface, such as a countertop, with nonstick cooking spray. By now the dough will have expanded into a wet, dimpled mass. Dump the whole thing out onto the oiled surface. Push it roughly into the shape of a ball and cover it again with a clean kitchen towel or plastic wrap. Let it sit for 1 to 2 hours. (If you don't get a chance to do this step or if it is cut short, that's okay, although the bread will be lighter and springier when it gets to rise a little more like this.)

3. When you're ready to bake the bread, preheat the oven to 450°F. Put the Dutch oven in the oven to get hot.

4. Pour or roll the dough into the hot pot. You may have to pry it or peel it off the countertop; the dough will be very wet. Don't worry if it looks like a mess as it's rolled into the hot pot. This is a rustic loaf! Cover the pot with a lid and bake for 30 minutes. Remove the lid and bake the bread for another 15 minutes to let it brown.

5. Remove the bread from the oven and immediately take it out of the pot, using potholders or a thick kitchen towel to handle it. If you have the time, let it cool for at least 30 minutes before slicing so that it can set. This is plenty of time to put a casserole into the oven and make a salad, so by the time the bread has cooled and is ready to eat, you should be able to have a complete meal on the table.

Taking Its Temperature

The best way to be sure that a loaf of bread is perfectly done inside and not gummy or underdone is to insert an instant-read thermometer into the side and take its temperature. This particular loaf will be done when the thermometer reads 210° to 220°F.

Even Quicker Soda Bread with Herbs

EVEN QUICKER AND MORE SPONTANEOUS than a simple no-knead bread, soda bread lets you decide to have bread with dinner not much more than an hour beforehand. This is a very basic soda bread recipe that is related to all those classic Irish loaves. If you want that authentic Irish taste, add a teaspoon of caraway seeds and a cup of raisins to the batter before baking. Serve with plenty of good butter. ○ *Makes one loaf, suitable for serving 4 people*

> **BAKING DISH:** 9 × 5-inch loaf pan
> **BAKE TIME:** 1 hour

3¾ cups all-purpose flour

2 tablespoons sugar

1 tablespoon baking powder

½ teaspoon baking soda

½ teaspoon salt

6 tablespoons unsalted butter, cut into small cubes

2 to 3 tablespoons chopped fresh herbs such as dill, thyme, or basil, chopped very finely

2 large eggs

½ cup buttermilk

1. Preheat the oven to 400°F. Lightly grease the loaf pan with nonstick cooking spray or butter.

2. In a large bowl, mix the flour, sugar, baking powder, baking soda, and salt. Mix in the butter, using your fingers or a pastry blender, until it is fully incorporated into the flour. The mix should resemble coarse bread crumbs or small peas. (You can also do this in the food processor. Pulse the flour and butter 3 to 5 times, or until they are mixed.) Blend in the herbs.

3. In a separate bowl, whisk the eggs with the buttermilk. Quickly stir this wet mixture into the dry ingredients, mixing just until combined. Press the dough into the prepared pan and cut a long slash down the center.

4. Bake for 60 minutes, or until a toothpick inserted in the center comes out clean. Let the loaf stand for 5 minutes in the pan, then turn it out onto a cooling rack. It can be sliced immediately or eaten cool.

Let It Be

One way to create a lighter loaf is to let the bread dough stand in the pan before baking. If you have time, put it in a warm place, loosely covered with a towel, for 30 minutes before you put it in the oven. You'll notice a lighter crumb and airier texture.

Dried Peach and Walnut Muffins

HOT, STEAMING MUFFINS broken open with a pat of butter tucked inside to melt are one of the greatest pleasures of the breakfast breadbasket. Here are muffins to serve with any of the eggy dishes in the breakfast chapter or to round out a meal of an autumn casserole and crunchy salad.

Makes 12 large muffins

BAKING DISH: 12-cup muffin pan
BAKE TIME: 25 to 30 minutes

1 cup dried peaches or apricots, chopped
2½ cups all-purpose flour
2½ teaspoons baking powder
½ teaspoon baking soda
½ teaspoon salt
½ teaspoon ground nutmeg
½ teaspoon ground cinnamon
⅔ cup packed light brown sugar
½ cup vegetable oil
1 cup milk
1 large egg, beaten
1 teaspoon vanilla extract
¾ cup toasted walnuts, chopped

1. Preheat the oven to 400°F. Line a muffin pan with paper liners or lightly grease each muffin cup with nonstick cooking spray or butter.

2. Put the dried fruit in a small bowl and pour boiling water over it to cover. Let steep while you prepare the muffin batter.

3. Mix the flour, baking powder, baking soda, salt, nutmeg, cinnamon, and brown sugar in a large bowl. Using a wooden spoon, beat in the oil, milk, egg, and vanilla.

4. Drain off the water from the fruit and stir the fruit into the muffin batter, along with the chopped walnuts. Drop heaping spoonfuls into the muffin cups and bake for 15 minutes. Lower the heat to 325°F and bake for another 10 to 15 minutes. Let cool on a rack for at least 15 minutes before serving.

Oat Muffins with Raisins

HERE IS ONE MORE QUICK AND EASY muffin recipe that goes very well with a supper casserole. My mother used to make very similar muffins for our family suppers, and I loved their soft, crumbly texture and the sweet raisins in the whole-grain bread. These are wholesome and delicious.

o Makes 12 large muffins

BAKING DISH: 12-cup muffin pan
BAKE TIME: 15 minutes

½ cup raisins
1 cup all-purpose flour
1 cup rolled oats, either quick-cooking or old-fashioned
¼ cup packed light brown sugar
1 tablespoon baking powder
½ teaspoon ground cinnamon
¼ teaspoon ground nutmeg
½ teaspoon salt
¼ cup vegetable oil
1 large egg, beaten
1 cup milk

1. Preheat the oven to 425°F. Line a muffin pan with paper liners or lightly grease each muffin cup with nonstick cooking spray or butter.

2. Put the raisins in a small bowl and pour boiling water over them to cover. Let steep while you prepare the muffin batter.

3. Mix the flour, oats, brown sugar, baking powder, cinnamon, nutmeg, and salt in a large bowl. Beat in the oil, egg, and milk with a wooden spoon. Drain the raisins thoroughly and mix into the batter.

4. Fill the muffin cups two-thirds full. Bake for 15 minutes. Let cool on a rack for at least 10 minutes before serving.

Stovetop Biscuits

HERE'S A QUICK RECIPE for easy dinner biscuits that come together in just a few minutes; they're nearly as quick (and not as nerve-wracking) as popping open a can of premade biscuit dough! They also have a twist: If your oven is full already with a casserole, vegetable side, and dessert, you can actually "bake" these on the stovetop. They will be a little denser than oven-baked biscuits, but they make up for it with a buttery pan-griddled taste.

○ *Makes about 20 biscuits*

2¼ cups all-purpose flour
1 tablespoon baking powder
½ teaspoon salt
5 tablespoons cold unsalted butter
1 cup milk or cream

1. If you are baking these in the oven, preheat it to 425°F. If you are using the stovetop, have a large cast-iron skillet ready with a lid or heavy baking sheet to cover it. Spray the skillet lightly with nonstick cooking spray.

2. Mix the flour, baking powder, and salt in a large bowl. Crumble in the cold butter. Using your fingers, work the butter into the flour, crumbling and squeezing it until it is fully incorporated into the flour and the mixture looks like coarse bread crumbs. (You can also do this in the food processor. Pulse the flour and butter 3 to 5 times, or until they are mixed.)

3. Stir in the milk just until it comes together into a rough dough. Do not overmix.

4. To bake in the oven: Drop the dough by heaping soup spoons onto a large, ungreased baking sheet and flatten each slightly with the back of the spoon. Bake for 10 to 12 minutes, or until golden brown. Serve immediately.

5. To cook on the stovetop: Heat the cast-iron skillet over medium-high heat. Take a spoonful of dough and lightly shape it into a small patty in your hand. Place the biscuits in the skillet 1 inch apart. Depending on the size of your skillet, you will probably be able to fit 4 to 6 biscuits at a time. Cook, partially covered, for 5 to 7 minutes on each side. Serve immediately.

Spice It Up

If you love onion soup and would like to try something a little different, add a warming spice to the soup as it simmers. An old *Gourmet* recipe I read recently calls for star anise, and when I tried it, the taste was so wonderful that I began to experiment with other spices. Try adding a few cloves, a stick of cinnamon, or a cardamom pod to the soup as it cooks.

Rich Onion Soup

ANOTHER VERY GOOD ACCOMPANIMENT to many of the casseroles in this book is soup. A simple, quick soup is a great way to start a meal on a cold winter's night. This onion soup will cook in the time it takes to bake a pasta or root vegetable casserole, and it's a wonderful way to start a meal on a cold night. Keep a few boxes or cans of store-bought broth around for impromptu soups like this. ○ *Serves 4*

2 tablespoons unsalted butter
2 large yellow onions, thinly sliced
½ teaspoon salt
2 tablespoons all-purpose flour
⅓ teaspoon freshly ground black pepper
½ teaspoon ground nutmeg
3 cups low-sodium broth, preferably beef, although chicken or vegetable will also do
1 cup white wine
Grated Parmesan or Swiss cheese
French bread slices

1. Heat the butter in a wide, deep skillet or sauté pan over medium heat. When the butter foams, add the onions. Sprinkle with the salt.

2. Cook the onions, stirring occasionally, for at least 30 minutes. Lower the heat if they begin to burn. Let them cook as long as you can; the longer they cook and the darker they get (without burning), the better they will taste. But if you have only 15 minutes, that's fine too; just cook them as long as you can.

3. Add the flour, pepper, and nutmeg and stir until the onions are coated. Add the broth and wine and bring to a boil. Lower the heat to a simmer and cover the soup. Let it simmer for another 10 minutes or so, lifting the lid at the end to let it reduce a little.

4. Taste and season with additional salt and pepper, if necessary. Serve with the grated cheese and good bread. If you would like to serve this in the traditional fashion, ladle soup into oven-safe mugs or bowls and top each with a piece of bread and a sprinkle of cheese. Toast under the broiler for 2 to 3 minutes, or until the cheese is melted. Serve immediately.

5-Minute Miso Soup

THE ONLY PLACE that many of us encounter miso soup is in sushi restaurants. But miso soup is the standard way to begin a meal in many Asian households, and its salty, savory goodness complements almost any meal. It goes with fresh spring dishes and rich autumn dishes, and it also makes a filling lunch on its own. This is traditionally made with a light broth made from seaweed and dried fish, but I simply use vegetable or chicken broth. ○ *Serves 4*

6 ounces firm or silken tofu
4 cups chicken or vegetable broth
3 tablespoons white or red miso paste
2 scallions, green tops only, thinly sliced

1. Drain the tofu and cut it into very small cubes, about ½ inch square. Set aside.

2. Bring the broth to a boil in a 2-quart saucepan. Lower the heat and let the broth simmer. Measure the miso paste into a small bowl, and pour a ladleful of broth over it. Whisk until the miso has softened and dissolved, then pour the mixture back into the broth. Whisk to combine.

3. Turn the heat to medium-low and add the tofu. Do not let the broth boil again; just simmer lightly until the tofu has warmed through, about 5 minutes. Add the scallions and serve immediately.

Measurement Equivalents

Please note that all conversions are approximate.

Liquid Conversions

U.S.	Metric	U.S.	Metric
1 tsp	5 ml	1 cup	240 ml
1 tbs	15 ml	1 cup + 2 tbs	275 ml
2 tbs	30 ml	1¼ cups	300 ml
3 tbs	45 ml	1⅓ cups	325 ml
¼ cup	60 ml	1½ cups	350 ml
⅓ cup	75 ml	1⅔ cups	375 ml
⅓ cup + 1 tbs	90 ml	1¾ cups	400 ml
⅓ cup + 2 tbs	100 ml	1¾ cups + 2 tbs	450 ml
½ cup	120 ml	2 cups (1 pint)	475 ml
⅔ cup	150 ml	2½ cups	600 ml
¾ cup	180 ml	3 cups	720 ml
¾ cup + 2 tbs	200 ml	4 cups (1 quart)	945 ml

(1,000 ml is 1 liter)

Weight Conversions

U.S. / U.K.	Metric	U.S. / U.K.	Metric
1/2 oz	14 g	7 oz	200 g
1 oz	28 g	8 oz	227 g
1 1/2 oz	43 g	9 oz	255 g
2 oz	57 g	10 oz	284 g
2 1/2 oz	71 g	11 oz	312 g
3 oz	85 g	12 oz	340 g
3 1/2 oz	100 g	13 oz	368 g
4 oz	113 g	14 oz	400 g
5 oz	142 g	15 oz	425 g
6 oz	170 g	1 lb	454 g

Oven Temperature Conversions

°F	Gas Mark	°C
250	1/2	120
275	1	140
300	2	150
325	3	165
350	4	180
375	5	190
400	6	200
425	7	220
450	8	230
475	9	240
500	10	260
550	Broil	290

Index